CHAMP19NS

CHAMP19NS

THE INSIDE STORY OF OUR HISTORIC 19TH LEAGUE TITLE TRIUMPH

WITH
STEVE BARTRAM

**SIMON &
SCHUSTER**

London · New York · Sydney · Toronto

A CBS COMPANY

First published in Great Britain by Simon & Schuster UK Ltd, 2011
A CBS COMPANY

3 5 7 9 10 8 6 4 2

Simon & Schuster UK Ltd
1st Floor
222 Gray's Inn Road
London
WC1X 8HB

www.simonandschuster.co.uk

Simon & Schuster Australia
Sydney

All photographs © Manchester United/Getty Images

A CIP catalogue record for this book
is available from the British Library

Hardback ISBN 978-1-84737-916-0

Typeset by M Rules
Printed in the UK by CPI Mackays, Chatham ME5 8TD

Contents

This book is dedicated to Norman Williams,
much missed by everyone at Manchester United.

Introduction

Only at Manchester United could one introduce a book about the season that has yielded a record-breaking 19th league title, yet still harbour regret with our Champions League final defeat to Barcelona so fresh in the memory.

But while it is impossible to ignore the disappointment of Wembley, it would be unforgivably remiss not to revel in the glory of becoming English champions again – especially given the significance of this particular success.

Two decades ago, United had won just seven titles. At the opposite end of the East Lancs Road, all-conquering Liverpool had amassed 18. The number was a byword for their superiority. But steadily, across two and a half decades, Sir Alex Ferguson has hauled this club out of their shadow, superseding them in the present over a long enough period to match their past successes.

'It's an absolutely massive achievement,' says Ryan Giggs, perched on the balcony at Carrington, reliving Old Trafford's comparatively barren decades of the 1970s and 1980s. 'I don't think anyone – Liverpool or United fans – would have seen us clawing it back so quickly. This season is extra special for those of us who have grown up watching Liverpool win everything.'

In time-honoured United fashion, history has been made the hard way. Another season of dizzying highs and gut-wrenching lows kept us guessing to the very end. In the most competitive Premier League season for years, Old Trafford became a citadel; the only island of consistency in a maelstrom of dropped points. Away from home was a different matter, yet the defining performances of the season were both staged outside M16, at Blackpool and West Ham where maximum points were procured from the brink of nothingness.

There have, of course, been tough times and disappointments. We have bidden farewell to Gary Neville, Edwin van der Sar and Paul Scholes, great servants to the club, and to Owen Hargreaves, who battled injury gamely for three years before being released to resurrect his career elsewhere. The inflamed sense of pride at becoming Premier League champions is underscored by a nagging wonder of what could have been, but for stinging cup defeats to Barcelona and Manchester City.

Those Wembley wounds will never completely heal. They will become scars to serve as reminders and motivation for Sir Alex and his squad. Nobody made history without looking forward, and the manager, his staff and players are the masters of consigning success to the past and staring down the future.

Steve Bartram, Manchester, 30 May 2011.

1

The Pre-season

'It runs through your head all summer, the disappointment of last year,' said Darren Fletcher, his 1000-yard stare betraying the fresh agony of three months earlier. 'Losing out in the Premier League and the Champions League ... you think about what you could have done better, moments that maybe cost you, different things like that. But the disappointments of last year will drive us on this year. Disappointment brings out a little more hunger in you.'

The 2009–10 season certainly had its disappointments. Seemingly on course for a fourth straight Premier League triumph and chugging along nicely in the Champions League, late hurdles proved United's undoing in a marathon campaign. Dropped points against Chelsea and Blackburn sent the title to Stamford Bridge, while Europe was agonisingly exited on away goals to Bayern Munich at the quarter-final stage. After back-to-back Champions League finals in 2008 and 2009, Fletcher and his colleagues who weren't involved in the World Cup were afforded a comparatively epic summer break.

'It can be a long summer,' he continued. 'Sometimes you have to try to switch off, and I managed to do that, but there are other times when you think things through in your head, about how you can improve yourself when you come back. It's a long summer when you've not achieved what you want to achieve. We achieved a little bit of what we wanted last season and hopefully the hunger the lads will have, plus not wanting to experience that disappointment again, will help us.'

'Like we say every year, the Premier League and the Champions League are the ones we really want to win, so we've got to come back better and stronger this season,' added Wes Brown, who was similarly itching to get back to business after a seven-week sabbatical. 'We were close last season, but it was never really in our hands. We've got to make sure it is this season. You do think about your disappointments, especially when the season's finished, but now it's completely new and we've got to put that behind us. We've got some new players and we can start again.'

Sir Alex Ferguson had moved swiftly to bolster his squad in readiness for the next silverware assault; he even secured two names before the 2009–10 campaign finished. In January Fulham's Chris Smalling chose to come to United after the season finished, ahead of interest from Arsenal, while in April Javier 'Chicharito' Hernandez was in the crowd for the Reds' Champions League exit against Bayern, the day before his covert deal was sprung upon the world. The little Mexican's involvement in the 2010 World Cup, however, meant he would have to wait a little longer before meeting his new team-mates in the summer. Of course, he wasn't the only United player on show in South Africa. Chicharito was joined by Wayne Rooney, Michael Carrick, Ji-sung Park, Nemanja Vidic, Zoran Tosic (sold to CSKA Moscow during the tournament) and Patrice Evra, who were all embroiled in varying degrees of success and controversy.

More of that later. Back in Manchester, Fletcher and Brown were among the majority of players who had reported back to the Reds' Carrington HQ to begin the long, arduous treadmill back to fighting fitness. But while the hard yards surely provoke hints of trepidation in a player's subconscious, fitness coach Tony Strudwick insists Sir Alex Ferguson's players all appreciate their necessity.

'They've all bought into what we've asked of them,' he says. 'Pre-season's a time where you have more exposure to the players and you can get more ideas and practices bedded in. There have been some changes over the last two to three years in terms of what we're asking the players to do more of. We changed the structure of how we worked and brought in some extra heads. We had a couple of injury issues last year and that became our primary focus this year – keeping the injuries down – plus increasing the players' strength and power.

'To help, we wanted them to do more exercises pre- and post-training, and we wanted more monitoring, so we needed their cooperation. We used things like GPS vests and heart monitors – they're very useful tools to assist in our decision-making. Consequently, we were getting reams and reams of data to help us make quality decisions on player management and to assist in identifying what players were at risk. Pre-season went very well. Gary Walker [first team fitness coach] and Richard Hawkins [head of human performance] were also on tour, so between us we were able to implement a lot of things. Effectively, you're trying to create a cultural change, but it's a really good bunch of guys we have here and they're always receptive. They always want to improve.'

In order to help and hasten the players' return to fitness, July's North American tour would take in Toronto, Philadelphia, Kansas City, Chicago and Houston. The trip would climax with stopovers to play curtain-raisers at new stadiums in Guadalajara and Dublin, but it was the three-week stint Stateside that most excited those inside the dressing room.

'I think if you had all the lads together and asked us which was our favourite place to go on tour, America would be the most popular choice,' says John O'Shea. 'The facilities are so good, the reaction of the fans is always good and it's a great place to relax after the hard work you do. It's just nice to be able to switch off and walk down the street and actually unwind a bit, because things aren't as intense as they are in some of the other places we visit.

'You get things happening that wouldn't happen elsewhere. I remember in Chicago, a few of us went for a walk, and Wes and Fletch were among the group. Wes had been hammering Fletch about how many lookalikes he has, because we'd been seeing them every ten minutes or so. Then Wes said nobody ever sees one for him, and literally around the next corner, within a minute, we bumped into the Reese's Pieces [an American sweet like Smarties] character – and he was the spitting image of Wes! You couldn't write it! We got Wes to pose for pictures with him. Those are things that mightn't happen in other countries because you can't switch off as much.'

Alongside the pursuit of fitness and match sharpness, the social aspect of pre-season tours is hugely important. New signings and youngsters promoted to senior duties are given their first taste of what representing Manchester United truly means.

'The size of the club can't be lost on you,' says Chris Smalling. 'Considering soccer isn't even a big sport over there, we were filling out the big American football stadiums and for us to have that big an impact, it just shows you how big United is. Personally, the tour was great. It lasted around three-and-a-half weeks, so obviously that gave me an opportunity to get to know a lot of the lads. A few of the boys were on World Cup duty, but I managed to get to know a lot of them really well and that was key for me in terms of settling in. Wes and Jonny Evans helped me early on, in particular. It was just the three of us in central defence during the tour, so being able to bed in alongside them was great.'

Northern Ireland international Evans also had an added role and responsibility on tour – that of protective sibling to younger brother Corry. 'It was probably the most I've seen him for a few years,' laughs Jonny. 'Obviously I see him day in, day out at Carrington, but we're often training with different teams. In America we were training together every day and I really enjoyed it. We could tell each other what we thought and had some really good banter. I think he really enjoyed it. It was a big test for him to see if he can handle it in that environment. It was the first time he'd been away with the first team over a sustained period, and it gave him a lot of confidence.'

Having come through the ranks himself and clambered into a position of seniority within the first-team squad, John O'Shea admits the more experienced players do take it upon themselves to help the younger lads integrate.

'Without a doubt,' he says. 'You help encourage them, especially if you've come through the club yourself with the youth team and the Reserves. The young lads the manager picks to come on tour are the lads who've done well the season before, and they're obviously there for a reason and the manager thinks they have a chance. He gives them that chance and you want to help – you encourage them to relax, to feel as if they're part of the group.

'That's the done thing at this club – you help out everyone who comes in, whether it be a new signing or a young lad coming through. Everyone chips in because it's to the benefit of the whole group if the young lads can help out when we're looking to win trophies. It's key because you know what you've been through yourself, and the players who've helped you out along the way. It's definitely good to pass on the knowledge.

'With me, the two Nevs – Gary and Phil – were brilliant, as well as Butty, Denis [Irwin] and Keaney, so I was spoiled for choice, really. But as well as that, you have to help yourself in terms of being confident enough to take part, whether it be in banter or at least being on the receiving end of it. It's just having the confidence to show your ability in training and show your character to the rest of the players and not be too shy about it. Although you look up to the senior players and have so much respect for them, you have to have your own bit of confidence and ability.'

Those two assets were certainly on show in the youngsters Sir Alex Ferguson took to the States. Danny Welbeck, Tom Cleverley, Kiko Macheda, Mame Diouf, Corry Evans, Gabriel Obertan and Ben Amos had all tasted varying degrees of first-team involvement previously, and their collective pluck impressed O'Shea.

'It just happens with kids in general – they're a lot more confident these days,' he laughs. 'Going back ten years to when I came through, you notice the difference. You still get the odd shy one, but the majority of them would have no problem coming in and training with the first team or travelling with them – they're just delighted to be involved.'

Two of the youngsters – Welbeck and Cleverley – were on target in United's opening tour game: a 3–1 win over Celtic in Toronto. The opening goal was scored by Dimitar Berbatov, the subject of intense media speculation for virtually half of his two-year United career to date. As the world's finest strikers were linked with big-money moves to Old Trafford, Sir Alex Ferguson publicly stood by the Bulgarian, insisting he was 'the right man' for the job.

Berbatov found the net again in an unlikely 2–1 defeat at Kansas City Wizards, after Gabriel Obertan had struck the solitary, clinical strike of a hard-fought win against Philadelphia Union. At the next stop, Houston, the Reds' newest striker finally got on board. Having shone with two goals and a series of electrifying displays for Mexico in South Africa, United's squad was abuzz in anticipation of meeting Chicharito for the first time. It didn't take the little Mexican long to make an impression in training.

'He was so sharp, it was incredible,' says O'Shea. 'Some of the finishes he was producing in training . . . we just knew straight away that we were glad to have him with us rather than against us!'

Hernandez marked his debut with a neat lob in a thumping 5–2 win over the MLS Allstars in Houston, where the remaining goals were provided by Kiko Macheda (2), Darron Gibson and Tom Cleverley. All talk post-match, though, was of the newcomer, and the spotlight's glare burned even brighter as United bade farewell to the States and crossed south of the border.

The Reds' maiden voyage to Mexico was agreed as part of the deal that took Chicharito from Guadalajara to Manchester, which stipulated that United would face the striker's former club, Chivas, in a friendly to open their new stadium, the Estadio Omnilife. It was agreed that Javier would play 45 minutes for each side and, inevitably, he was the centre of attention before, during and after the game. His every move was shadowed by adoring supporters, while a Nike signing session in Guadalajara was attended by more than 2,000 fans, despite no advertising of the event.

'We all knew Mexico loved Chicha, especially after the World Cup, but it was incredible to see how big he really is out there,' says Chris Smalling. 'The people were going crazy! The stadium was great, the atmosphere was buzzing and the game itself was a good test as well – there was a bit of a downer because we lost 3–2, and Chicha scored against us after about ten minutes!'

'We arranged that for him beforehand,' adds John O'Shea, laughing. 'We just wanted to make sure Chivas were able to send him off on a high. And, having played against him, even for forty-five minutes, I think we were all delighted that he'd be with us for the rest of the season, rather than against us!'

After almost a month on a different continent, United's weary squad were homeward bound, albeit with one final commitment: opening the Aviva Stadium in Dublin against an Airtricity League XI. The tour party was met in Ireland by the returning World Cup contingent of Wayne Rooney, Michael Carrick, Ji-sung Park and Nemanja Vidic, while Antonio Valencia and Michael Owen made long-awaited returns from injury. United's bolstered ranks were merciless in racking up a 7–1 victory, with goals from Park (2), Owen, Chicharito (with his first touch as a substitute), Valencia, Jonny Evans and Nani.

The World Cup had provided differing experiences for United's contingent. Chicharito had announced himself on the global stage and confirmed his status as Mexico's greatest hope, Ji-sung Park and Nemanja Vidic had shone in solid showings for South Korea and Serbia, while Rio Ferdinand and Nani had their campaigns curtailed by injury before they could even kick a ball. Michael Carrick was also deprived of any action, but still featured in every squad throughout England's dismal campaign. A nation's hopes had rested on the broad shoulders of Wayne Rooney, but the striker couldn't find the form or service that made him such a devastating marksman in United's 2009–10 campaign. But, for all the media musings over Rooney's form and England's meek surrender to Germany in the second round, from a United perspective the most eventful tournament was endured by Patrice Evra.

As captain of France, Evra led *Les Bleus* into what appeared a comfortably navigable group containing South Africa, Uruguay and Mexico. However, simmering unrest under the management of Raymond Domenech spilled over after the coach dismissed Nicolas Anelka from the squad following defeat to Mexico. Evra was prominent amid a squad boycott of training, a revolt that led to several players being benched for the final group game against the tournament hosts. France lost the game and crashed out of the competition. Subsequently banned from representing his country for five matches, Patrice's World Cup had been a disaster.

'It was a nightmare,' he says. 'I will never accept that I was given a five-game ban. I want to play to the highest level, and that's being at the top with your club and playing for your country. Maybe one day I will feel I don't have the quality to play at that level, and I will say: "That's enough." But until then, I will work hard in training and aim to play again for my country. To play just for United, not for France, is only doing half a job.

'I will never accept it throughout my career. Every player and every member of the staff in the French squad would say that I was a good captain. No one can say I was a bad captain, and that's why people tell me that I must love my country, to fight the decision like I did. But this is me. I think I'm lucky to be playing football, and I will fight to do my job. I'm not fighting for something big – just to play football. That's it.

'After everything, though, it was a relief to get back to Carrington. People may say I'm crazy, but even on holiday after the World Cup I was in the gym, working hard. I didn't do anything in pre-season with United, but during my holiday I was focused on

Manchester United. Everything happened, I had one week of rest and then for four weeks I was working hard in the gym to get fit and ready for the new season because I wanted to be ready for the first game against Newcastle.'

Sir Alex Ferguson publicly ruled Evra out of contention to start against the Magpies, and the preceding Community Shield curtain-raiser against Chelsea, but the United manager would soon be handed a bombshell that overshadowed all other pre-season preparations.

2

August

There was no hint of the tumult and upheaval that loomed as August began.

Sir Alex was looking forward to testing his squad against the domestic benchmark – 2009–10 Double-winners Chelsea – with a trip to Wembley for the Community Shield, while chief executive David Gill was left to reflect on a successful pre-season tour.

'The tour went very well,' he says. 'It was the first time we'd been to America since 2004. Clearly it wasn't the full squad, because the World Cup players weren't there, but we had people like Dimitar Berbatov and Ryan Giggs, who had retired from international football. To go to the States was fantastic. The manager, in the first instance, likes going there. The players can walk down the street, go shopping or go out for a meal without being disturbed, which is great. And the facilities are fantastic.

'The other thing that was good this time around was that it was organised in conjunction with the MLS [Major League Soccer]. We played American teams and then featured in the All-Star game. In the past, we'd merely played European teams over in America. This time we were integrated and it was interesting to see how soccer's being developed over there. They've got soccer-specific stadia – we didn't play in them, but at Philadelphia, for example, we trained there. It was great and the crowds were really appreciative, too. It was thumbs up all round.'

When Sir Alex arrived at Wembley for the season's traditional curtain-raiser, he did so with a number of players in tow who'd missed the tour through injury or international duty. And yet he still had to take on Carlo Ancelotti's side without a full complement of players. Anderson, for example, had never been in contention to face the Blues, as he was still recovering from knee ligament surgery, although at this juncture the Brazilian international was just thankful to have escaped unscathed from a serious car crash in Portugal a week earlier.

Back in light training after six months on the sidelines, the Brazilian was on the verge of rejoining his team-mates for full sessions. Sir Alex was hopeful that the time spent reflecting and refocusing had given Anderson a fresh perspective on life at United after the midfielder had voiced a desire for a fresh start midway through the 2009–10 season.

'Anderson has an incredible talent,' said the manager. 'He loves training and playing. He wants to play every game and train every day. But that's a problem for me because at twenty-two he hasn't got the maturity to understand we operate a squad here. When he does understand that he'll be a fantastic player. But last season he was talking about leaving because he wasn't playing in every game. Maybe it's a good thing he's been injured for a spell because he can look at the situation.

'It's wonderful to see someone who wants to play every minute of every day. If you have someone with that enthusiasm, you have to be careful you don't check it to the point when you lose it. I didn't talk to him about leaving. I just let him get it out of his system. Maybe the injury has quelled the storm in his body, because he came back here with the same enthusiasm.'

Like Anderson, Rio Ferdinand was at Carrington, but still some way off returning from a knee injury. The da Silva twins had food poisoning, Michael Carrick and Gabriel Obertan were carrying ankle knocks and Owen Hargreaves was in America, continuing his recovery from knee tendonitis. None appeared in contention to face Chelsea.

Nevertheless, the smell of silverware proved alluring for all concerned. 'Going back to Wembley is an occasion for everybody – supporters as well as players,' assistant manager Mike Phelan said. 'We'll put a side out that can hopefully do the job. I think both teams will still be in a recovery phase and getting everybody ready for the start of the season. But it'll be a good showing.'

'There are more players to choose from now,' added Nemanja Vidic. 'Last year we had injuries and, for a period, a few midfield players had to come into the defence, which wasn't good. Now we have a lot of options in each position, which is important because we are looking to win all the trophies this season.

'It hurt to lose the title last year, especially as it was very close. We finished just one point behind Chelsea and were very disappointed. But this is a new season and we have to forget what happened last year . . . and the three seasons before that, if I am truthful. Our targets do not change. We have to win the league again and now we are stronger.'

Community Shield

Wembley Stadium | Sunday 8 August 2010 | KO 4.00pm |
Attendance: 84,623 | Referee: Andre Marriner

Chelsea 1 (Kalou 83)
Manchester United 3 (Valencia 41, Hernandez 76, Berbatov 90)

Chelsea swept up three of the four pieces of domestic silverware on offer in 2009–10, but United moved quickly to nab the first pot of 2010–11 with a deserved victory at Wembley.

Antonio Valencia's opener and a bizarre competitive debut goal for Javier Hernandez put the Reds well in command. Salomon Kalou halved the deficit, but Dimitar Berbatov's graceful late lob sealed a record-extending 18th Community Shield triumph.

The Reds' dominance owed much to the surprise selection of Michael Carrick, who had been rated doubtful to make the start of the Premier League season, let alone the Wembley showpiece. The England midfielder's display, allied to another majestic showing from cohort Paul Scholes, allowed United to seize control of matters in the centre of the park. The latter might have opened the scoring after eight minutes, but blazed his 15-yard volley over the bar.

Another veteran, Edwin van der Sar, turned away Branislav Ivanovic's header in a rare Chelsea attack, before Michael Owen's lob narrowly missed the target and Wayne Rooney shot just past the post. The England striker, roundly booed by the Chelsea supporters for his role in England's dismal World Cup campaign, then brilliantly teed up Valencia with a first-time cross that the Ecuadorian clinically slotted home.

Chelsea's response was to up the ante after the break, as the game slowed in the baking sunshine. But while the Blues enjoyed the better of the posturing, they never came close to landing a telling blow. Exploiting the space left behind the pressing Blues, United's lead was doubled when Valencia outstripped Ashley Cole and crossed for substitute Chicharito, who somehow contrived to bundle the ball into the goal via his face.

United's jubilation was tempered when Chelsea, galvanised by substitute Danny Sturridge, pulled a goal back through Kalou, but the final word belonged to the Reds. An epic passing move culminated in Nani releasing Berbatov and the Bulgarian beautifully lobbed the advancing Hilario to wrap up the match, the silverware and the latest instalment of the sides' Wembley rivalry.

John Terry and his team-mates were forced to watch Nemanja Vidic lead the Reds up to the Royal Box and lift the Community

Shield. Though the Blues' irritation would be short lived, with attentions soon switching to Premier League matters, United had quickly made a statement of intent for the coming season.

The Teams

Chelsea: Hilario, Ferreira (Bruma 79), Ivanovic, Terry, Cole (Zhirkov 79), Essien, Lampard, Mikel (Drogba 60), Kalou, Anelka (Sturridge 60), Malouda (Benayoun 72)
Subs not used: Turnbull, van Aanholt

Manchester United: van der Sar, O'Shea, J.Evans, Vidic, Fabio (Smalling 71), Valencia, Scholes (Fletcher 80), Carrick (Giggs 79), Park (Nani 46), Owen (Hernandez 46), Rooney (Berbatov 46)
Subs not used: Kuszczak

'Chelsea are a good team and at times we made them look ordinary,' beamed Ryan Giggs in his post-match interview, having picked up the 32nd senior team honour of his epic career. 'I felt we controlled the game. It's always nice to win in this manner and that is what we'll take out of it. The aim of pre-season is to get through with no injuries, but obviously you want to win games as well. We're confident, our pre-season has gone well and we've topped it off with a good show.'

Much of the post-match debate centred around the work of two of United's half-time substitutes: Dimitar Berbatov and Chicharito. The former modestly played down the brilliance of his clinching goal, saying: 'We have a great team spirit. Everyone is like a big family. That goal relaxed everyone and we won.' Sir Alex Ferguson was less inclined to understate, branding the Bulgarian a genius.

Mexican striker Hernandez, meanwhile, quickly drew comparisons with Ole Gunnar Solskjaer from Paul Scholes. 'He looks like an out-and-out goalscorer,' said the veteran midfielder. 'He's a threat in behind defenders and hopefully he'll score a lot of goals this year. People say he's like Ole, and I thought that the first time I saw him in training. We did a finishing session and everything was in the bottom corner. He scores whenever he gets a chance. If he's anything like Ole, we'll take that!'

Privately, Scholes had already made an uncharacteristically bold assertion about Chicharito. After the Mexican's first outing for the Reds, a goalscoring cameo against the MLS All-Stars, the midfielder told Sir Alex he expected the new signing to hit 25 goals in his first season. 'Paul is a quiet lad and doesn't say a lot, but he's a fantastic judge,' said the boss. After his first competitive goal in his first competitive appearance, Scholes' boldness appeared well founded.

Such optimism was commonplace around Carrington as United looked forward to hosting Newcastle United in the closing slot of the opening round of Premier League fixtures. But if Sir Alex and his players were hopeful of a serene build-up to the Monday night resumption of league matters they were very much mistaken.

First, Wes Brown announced his retirement from international football, stating: 'After a lot of thought and with a very heavy heart, I have decided the time is right [to retire]. At the age of thirty, I feel it's time to stand aside and let younger players come through, which allows me to concentrate on my club career. I regard it as an honour and a privilege to have represented my country at every level from Under-15s upwards.'

At the opposite end of the age scale, Danny Welbeck, Mame Biram Diouf and Joshua King embarked on loan deals with Sunderland, Blackburn and Preston respectively. Meanwhile, Craig Cathcart became a permanent signing for Ian Holloway's Blackpool and made his Premier League debut in the Tangerines' stunning opening-day win at Wigan.

Despite widespread insistence there would be no further additions to his squad, Sir Alex caught everybody on the hop with the shock signing of an almost total unknown. Twenty-year-old

Portuguese winger Bébé had barely any reputation in his homeland, yet United moved swiftly to snap him up after receiving a tip-off of a raw talent who had, until a move to Vitoria Guimares a month earlier, been plying his trade in Portugal's third tier.

'We were looking at him and we got advised on him that there was an opportunity,' recalls David Gill. 'Alex spoke with Carlos Queiroz and we went out quickly to secure him. There were other clubs interested. Clearly it's created a lot of interest in terms of how the deal came about and Alex confirmed he hadn't seen him in the flesh. But we had done our homework and we moved quickly. He's a late developer in football terms – he's come up through the Portuguese leagues quite quickly – so it was an interesting deal. But that's what Manchester United is about. We took a bit of a risk. We'll see what happens, but hopefully he'll fulfil his potential.'

As details of the hitherto unknown winger's background emerged in the media, the deal was soon labelled a fairytale, as Bébé had been brought up in an orphanage and spent part of his upbringing in a shelter.

'I don't think it's a risk or a fairy story,' protested Sir Alex. 'It's just an incentive to all young players who haven't necessarily had the best start to their careers. There are plenty of good young players who don't get the breaks, or the right opportunities right at the outset, but get noticed in the end. Stuart Pearce was one of them. Bébé is still young and when you get players at that age you can give them time. With all the experience we have in our first-team squad, we don't need to rush them.

'Sometimes you have to go on instinct and sometimes you have to trust your staff. This was a first for me, but we rate our scouting department very highly and our scout in Portugal was adamant we needed to do something, and quickly. I know Real Madrid were hovering and so were Benfica. It was one of those decisions that had to be made quickly, so I made it quickly.'

Almost as soon as the United manager had welcomed his newest player to the club, he was handed a totally unforeseen bombshell from one of those he valued most. Contract talks with Wayne Rooney had been put on hold during the World Cup, with a view to resuming after the striker had returned to Manchester. Instead, on 14 August, David Gill received a phone call from agent Paul Stretford that stunned the Reds' chief executive.

'We already had discussions going on, then I had a call indicating Wayne didn't want to sign the deal,' recalls Gill. 'He had some issues and didn't want to sign a new contract. That was the first we'd heard of it, because there had been discussions going on to a timetable that had been agreed. It was a bolt from the blue. I was pretty shocked, to be honest. I had a good working relationship with Paul Stretford, having done deals with him over a number of years, and there was never any indication that this was the call he was going to make. But you look at reasons and try to understand it, address some of the concerns and try to work through the issues one by one to try and solve them.'

The chief executive's next move was to telephone Sir Alex Ferguson and swiftly arrange a meeting. 'David came across to see me,' says the United manager. 'He said he couldn't believe it, and neither could I. I was dumbfounded. I couldn't understand it at all, because only months before Wayne had said he was at the biggest club in the world and he wanted to stay for life. We just didn't know what changed the boy's mind. David was shocked; I was shocked. I then had a meeting with the boy and he reiterated what his agent had said. He wanted to go. I said to him, "Just remember one thing: respect this club. I don't want any nonsense from you; respect your club."'

Though his pre-season preparations had been unexpectedly rocked, the boss soon had plenty more to occupy his thoughts. The Rooney call had fallen on the same day as the start of the new Premier League season, and champions Chelsea had laid down an impressive marker with a crushing 6–0 victory over promoted West Brom. No matter, the show had to go on.

Barclays Premier League

**Old Trafford | Monday 16 August 2010 | KO 8.00pm |
Attendance: 75,221 | Referee: Chris Foy**

Manchester United 3 (Berbatov 33, Fletcher 41, Giggs 85)
Newcastle United 0

United's Premier League assault began in solid fashion, as Chris Hughton's Championship winners were gradually overpowered on a balmy evening at Old Trafford.

The Magpies proved worthy opponents, especially in the opening half-hour, as Andy Carroll wastefully headed wide from close range. But quickfire goals from Dimitar Berbatov and Darren Fletcher settled the outcome before the break and Ryan Giggs added a sublime late third.

Though the Reds enjoyed the lion's share of possession throughout, Newcastle defended stoutly and carried a real menace at set-pieces, most notably after ten minutes when Carroll rose to meet a Joey Barton corner and powered his header off-target from six yards.

With the game tantalisingly poised just after the half-hour, United forged ahead. Jonas Gutierrez was caught in possession, John O'Shea found Paul Scholes and the midfielder quickly ferried a ball through for Berbatov. Though Luis Enrique almost intercepted the pass, the Spaniard's touch merely helped the ball into the Bulgarian's stride and his unerring finish shot inside Steve Harper's right-hand post.

Newcastle's poise disappeared and the game was effectively over when Fletcher bagged a second goal just before the interval. Patrice Evra's surge and shot culminated in the ball ricocheting to the Scot, who swivelled to fire in from four yards.

Despite being two goals clear at half time, there was still room for improvement in United's display and the Reds set about completely dominating matters after the interval. Both Harper and his post conspired to twice deny the scintillating Berbatov before the game's final flourish was provided by United's old stagers. After substitute Chicharito had nicked possession, Scholes beautifully flighted a ball to the far post, where the lurking Giggs drilled a low volley inside Harper's left-hand upright to set the seal on a textbook start to the season.

The Teams

Manchester United: van der Sar, O'Shea, Vidic, J.Evans, Evra (Rafael 87), Valencia, Fletcher, Scholes, Nani (Giggs 71), Rooney (Hernandez 63), Berbatov
Subs not used: Kuszczak, Carrick, Smalling, Macheda
Booked: Fletcher, Scholes

Newcastle United: Harper, Perch, Williamson, Coloccini, Enrique, Routledge, Barton, Smith, Nolan (Ameobi 71), Gutierrez (Xisco 81), Carroll
Subs not used: Taylor, Tavernier, Vuckic, Krul, Ranger
Booked: Barton, Perch

Clutching Sky Sports' man of the match champagne, Paul Scholes declared himself more than satisfied with a triumphant start to the season. 'The most important thing is to win the game,' he said. 'Maybe we could have scored more, but we'll take a 3–0 win on the first day of the season. Newcastle came, set their stall out and defended deep. Once we got the goal, we were a constant threat. A lot of teams come here and try to make it difficult. We just had to tire them out as much as we could. I really enjoyed the second half, especially ... creating chances, looking like we were going to score whenever we went forward.'

Though Scholes remained ever-reluctant to bathe in the limelight, there were plenty of others willing to hog it in tribute to him.

'Anyone who gets to that age and retains that level of performance like he and Ryan Giggs have ... you have got two players with something special,' marvelled Sir Alex.

'Scholesy is probably better at controlling the tempo of a game than anyone else in the league,' added Darren Fletcher. 'He can speed it up or slow it down as he wishes. His range of passing is second to none. His touch and awareness are amazing. He can just sit in midfield and control teams. He dominates and plays killer passes. He is like a deep-lying quarterback. Thank goodness the manager talked him into carrying on.'

The boss's powers of persuasion were elevated for further praise later that week when defender Nemanja Vidic signed a four-year contract extension. The Serbian powerhouse had been linked with a move to sunnier climes for more than a year in persistent tabloid rumours, so his decision to remain at Old Trafford was regarded at the club as one of the biggest signings of the summer.

'There had been a bit of speculation in the media about him leaving,' says Jonny Evans. 'There was a lot of talk, so when you see big-name players committing their future to the club, it gives everyone around the place a lift. People might say it doesn't, but these guys want to be here and they can see successful years ahead of them, otherwise I don't think they'd sign a new contract. You could sell him and get replacements in, but he knows the club inside out and he's a magnificent defender, so keeping Vida was a huge boost for everyone at the club.'

With one key signing made, it was time for United to unveil the three newest recruits, as Bébé, Chicharito and Chris Smalling were paraded at a Carrington press conference. Although he had been linked with more than £1 billion of spending on a host of big names during a summer saturated by fantasists' fare, Sir Alex insisted he was certain his policy of making stars, rather than buying them, was the right way to do business.

'We could have bought players in the summer for a lot of money,' he said. 'But I didn't think they would have made a big difference.

They wouldn't have done what Cantona, Rooney or Ronaldo did for us. They wouldn't have given us that quantum leap.

'It's one of our policies – one of our important policies – to identify young players that can grow into the club and develop here. We've always worked on the age-factor here. We have several players in their thirties, a few in the mid-twenties to late-twenties, and the rest are all young players who are improving all the time.

'So I feel it's the right policy for Manchester United. We're good at producing our own young players and we're also good at developing young players. By getting younger players now – at twenty or twenty-one – they have time and we don't need to rush them. They can develop to be the players we want them to be.'

The manager's excitement was shared by the trio of young men alongside him. 'There's a crop of youngsters who are looking to earn the manager's faith as the season goes on,' said Smalling. 'There are a lot of games, and if we all work hard from day to day we can take that chance when it comes. I think the chances are there if you're working hard.

'When you go out on the training field, there's a bunch of players who have played the game at the highest level and I think that spurs you on,' he says. 'I'm just starting out in my career, and seeing the players here who've established themselves and had the consistency to play at this level for many years, that's obviously an aim for myself.'

'It is like a dream,' added Chicharito, sporting a broad grin that had already become his signature around Carrington. 'I am living the dream that I had when I was ten years old when I loved this team and these players like Giggs and Scholes. All the players at United were heroes to me, from Cantona to Ronaldo. I liked Ole Gunnar Solskjaer a lot as well. They are all good players. I wanted to be like them. I am here now and I want to enjoy it and take this opportunity and to grow up as a human and as a player. Most importantly, I want to win things.'

'To come to a team like Manchester United is a dream come true for any player,' concurred Bébé. 'The Portuguese factor at Old Trafford was a motivation for me. You have very big names like Cristiano Ronaldo, who has played here and is a very big player now. Nani and Anderson [who played in Portugal before signing for United] are still at the club. I want to become like them and I will work hard to become a top-quality player.'

With ambition, confidence and spirits brimming among the new boys and the Carrington camp as a collective, the mood was well set for a tough opening away assignment at Fulham. For so long a happy hunting ground, Craven Cottage had hosted two successive defeats for United: 2–0 and 3–0 losses in the previous two seasons. The Reds had much to ponder ahead of an increasingly taxing trip to West London, especially up against Mark Hughes, who was taking charge of his first home game as the Cottagers' manager.

Sir Alex's team selection was also uncertain, with Wayne Rooney dropping out of contention at the last moment. Just prior to the squad leaving for London, the striker – who had just been shortlisted for the UEFA Club Player of the Year award – had been struck down by a virus and was left behind in Manchester.

Barclays Premier League

Craven Cottage | Sunday 22 August 2010 | KO 4.00pm | Attendance: 25,643 | Referee: Peter Walton

Fulham 2 (Davies 57, Hangeland 89)
Manchester United 2 (Scholes 11, Hangeland o.g. 84)

So soon after failing to make history by a single point, Sir Alex Ferguson and his side were well aware of the ramifications individual moments can have.

With three minutes of normal time remaining and United ahead – perhaps a touch fortunately – Damien Duff was penalised for handball inside his own area. Nani's subsequent spot-kick was saved by rookie goalkeeper David Stockdale, and two minutes later Brede Hangeland headed home an equaliser to deny United two invaluable points.

The Norwegian had inadvertently put the visitors into the lead five minutes earlier, slicing Nani's corner past Stockdale. Fulham were worthy of a point, having created the greater openings and drawn level through Simon Davies' strike to negate Paul Scholes' powerful early opener.

The veteran midfielder drilled home a scorching, low effort from 25 yards after being teed up by Dimitar Berbatov, but that excellent effort was a rare example of attacking fluency in the first period. Though Berbatov's scissor kick also prompted a smart save from Stockdale, Fulham roared back, flew into challenges and allowed United no opportunity to settle into a rhythm.

It took a magnificent double save from Edwin van der Sar to preserve the Reds' interval lead; the big Dutchman parried Dickson Etuhu's shot and then somehow pawed the midfielder's follow-up over the bar, despite still being grounded.

Those heroics were in vain just short of the hour-mark when Davies drew Fulham level, sweeping home Bobby Zamora's pull-back after lax possession play from the Reds.

Both sides put forward convincing cases for the three points and United looked to have pinched them when Hangeland put through his own goal. But after Stockdale's heroics had denied Nani from 12 yards, the giant Norwegian rose to ensure a share of the spoils. A fair result, but a frustrating one.

The Teams

Fulham: Stockdale, Pantsil, Hangeland, Hughes, Konchesky, Davies (Gera 90), Etuhu, Murphy (Greening 81), Duff, Dempsey (Dembele 61), Zamora
Subs not used: Zuberbuhler, Kelly, Baird, Riise
Booked: Duff, Greening

Manchester United: van der Sar, O'Shea, Vidic, J.Evans, Evra, Valencia (Giggs 74), Fletcher, Scholes, Park (Nani 67), Berbatov, Hernandez (Owen 75)
Subs not used: Kuszczak, Smalling, Carrick, Rafael
Booked: J.Evans, Valencia

'It's a bad result, especially when we had a good result in the last minutes of the game,' rued Nemanja Vidic. 'A draw is difficult to take and we feel real disappointment about what happened in the end, but I hope we take some points from the goal we lost and it doesn't happen again.

'It's hard to take. I think we would have been happy with the result – if not the performance – had we won, but there are definitely some points to take from the game. The goal we lost at the end was a shame and we probably need to improve at set-pieces. We shouldn't allow them to score again two minutes from the end. That's why we're disappointed. But we've had some bad results at the beginning of seasons and we don't want to get down after this result. I hope in the next game we will be stronger.'

Sir Alex Ferguson could not avoid citing Nani's penalty miss as a pivotal moment in the match and questioned the on-field debating process over which player would take the spot-kick.

'We should be going home with three points,' he said. 'To miss a penalty kick to make it 3–1, you've thrown two points away there, I'm afraid. I don't think we deserved to be in front at 2–1 – when we got the second goal, I thought, "We've escaped here." But when you get the opportunity to seal the game with a penalty, you should be home and dry. I thought Ryan Giggs should have taken it, because he scored two penalties in the home game against Tottenham towards the end of last season. Nani was on the pitch that same day. So maybe Ryan should have taken it.

'Our miss galvanised Fulham. It got their crowd up and they equalised. Hangeland's header was good and Edwin [van der Sar] just didn't get enough of his hand on it to knock it away. You've got to give Fulham credit because they deserved a point. They upped their game and played very well in the second half – better than us. They caused us a lot of problems.'

The glaring positive to take from the afternoon was another sterling shift from Paul Scholes, who hammered home his 150th goal for United to open the scoring. With the post-mortem of England's World Cup failure still ongoing, the revelation that Scholes had turned down a last-gasp call-up to the squad continued to fill column inches – as did sustained shouts for him to still make a belated return to Fabio Capello's squad, aged 35. Even though the veteran midfielder conceded he harboured some regrets over not going to South Africa, he stood firm and rejected a second attempt from Capello's right-hand man, Franco Baldini, to coax him back into the fold.

The closest Scholes would be coming to a globetrotting lifestyle was in United's next assault on the Champions League. The club's small band of officials travelled to Nyon in Switzerland for the annual group-stage draw and returned bearing news of looming ties with Valencia, Rangers and Bursaspor – a trio that filled Sir Alex Ferguson with confidence.

'You can't complain about that – it's a good draw for us,' he said. 'You always look at the travelling side of it, and the only one that's of any great distance is the trip to Turkey. Walter Smith's already been on the phone, talking about tickets for the Rangers game at Old Trafford! Like me, he's really looking forward to our games against each other.'

The Reds' Champions League programme wouldn't commence until mid-September. More pressing was the Premier League visit of West Ham, who had lost their opening two games of the season and looked set for a difficult campaign under the fresh stewardship of Avram Grant.

Sir Alex was handed a series of timely boosts ahead of the Hammers' visit, with Rio Ferdinand moving ahead of schedule and Anderson reacting positively to a Reserve team outing against

Manchester City. But only Michael Carrick was expected back to bolster the ranks against his former side.

Barclays Premier League

Old Trafford | Saturday 28 August 2010 | KO 5.30pm |
Attendance: 75,061 | Referee: Mark Clattenburg

Manchester United 3 (Rooney (pen) 33, Nani 50, Berbatov 69)
West Ham United 0

The Reds enjoyed an early-evening stroll against Avram Grant's Hammers, as Wayne Rooney ended his goal drought with a first-half penalty, before Nani and Dimitar Berbatov capped excellent individual displays with stunning second-half strikes.

Sir Alex Ferguson's side was rarely troubled, as Nemanja Vidic extended his own impressive start to the season with a mountainous display at the back to entirely negate the Hammers' faint menace.

Rooney was back to partner Berbatov after recovering from a stomach bug, while Nani and Ryan Giggs returned to the wings at the expense of Antonio Valencia and Ji-sung Park.

The first opening of the game came after ten minutes, when Rob Green clutched Rooney's low, skidding effort. The England stopper then produced a marvellous save to tip Nani's scorching effort onto the crossbar and away to safety.

Parity never looked like a permanent arrangement, and the half-hour had scarcely passed when Giggs tormented Jonathan Spector before drawing a foul from the former Red. It was a clear penalty and one Rooney duly dispatched past Green for his first competitive goal since putting United ahead at Bayern Munich five months earlier.

Insatiable, United continued to press. Green denied Fletcher's 25-yard shot and Nani lobbed heavily over the bar when released by a wonderful Giggs pass. But the Portuguese winger made amends within five minutes of the second period starting; he cut in from the right wing, slalomed between defenders and thundered an unstoppable shot past Green at the Scoreboard End.

West Ham's dormant threat briefly bubbled into life when Kieron Dyer slid a shot against the outside of Edwin van der Sar's post, but United's control of the game was almost entirely unchallenged. Nani and Berbatov tormented the visitors throughout, and the duo combined to end the contest as the former crossed from the right and the latter buried a magnificent scissor kick into the roof of the net.

With victory assured, Sir Alex Ferguson introduced Chris Smalling for his home debut, Michael Owen for his first Old Trafford outing since February and Michael Carrick at the expense of the ageless Paul Scholes, who again pulled all the strings in his 74-minute outing.

The three substitutes met little opposition and sailed through the remainder of the game, with West Ham's resistance long-since extinguished.

The Teams

Manchester United: van der Sar, O'Shea, Vidic, J.Evans (Smalling 74), Evra, Nani, Fletcher, Scholes (Carrick 74), Giggs, Berbatov (Owen 74), Rooney
Subs not used: Kuszczak, Hernandez, Rafael, Valencia
Booked: Berbatov

West Ham United: Green, Spector, Upson, Gabbidon, Ilunga, Faubert (Barrera 61), Dyer (Piquionne 75), Parker, Noble, Boa Morte (Stanislas 90), Cole
Subs not used: Stech, Kovac, McCarthy, Da Costa
Booked: Noble, Upson

Wayne Rooney was back among the scorers, which meant talk of his goal drought was off the agenda. Instead, positivity reigned in the Reds' post-match post-mortems.

'It's only the third game of the season, and he's only played in two of them, but a goalscorer is a goalscorer and, especially with the season he had last year, he was keen to get off the mark,' admitted Ryan Giggs. 'I'm sure he'll start putting the ball away quite regularly now.'

'It was important he scored,' added Nani. 'He's a player who needs goals. This goal will give him more confidence for the games coming up.'

'Strikers want to score and he took his penalty well,' continued Sir Alex. 'But it's his performance we should be talking about. He needs football; he needs games. That ninety minutes will do him no end of good. He'll get a couple of games for England now, too, and that will help him for when he returns for some big games.'

Though Rooney had broken his duck for the season, Giggs was keen for United's collective power to compensate while the England striker picked his way back to top form – not least because they had over-relied on Rooney's goalscoring prowess during 2009–10.

'We can't just rely on Wayne like we did last season,' said the winger. 'Berba has started on fire – in the games so far, he's had a lot of chances and he's putting them away. But everyone needs to chip in: midfielders, defenders, everyone. As a team, we need to score a lot more goals from different areas on the pitch.'

'We always enjoy ourselves when we're scoring,' said Nani. 'We had a draw last week and we were focused on getting the win today. We played some good stuff and we won, so we're happy. We could have scored a couple more goals, but the result is good for us.

'I was so excited to score. I've missed a few opportunities, so I was really hungry to get my goal and I want to continue to get goals to help the team. I want to push on this season and I've been really looking forward to it. That's why I'm working so hard.

'Chelsea and the other teams are doing well, so we need to keep up with them. We have to keep up with Chelsea. If they win, we have to win as well. We don't want to lose any points, so that is why we are working hard to win every game.'

Though the late slip at Fulham had blunted hopes of a perfect start, the Reds, with seven points from three games, could reflect on a positive opening to the Premier League season as the players disbanded for an extended international break.

3

September

True to the word of Sir Alex Ferguson and David Gill, there were no last-gasp arrivals before the close of the transfer window. There was, however, the conclusion to a summer-long saga concerning the future of Tom Cleverley. The England Under-21 international midfielder had impressed so much in United's pre-season campaign that Sir Alex wanted to keep him at Old Trafford on the basis that he would be given enough senior squad openings to further himself.

After failing to make a single competitive Reds squad in August, however, Cleverley met with his manager and the pair concluded a Premier League loan deal would be the best way to offer the midfielder the top-level experience he required. Almost immediately a queue formed, with several clubs jostling, before he was snapped up by Wigan Athletic for the remainder of the season.

'This was the right step for me,' said Cleverley. 'Sir Alex had said he wanted to keep me, but looking at the size of United's squad and the quality of the midfielders, I worried I might not get many chances. Wigan suits me down to the ground. I would have loved to have stayed at United, but I had to be realistic. This is the best approach. I felt ready to give the Premier League a go. My aim is to prove myself at this level and then hopefully next season it could be the Champions League with United. I needed the week-to-week test of the Premier League if my game was going to keep on the up.'

Cleverley had been honing his sharpness in Ole Gunnar Solskjaer's Reserves during August, and soon after his departure an even higher-profile name bolstered the second string. Having recovered from a summer knee injury and undergone intensive fitness work to bring him up to speed, England skipper Rio Ferdinand made his long-awaited return in the relatively modest surroundings of Moss Lane, in a Manchester Senior Cup clash against Oldham Athletic.

After strolling through a routine victory, in which Anderson, Wes Brown and Kiko Macheda also featured, Ferdinand said: 'It's been well documented that in the past I've rushed back too many times and broken down, but hopefully this time I have done it the right way. I have had that many games on the sidelines that I would just like to get back and have that release and satisfaction of playing football again.'

In keeping with his 'softly softly' comeback, Ferdinand was not considered for Fabio Capello's squad for England's vital Euro 2012 qualifiers against Bulgaria and Switzerland. The Three Lions' only representatives from United were Wayne Rooney and Michael Carrick, with the former dogged by tabloid rumours about his private life and the latter struggling with a niggling Achilles injury. England won both matches, with Rooney opening the scoring in Zurich, but the media continued to whip up a public storm. The striker's private impasse at Old Trafford was similarly prolonged.

When Rooney returned to Carrington, further meetings were held with the club, as Sir Alex Ferguson and David Gill sought to assure the striker that his future should lie with United. 'I wouldn't say there were discussions every day, but there was regular contact,' says Gill. 'It was always there, but it wasn't perpetually on the agenda. There were talks around the time he had some of his personal issues and we kept trying to work through the issues that he had with the club.'

As fate would decree, United's next fixture promised a stern examination of Rooney's mental fortitude: Everton at Goodison Park. Given the circus surrounding the striker's every move, a return to his former club was a troublesome prospect for Sir Alex to consider. He refused to discuss the matter at his pre-match press conference, but did confirm the enforced absence of Michael Carrick, who had again reported Achilles trouble upon returning from international duty. The midfielder visited a specialist in London, where he received an injection to calm the injury and was advised to sit out the next three weeks. Anderson was also out of contention for Goodison, after picking up a slight knock in another Reserves outing.

Barclays Premier League

Goodison Park | Saturday 11 September 2010 | KO 12.45pm |
Attendance: 36,556 | Referee: Martin Atkinson

Everton 3 (Pienaar 39, Cahill 90, Arteta 90)
Manchester United 3 (Fletcher 43, Vidic 47, Berbatov 66)

United are no strangers to late drama, but for once the Reds were on the receiving end of an unlikely plot twist.

Sir Alex's men appeared to have sewn up victory just after the hour mark at Goodison Park, but twice conceded in injury time to gift Everton a point. Darren Fletcher had cancelled out Steven Pienaar's first-half opener for the hosts, before second-half goals from Nemanja Vidic and Dimitar Berbatov put United in a commanding position.

The Reds spurned several chances to run up a handsome victory, however, and then lost concentration during added time, as Tim Cahill powered home a header, then teed up Mikel Arteta to blast home an equaliser and send Goodison Park into delirium.

Sir Alex Ferguson, who omitted Wayne Rooney from his squad after a testing week, was left mystified by his side's late lapses, especially after a performance that had, for long periods, oozed authority, despite the continued absence of Rio Ferdinand, plus the strategic resting of Antonio Valencia and Chicharito after their mid-week international exertions. In their stead, Berbatov shone as a lone striker.

Early on, however, it was the hosts who made all the running, and Everton nearly forged ahead when Arteta's free-kick clipped the top of Edwin van der Sar's bar. In response, makeshift midfielder John O'Shea sent a stunning 25-yard effort searing wide, via the outside of Tim Howard's post. The American then produced a wonderful save to keep out Paul Scholes' deflected shot, before denying Ryan Giggs from close range.

Immediately, Everton broke and took the lead as Arteta led a charge. Though the Spaniard was denied by van der Sar, Leon Osman quickly ferried the loose ball to Pienaar for a simple tap-in. United hit straight back and drew level when Fletcher volleyed home Nani's wickedly curling cross.

Within two minutes of the second period, the Portuguese winger had another assist; this time he crossed for Vidic to glance home his first goal of 2010. Thereafter, the Reds defended stoutly and always looked to exploit the hosts' high defensive line. Another break-through came shortly after the hour mark.

Scholes' superb 50-yard pass caught Sylvain Distin out of position, and Berbatov's immaculate first touch removed the defender from play. The Bulgarian then caught Howard cold by taking an early shot with the outside of his right boot and seemingly put United out of reach.

The points should have been sewn up after further openings for Scholes, Berbatov and Nani, but the two-goal cushion seemed more than comfortable as injury time began. Instead, the game underwent a stunning transformation. First, Cahill rose to thump home a header from Leighton Baines' left-wing cross. Then, as United retreated, another Baines cross landed at the feet of Arteta and the Spaniard smashed in a leveller.

In a breathless finish to the game, United poured forward in desperate search of victory and were almost caught on the break. Referee Martin Atkinson sounded his final whistle as Phil Jagielka bore down on goal, although van der Sar produced a smart save to deny the defender anyway.

David Moyes was livid with the official for halting the game mid-attack, but his demeanour was positively beaming in comparison to that of Sir Alex Ferguson.

The Teams

Everton: Howard, Hibbert (Coleman 69), Jagielka, Distin, Baines, Osman, Arteta, Heitinga (Yakubu 69), Pienaar, Fellaini, Cahill
Subs not used: Mucha, Neville, Beckford, Bilyaletdinov, Gueye
Booked: Heitinga

Manchester United: van der Sar, Neville, Vidic, J.Evans, Evra (Park 81), Fletcher, Scholes, O'Shea, Nani, Berbatov, Giggs
Subs not used: Kuszczak, Owen, Smalling, Rafael, Macheda, Gibson
Booked: Giggs

'The manager was really disappointed and made it clear in no uncertain terms what is expected at this club,' confirmed Darren Fletcher. 'The game was fizzling out, but once you give a team like Everton a bit of hope it lifts the whole place. They found that extra bit of energy and threw men into the box in the last minute. You can't afford to give teams at their home ground any sort of momentum or confidence, a half-chance or a goal, because in the end you suffer for it.

'We should have learnt from the Fulham game and we didn't. We really have to learn from this game if we want to take it forward this season and win the league. We can't afford to throw away points as we have done in the two away games so far. It just shows you that you may be winning 3–1 and think you can take it easy, but you've got to keep taking your chances and finish the game off. The more confidence you give to teams, showing them things like that, the more confidence they will get to say "Keep on right till the end against Manchester United." We need to put that to bed and get away from it as soon as possible. There is no vulnerability – it's just simple mistakes that we need to eradicate quickly.'

Looking back, Edwin van der Sar concedes the Goodison capitulation, coming hot on the heels of a similar late slip at Fulham, laid the foundations for an away-day neurosis that would permeate the first half of United's campaign.

'Of course, at the time you want to say it's not an issue,' says the Dutchman. 'You want to keep clean sheets, win games easily and be full of confidence, but we were giving some points away early on in the season away from home. That's never a good sign and it was a concern.'

Once the dust had settled on a dramatic denouement to the Goodison game, Sir Alex Ferguson's decision to omit Wayne Rooney became the major post-match talking point. The boss said: 'We made the decision simply because he gets terrible abuse here. We don't want to subject him to that,' before confirming the striker would be back in action in United's next outing, the Champions League opener against Rangers in the altogether more forgiving environment of Old Trafford.

The Champions League continued to provide a source of inspiration and, on occasion, irritation. The Reds' dramatic and agonising failure to negotiate a route past Bayern Munich in the 2009–10 quarter-finals was still fresh in the memories of everyone at the club.

'Last year still plays on my mind, that Bayern Munich game,' admitted Sir Alex. 'I'm still not sleeping after that! I keep thinking about that game and keep getting angry about the way we lost it. We were in complete control until Rafael was sent off and then they came back into it. That result hurt and still does. If we'd got past Bayern Munich, I think we would have reached the final last year and I'd have fancied us against Inter Milan.'

For young Brazilian defender Rafael, the guilt lingered. 'It was the worst experience I've had in all my life,' he said. 'That night I learnt that in football you can go from heaven to hell in a matter of minutes. If I hadn't have been sent off, we almost certainly would have won the match and my life would be much easier now. It would have taken a lot of weight off my shoulders. Now I feel like I have to prove myself all over again and show everybody I'm capable of being a Manchester United player.'

Rafael would have to wait for his chance to make amends on the European stage, as he was missing from the squad to face the Scots. Much of Sir Alex's pre-match thinking centred on how to overcome Walter Smith's side – who he expected to come to Old Trafford and display their trademark grit and organisation – while still keeping one eye on the looming visit of Liverpool five days later.

'You've got to respect Rangers and, with their history, you can't take them for granted,' said the boss, himself a boyhood Gers fan and an ex-striker at the club. 'I know Walter well and just how organised and difficult to beat his side will be. He will get a good glass of wine after the match but, hopefully, that's all he'll get!'

Champions League Group C

Old Trafford | 14 September 2010 | KO 7.45pm | Attendance: 74,408 | Referee: Olegario Benquerenca

Manchester United 0
Rangers 0

Rangers turned in a masterclass of dogged defending to ensure a frustrating resumption of Champions League duties for United, but the Reds' main concern post-match was for the welfare of Antonio Valencia, who suffered a serious ankle injury.

The Ecuadorian was quickly diagnosed with a broken ankle and damaged ligaments after an innocuous challenge from Gers defender Kirk Broadfoot, and the winger's withdrawal further dampened the mood on a dour night at Old Trafford.

The inevitable 'Battle of Britain' tag that pre-empted the game proved rather misleading, as Rangers were happy to surrender ground and defend the stronghold of their own penalty area. In 90 minutes, United scarcely made a chance of note, despite bossing possession throughout.

Sir Alex Ferguson made ten changes to the side that drew at Everton, retaining only Darren Fletcher, and handed Champions League debuts to Chris Smalling and Javier Hernandez. Rio Ferdinand, Wes Brown and Darron Gibson all made their first appearances of the season.

With some ring-rust evident in United's early play, Rangers appeared comfortable and even mustered the game's first shot on target: a flicked header from David Weir that posed Reds goalkeeper Tomasz Kuszczak no trouble.

As United slowly clicked into gear, Chicharito headed just wide from Fabio's cross, before Rooney's errant pass spurned a clear opening for the Mexican. With few gaps appearing behind Rangers' five-man defence, long-range shooting seemed a logical solution. Gibson, never shy of chancing his arm, came close twice in quick succession, as one effort scorched just wide and the other thudded straight into goalkeeper Alan McGregor.

The Republic of Ireland international then volleyed narrowly over with the first effort of the second half, and he dictated United's attacking tempo as the visitors continued to sit back and invite pressure. But just as the Reds were building up a sustained spell of pressure, disaster struck.

A strong but routine challenge from Broadfoot on Valencia sent the ball hurtling into touch. The Gers defender emerged unscathed, but the United winger lay writhing in agony, his left ankle hanging at an unnatural angle. After lengthy treatment, Valencia was stretchered from the field, taking in oxygen as he went.

Though Ryan Giggs entered the fray, United's attacking momentum waned. The visitors almost sprung an almighty shock when Broadfoot tumbled under Smalling's trailing leg in the United area, but the rookie defender breathed a sigh of relief when his trip went unpunished.

Rangers were similarly relieved when Maurice Edu escaped censure for a clear handball inside his own area as he tangled for possession with Giggs. But even though United had dominated almost from start to finish, a late concession would have been unfair on the visitors and flattering of the hosts.

The Teams

Manchester United: Kuszczak, Brown, Smalling, Ferdinand, Fabio (J.Evans 76), Valencia (Giggs 63), Fletcher, Gibson, Park (Owen 76), Rooney, Hernandez
Subs not used: van der Sar, Anderson, O'Shea, Macheda
Booked: Giggs

Rangers: McGregor, Whittaker, Bougherra, Weir, Papac, Broadfoot, Davis, Edu, McCulloch, Naismith, Miller (Lafferty 81)
Subs not used: Foster, Hutton, Weiss, Little, Beattie, Alexander
Booked: McCulloch, McGregor

'As long as I've been playing football, I've never seen anything like Antonio's injury before,' says Darron Gibson. 'It really wasn't a pretty sight and you'd never wish that kind of thing on anyone. It does affect everyone at the time, but you just have to rise above it and get on with the game. I thought we played well enough and totally dominated the game, but they defended well and we had to make do with a point. It wasn't ideal, but everybody's main concern was for Antonio.'

While shocked by the severity of the Ecuadorian's injury, Valencia's team-mates were well aware his rehabilitation would be facilitated by the determination and single-mindedness evident in his play since he arrived at Old Trafford. 'It looked really bad,' admitted Darren Fletcher. 'He had a great first season and was looking to push on this year. That is why the injury is a real blow. He's only just got back from the injury he suffered at the end of last season, too. He's a strong character, a good lad, has real determination and works hard. He'll be back, I'm sure. He will have a long future at Manchester United.'

The following day brought successful surgery and the insertion of a metal plate in Valencia's ankle. While the winger's compound fracture provided a disturbing image, it was the dislocation and subsequent ligament damage that posed the greatest challenge. Nevertheless, the no-nonsense Ecuadorian was, according to a club statement, 'perfectly fine, very positive and very determined', despite realising he would miss the majority of the season.

Just as the Rangers draw had marked the start of a long, arduous journey for Antonio, it heralded the end of the comeback road for Rio Ferdinand, who was understandably delighted to be back in action. 'It was great to be back and playing again,' beamed the England skipper. 'Getting through the ninety minutes is fantastic and I'm looking forward to the next game. Rangers came here and set up their stall to defend and maybe go on the counter-attack. You have to respect that. They've done well at what they came to do.'

With so little to take from a monotonous Champions League opener, it didn't take long for attentions to switch to the rather more enticing prospect of hosting Roy Hodgson's Liverpool at Old Trafford. 'This kind of game is always good for galvanising spirit and belief,' said Rio. 'You'd be beating one of your closest rivals, so to win this game would be great for team morale. Hopefully it will put us on the crest of a wave.

'There is a frustration with our results but not with our perform-ances. We have been in commanding positions, so to not come away with six points from those two away games [in the Premier League] is disappointing. But, overall, we are pleased with the way we are play-ing. We have been scoring goals freely, including five in two games away from home. The main point is that we have to finish them off.'

Before the Merseysiders' visit, the spotlight briefly shone on United's second string. Having failed to feature for either the first team or Reserves since signing back in mid-August, Bébé was the subject of intense speculation as the media continued to fan the flames of his engaging story, with some outlets suggesting he was struggling to reach the Reds' standards in training. Sir Alex took exception to the daily probing of and speculation around his newest arrival, and made his feelings clear.

'I know he's had a couple of vicious attacks on him for why he wasn't playing in the last Reserves game, but he was never going to be playing then,' snapped the boss. 'The boy did not deserve that. He is a young man trying to make his way in football. The [media] didn't need to do that. It was a really bitter attack. Ability-wise he is excellent. He is a terrific finisher. We have been very impressed with that. It is just the fitness levels he needs to get to.'

Having completed an intense programme designed to boost his physical endurance, Bébé made his Reserves debut the night after Rangers' visit. Although Aston Villa's impressive young crop posted a resounding 4–1 win at Moss Lane, the winger showed glimpses aplenty of his physicality, pace and power in a solid first appearance. Following the serious injury to Valencia, the form of fellow wingers Bébé and Gabriel Obertan was a subject of Sir Alex's keen interest.

With Liverpool's visit edging ever closer, the manager also sought to clear up the ongoing matter of the United captaincy. Club captain Gary Neville was stripped of the matchday skipper's role on the grounds that Sir Alex needed consistency. 'Over the last two or three years we've had to pass the baton along the line a few times,' Sir Alex explained. 'We've not had a consistent captain because Gary's injuries have prevented him playing all the time. If he were available all the time, he would be the captain. With all due respect to Gary's time at United, he knows and I know that we don't play him every week and I am looking for someone who does.'

The catalogue of contenders could barely be deemed a shortlist. Rio Ferdinand, Ji-sung Park and Patrice Evra – until his World Cup problems – were all incumbents of their international team's captaincy. Ryan Giggs, Dimitar Berbatov and Edwin van der Sar had also occupied the role prior to their international retirement, while

Wayne Rooney had long since been touted as a potential England skipper. It takes a special personality to lead a team of leaders, but the front-runner soon emerged after discussions between Sir Alex, his coaches and a handful of senior players.

'There was sort of a question-and-answer session as far as the staff went, to find out who was the one we all thought should do the job,' reveals assistant manager Mike Phelan. 'The final decision is the manager's, but there were a few opinions sought. It was discussed among the players as well ... not who they would like, but the names of the people in contention and if they would be happy with that.

'Nemanja Vidic was an obvious choice, really, when you factor in his appearances, his consistency and his strong mentality and approach. He's conscientious and not only wants to do well for himself but for the team as well; he's very team-orientated. The decision was made purely on consistency; he's a consistent performer. He's conscientious of what he brings to the team and he was the choice the dressing room felt most comfortable with.'

Though he had captained the Reds for the majority of the season to date, Vidic could barely contain his pride at being officially named United skipper, saying: 'It's a big achievement for me. No one is going to say they don't want to be the captain of Manchester United and I'm very happy with it. It is a major responsibility but I have always liked responsibility. I'm not a player who shies away from it. Nothing has really changed in that respect.'

His first official outing as captain could hardly have been bigger: Liverpool at Old Trafford.

Barclays Premier League

Old Trafford | Sunday 19 September 2010 | KO 1.30pm | Attendance: 75,213 | Referee: Howard Webb

Manchester United 3 (Berbatov 42, 59, 84)
Liverpool 2 (Gerrard 64 (pen), 70)

Dimitar Berbatov sealed the points and his place in United folklore with a wonderful hat-trick against Roy Hodgson's Merseysiders.

United again squandered a two-goal lead, despite assuming a position of complete control after Berbatov followed his first-half header with a breathtaking overhead kick early in the second period. Steven Gerrard struck twice in a madcap six-minute spell for the visitors, only for Berbatov to head a late winner and deservedly clinch victory.

Though there was cause for concern in the way United somehow allowed Liverpool back into the game, Berbatov's happy ending capped a wonderfully entertaining encounter at a rain-sodden Old Trafford.

United's hopes were dealt an unexpected pre-match blow when Rio Ferdinand reported flu-like symptoms, prompting the return of Jonny Evans alongside Nemanja Vidic in the heart of defence. John O'Shea returned to a familiar full-back role, with Gary Neville dropping out of the squad altogether and Nani replacing Antonio Valencia.

Liverpool's stuttering start to the season had yielded a win, two draws and a defeat, and they began the afternoon in nervy fashion, sitting deep against a United side happy to dictate play. Vidic headed just over from a corner, and Nani and Wayne Rooney were crowded out by a desperate visiting defence. Although Glen Johnson fired just wide from outside the area in a rare Liverpool foray, it was no surprise when United took the lead shortly before the break, as Berbatov held off Fernando Torres to arrow a header between Pepe Reina and his post.

The interval did little to curb United's dominance. Nani rattled a post with a scorching effort, then turned provider just before the hour mark. Technically, the Portuguese totted up another assist, but really the goal was entirely down to the genius of Berbatov, who used his thigh to control Nani's floated cross, creating time and space to hook a wonderful overhead effort in off the underside of Reina's crossbar.

As Liverpool reeled, Old Trafford rocked. Briefly. Edwin van der Sar had been a spectator all afternoon, but found himself facing a penalty after Torres tumbled under Evans' rash challenge. Gerrard comfortably dispatched the spot-kick, then doubled his dead-ball tally five minutes later by curling a 20-yard free-kick through a ramshackle defensive wall. United now had to win the game all over again.

Fittingly, the plaudits were hogged by Berbatov when, with six minutes remaining, he outjumped Jamie Carragher and met O'Shea's excellent cross to plant a powerful header in the bottom corner at the Stretford End. The Bulgarian, his colleagues and the vast majority of fans inside Old Trafford went wild, yet retained enough composure to see out the final few minutes without further incident.

The Teams

Manchester United: van der Sar, O'Shea, Vidic, J.Evans, Evra, Nani (Anderson 88), Scholes, Fletcher, Giggs (Macheda 82), Berbatov (Gibson 88), Rooney
Subs not used: Kuszczak, Brown, Owen, Smalling
Booked: J.Evans, O'Shea, Rooney, Scholes

Liverpool: Reina, Johnson, Carragher, Skrtel, Konchesky (Agger 82), Gerrard, Poulsen, Rodriguez (Ngog 62), Meireles (Jovanovic 79), Cole, Torres
Subs not used: Jones, Babel, Lucas, Kyrgiakos

'I didn't know it was such a long time since any United player had scored a hat-trick against Liverpool,' grinned Dimitar Berbatov, scorer of the Reds' first treble against the Merseysiders in 64 years. 'I felt so proud. It was a magical day for me. It's not every day you score three goals against a team like Liverpool. But the most important thing was that we won. If the game had finished 2–2, even if I had scored two goals, it wouldn't be pleasant. It was a great game and I hope everyone was entertained.'

Try as he might to shift the focus back on to the collective effort that yielded victory, Berbatov couldn't avoid being grilled about his jaw-dropping overhead effort that had established the Reds' two-goal lead early in the second period.

'Sometimes you think for a second, "What if I do that?" You've never tried it before but you just try,' he said. 'I thought, "Well, you never know." I already felt in that game that if I shot from the half-way line I was going to score. Honestly, you get some games like this where you feel everything is working for you and you feel powerful.

'I was just in the box and I saw Nani's cross coming. Wayne Rooney was in front of me and he was going for the ball, so I was screaming for him to leave it. I think he heard me. Afterwards in the dressing room he said he did and that's why he left the ball at the last minute. I saw the ball drop and there was no other way to control it except with my thigh, and I just tried to do something different. You don't have much time to think. The first thing that came into my mind was to take it on the thigh and try to hit it. Even when I did it, I didn't know the ball was in. I was on the ground, turning around, and then I heard the crowd screaming. After that I knew something special had happened.'

According to Sir Alex Ferguson, that extraordinary act – within another superb afternoon's work – provided glaring affirmation of Berbatov's worth to the United cause. 'He had a lot of criticism last season from the media and that happens when we buy a player for a lot of money and he's not scoring a hat-trick in every game,' said the boss. 'That's the way of the world for some players who come here. I have never had any doubt about the quality of the man, and you've seen it again today.'

Continuing to dissect the game, Sir Alex added: 'Liverpool didn't really offer anything, did they? They depended on two decisions from the referee and linesman to get them back in the game: a penalty kick and a free-kick. I've watched the free-kick since, and Torres definitely made a meal of it [John O'Shea's challenge]. There's absolutely no doubt. He tried to get our player sent off.'

Upon reporting to Carrington the following morning and

finding the back pages dominated by his comments about Torres – spun in some instances to be seen to brand the Spaniard a 'cheat' – rather than focusing on Berbatov's virtuoso display, Sir Alex was livid and enforced a blanket ban across external media, meaning no interviews in advance of the Reds' Carling Cup trip to Scunthorpe.

After seeing off Tottenham and Aston Villa in successive finals, the Reds were bidding to win the trophy for a third successive year, a feat that had never been achieved in the club's history. Paul Scholes, for one, was well aware of the competition's importance.

'You do get high-intensity games in the Carling Cup and maybe in other countries cup competitions are not as important,' said the midfielder. 'But it is in our nature to want to win every game. Winning trophies is all about getting to the latter stages of competitions and having big games at the end of them. We want to win this, just as we want to win every other tournament we enter. But Scunthorpe are a very good team at home. Anything can happen at places like that, so I just hope we can get through to the next round.'

As ever, Sir Alex was expected to shuffle his pack in order to rest some senior players and hand valuable playing time to members of his squad who were action-starved or chasing full fitness. Bébé was one of them, and the Portuguese joined the squad for his maiden taste of first-team football. In an unexpected move, however, there was even a rotation in the managerial hot-seat, with Mike Phelan taking charge as the boss jetted to Spain to watch forthcoming Champions League opponents Valencia take on Atletico Madrid.

Carling Cup third round

Glanford Park | Wednesday 22 September 2010 | KO 7.45pm |
Attendance: 9,088 | Referee: Mike Dean

Scunthorpe United 2 (Wright 19, Woolford 90)
Manchester United 5 (Gibson 23, Smalling 36, Owen 49, 71, Park 54)

The Carling Cup holders marched on, but not without undergoing a stern examination from a spirited Scunthorpe side, who took a deserved early lead at Glanford Park.

United hit back and were ahead by the interval through goals from Darron Gibson and Chris Smalling, before a Michael Owen brace and Ji-sung Park's first goal of the season wrapped up a convincing victory for the Reds.

Goalkeeper Tomasz Kuszczak was kept busy enough to earn the man-of-the-match award from Sky Sports, even though he was beaten again in injury time as the hosts deservedly attained further consolation.

Despite an entirely different line-up from that which overcame Liverpool, the Reds still featured nine senior internationals in the starting XI. Nevertheless, the hosts had the game's first noteworthy effort – a ferocious first-time strike from left-back Eddie Nolan that tested Kuszczak – and then took the lead in stunning fashion when Josh Wright fired a scorching drive into the top left-hand corner.

Shaken from a sloppy start, United were soon moving up through the gears. It took just four minutes for Darron Gibson to beautifully lob home Chris Smalling's expert long pass, and before half time the defender latched on to Park's cross to volley smartly his first goal for the club.

Scunthorpe continued to press gamely in the second period, an approach that left gaps at the back. They were exploited when Kiko Macheda released Owen and the veteran striker buried an unerring finish. Owen then turned provider for Park, heading down for the Korean to lash in a low shot through a thicket of bodies, before poaching his second goal from close range when Park's shot was spilled.

Though there were no further United goals, the away support were treated to a lively, direct cameo from debutant Bébé. It was Kuszczak who sprung to the fore once more, though, making a string of saves before Martyn Woolford slid in an injury-time strike.

The Reds' bid for a third straight Carling Cup was off and running, and further boosted on a night on which Chelsea, Liverpool and Manchester City all exited the competition.

The Teams

Scunthorpe United: Murphy, Nolan, Byrne, Mirfin, Canavan, Woolford, Togwell (Collins 72), O'Connor (Grant 61), J.Wright, Dagnall (Godden 81), Forte
Subs not used: Slocombe, A.Wright, Jones, Raynes
Booked: J.Wright

Manchester United: Kuszczak, Brown, Ferdinand, Smalling, Rafael, Park (Bébé 74), Anderson, Gibson, Macheda, Owen, Hernandez (Obertan 68)
Subs not used: van der Sar, O'Shea, De Laet, C.Evans, Eikrem

Manager for the evening Mike Phelan was delighted to reach the fourth round of the competition, but soon found himself explaining Sir Alex Ferguson's decision to scout Valencia rather than guide his own team at Glanford Park. 'He had to make some priorities and he left it to his other people to do,' admitted Phelan. 'He had to go and watch Valencia. It's important after the Rangers game, with the draw, that we prepare properly and we get a good view of Valencia, who have started their season very well.'

'It was the right thing to do,' Sir Alex confirmed the next day. 'Drawing with Rangers makes the Valencia match far more important than it would have been. It was a great opportunity to see Valencia in a really hard match. I wanted to see my younger players at Scunthorpe, but Mike Phelan has been working with me for fifteen years, so why shouldn't I trust him?'

While the Carling Cup has often been regarded as a proving ground for youth, for Michael Owen the two-goal outing at Glanford Park was reward for his patience in a barren start to the season. As ever, the striker remained philosophical. 'It's been a strange start to the season,' he smiled. 'We've played weekend-weekend-weekend and then into a double-header international break, so the manager's kept a similar team through those three games.

'It's a difficult juggling act for the manager, because he's got young kids he wants to bring through and learn a thing or two, then there are players who have been injured and are coming back into the action, players who have been fit but need games . . . it's par for the course at Manchester United.'

With doubts persisting over the full fitness of Wayne Rooney, it looked likely that Owen would be involved in some capacity four days later when United travelled to face Bolton Wanderers. In their first full season under Owen Coyle, the Trotters were gradually moving away from their long-standing stereotype of being an imposing kick-and-rush outfit. That didn't mean they'd lost their physical edge, though.

'Maybe they are more of a footballing side, but they still have that physical threat,' Darren Fletcher said. 'Owen Coyle is trying to stamp his mark on the team, but the personnel is more or less the same. When you have two strikers like Kevin Davies and Johan Elmander, who are big and strong and powerful in the air, they are bound to try to get the ball into our penalty box from wide positions as quickly as possible. That is their strength and we will have to deal with it. A trip to Bolton is always difficult. When Manchester United are in town, the fans get up for it and the players get up for it. At Bolton, taking our scalp means a lot. We know what to expect from them.'

While the challenge awaiting United had long since been laid bare, the Reds were handed added motivation by a first league defeat of the season for Chelsea. Five successive wins had given Carlo Ancelotti's side a menacing air in the early weeks of the campaign, but the Blues came unstuck at Manchester City. Already trailing the champions by four points, the chance to pick up some slack beckoned.

Barclays Premier League

**Reebok Stadium | Sunday 26 September 2010 | KO 12.00pm |
Attendance: 23,926 | Referee: Phil Dowd**

Bolton Wanderers 2 (Knight 6, Petrov 67)
Manchester United 2 (Nani 23, Owen 74)

Though a sustained failure to win away from home seemed cause for frustration, United could extract a degree of satisfaction from a gutsy fightback at the Reebok Stadium.

Michael Owen again showed his worth, heading a clinical leveller after Martin Petrov had put Bolton in charge midway through the second period. Earlier, Nani had scored an outstanding solo equaliser to cancel out Zat Knight's opener for the hosts.

The Reds were dealt further setbacks through the loss of Ryan Giggs and Wayne Rooney to injury, but digging in and taking a point without their attacking craft, and in the face of a determined Trotters display, warranted a fair return.

United lined up with the same XI that had beaten Liverpool at Old Trafford a week earlier. Rio Ferdinand missed that clash with a virus and on this occasion he was rested, with Sir Alex clearly respectful of the need for his most experienced defender at Valencia the following week.

Following late lapses at Fulham and Everton, the boss described Liverpool's two-goal fight-back at Old Trafford as 'a final warning'. For Bolton then to forge ahead within six minutes suggested the alert had gone unheeded, especially given the ease with which the unmarked Knight flicked home a corner.

Another warning was required to shock the Reds into life, as Edwin van der Sar thwarted a close-range shot from Johan Elmander. The situation demanded somebody step forward, and Nani duly did. The winger embarked on a weaving run through the midfield and towards the edge of the Bolton area, where he drilled a superb low finish into the bottom corner.

Liberated by the leveller, Giggs, Rooney, Dimitar Berbatov and Nani served up some neat approach play but, fronted by the hosts' energetic closing-down, chances were at a premium throughout the remainder of the first half and the opening stages of the second.

United's approach was soon rejigged by the enforced removal of Giggs, victim of a hamstring strain, and Rooney, who was limping heavily on the ankle he damaged against Bayern Munich towards the end of the 2009–10 season. The pair were replaced by Ji-sung Park and Kiko Macheda, and as the Reds' attack adjusted, Bolton pounced, retaking the lead when Petrov's shot took a telling deflection off Darren Fletcher and flew past van der Sar.

The Scot soon made way for Owen as Sir Alex went for broke. The gamble paid almost instant dividends as the striker rose to guide Nani's free-kick into the far corner with an expert header, much to the delight of the travelling supporters behind Jussi Jaaskelainen's goal.

Despite the brief flurry of goalmouth incident, there were no further opportunities for either side to snatch all three points. Perhaps that failure to kick on and build on Owen's leveller was cause for irritation, but the pluck shown to twice peg back the hosts hinted at the bloody-mindedness Sir Alex Ferguson demands of his sides.

The Teams

Bolton Wanderers: Jaaskelainen, Steinsson, Knight, Ricketts, Robinson, Lee (Blake 90), Holden, Muamba (M.Davies 64), Petrov (Taylor 90), Elmander, K.Davies
Subs not used: Bogdan, Klasnic, Moreno, Alonso

Manchester United: van der Sar, O'Shea, Vidic, J.Evans, Evra, Nani, Fletcher (Owen 71), Scholes, Giggs (Park 53), Berbatov, Rooney (Macheda 61)
Subs not used: Kuszczak, Anderson, Smalling, Rafael
Booked: Scholes, Vidic

The boss was in relatively chipper post-match mood, despite having seen his side drop two points on a usually fruitful hunting ground. 'In the first half we should have done better, but we did well to come from behind,' he proffered. 'The second half was very even. Bolton were a real handful and our chances were reduced, but we must take credit for coming back again. It shows a bit of character.'

The frustration was evident within the United dressing room, though. A third away game had passed without victory, punctuated by more uncharacteristically sloppy defending and a missed chance to climb the table. 'We're disappointed because we wanted to win this game, especially because Chelsea and Arsenal dropped points,' Nani sighed. 'It was a great opportunity for us. We want to fight for that top spot. Our rivals lost and this was a good chance to get closer to Chelsea. We now have to look forward to the next game.'

For the winger, his part in both United strikes took his early-season haul to two goals and six assists from the opening six Premier League games, continuing his magnificent form from the start of 2010. 'I feel more confident now than at any stage in my career,' he admitted. 'I know I'm at a very good moment in my career and my performances have been at a high level. I am doing well and am playing at an important level for my team. That's making me confident in every game and I hope to continue that.'

The growing importance of an on-song Nani was underlined by the injuries to fellow attackers Rooney and Giggs. The former was initially rated as a possibility to face Valencia in the Estadio Mestalla, but was ultimately left behind in Manchester as a precaution; the latter was ruled out for a fortnight. Furthermore, fellow veterans Paul Scholes and Gary Neville were also missing from the Spain-bound squad. On the way back into contention, however, were Rio Ferdinand and Michael Carrick.

With Valencia occupying top spot in La Liga and Group C, the United squad was in no doubt of the enormity of the task before them. 'The gaffer going out there to watch them last week shows what he thinks of it,' said Wes Brown. 'We know it'll be difficult. We know what we have to do. The challenge is going out there and doing the business on the pitch.

'We'd like to get the win, and if we don't then a draw wouldn't be a bad result as Valencia are a good side – they're top of the league in Spain, they had a convincing win away to Bursaspor and they're top of the group. Valencia will be confident, not least because they're at home. They'll make it difficult, but we've got to try to stop them playing. We need to frustrate them as the home team. It'll be hard, but we always feel confident we can get a result and that would really get our European campaign going. They're a good team, but we'll go there to win.'

The greatest tests invariably bring out the best in Sir Alex and his players, and the boss was in upbeat mood when he conducted his pre-match press conference in Spain. 'The Champions League is the biggest challenge, simply because you are playing the best teams,' he beamed. 'You want your team always to be classed alongside the great ones who have won this tournament so many times. There is a demand and expectation for us to do well in Europe, which I quite agree with.'

United went into the game with just one win from 18 games on Spanish soil. 'When you look at that statistic, obviously it is the hardest place for us to go,' he added. 'But we can change that.'

Champions League Group C

Estadio Mestalla | Wednesday 29 September 2010 | KO 7.45pm |
Attendance: 52,689 | Referee: Viktor Kassai

Valencia CF 0
Manchester United 1 (Hernandez 85)

United produced a textbook European away performance to take all three points from Valencia, as Javier 'Chicharito' Hernandez announced himself to the world with a clinical late winner.

If the little Mexican's World Cup exploits were not enough to build him a reputation, the stunning way in which he pilfered the points for United surely laid the foundations for one.

He needed just eight minutes to make his mark in the Mestalla. After coming off the bench and hitting a post with his first effort, he then drilled home a low left-footed shot from just inside the area to secure the Reds' second-ever victory in Spain and take United to the top of Group C on four points.

Although the hosts enjoyed long spells of possession, United's resilience held firm throughout – and the discipline and cool heads on show were all the more impressive for coming without the veteran trio of Giggs, Scholes and Neville.

The presence and form of Rio Ferdinand were key to United's victory, while Nemanja Vidic was also in imposing form in the heart of defence. On the right flank, Rafael made only his second start of the season – his first Champions League outing since his red card against Bayern Munich – and shone.

Lone striker Dimitar Berbatov shouldered much of the Reds' attacking burden, and fired off the game's first shot on four minutes, capping a slaloming run with a 25-yard strike that passed just the wrong side of the woodwork. Valencia might have taken the lead in bizarre circumstances when Edwin van der Sar missed a floated cross, but Roberto Soldado clumsily headed over the unguarded goal.

Pablo Hernandez flashed a shot across goal just after the second half began, and Manuel Fernandes stung van der Sar's palms with a ferocious shot, but that was the sum of Valencia's meaningful efforts on goal. Conversely, United grew in menace. Berbatov surged into the box and forced a fine save from Cesar Sanchez, Carrick fired over from distance and Park just failed to reach a curling Nani cross.

Never afraid of a bold substitution, Sir Alex threw on Hernandez and Kiko Macheda in search of victory. Moments after Chicharito had diverted Carrick's cross on to the post, Macheda teed up the Mexican on the edge of the Valencia area. He needed just two sublime touches: one to control the ball beautifully on the bobbling pitch, another to rifle it into the bottom corner and post a memorable away win.

The Teams

Valencia: Cesar, Miguel, Navarro, Maduro, Mathieu, Hernandez, Albelda (Topal 86), F.Costa (Fernandes 74), Mata, Dominguez (Aduriz 59), Soldado
Subs not used: Moya, Bruno, Feghouli, R.Costa

Manchester United: van der Sar, Rafael (O'Shea 90), Ferdinand, Vidic, Evra, Fletcher, Carrick, Anderson (Hernandez 77), Nani, Berbatov (Macheda 85), Park
Subs not used: Kuszczak, Owen, Smalling, Gibson

'When Chicharito took his chance, it was like he was shelling peas,' marvelled Sir Alex of his match-winner. 'It was so natural to him. The form of Dimitar Berbatov has delayed his appearances this season and, of course, playing Wayne Rooney and Berba has been a natural choice. It's meant Javier's not had a lot of football. But he's young and getting a lot of strength in the gym because, with his physique, he needs to work on that.'

The Mexico international had already made a positive impression on everyone at Carrington with his cheery demeanour, but his smile beamed even brighter after his first goal for the club. 'I used to watch the Champions League at home in Mexico,' he said. 'It is one of the most important tournaments in the world and to score in it, so early in my United career, is a dream come true and a big boost. It will give me so much confidence. I'm settling in well in Manchester. I've been learning and working hard because I want to do well here. I'm enjoying it – it's great to be a United player and I want it to continue for a long time.'

The first flash of Chicharito's brilliance had secured a happy ending to a solid September, but the 'little pea' would have an even bigger impact in October.

4

October

There have certainly been quieter months in Manchester United's history.

Chelsea's charge at the head of the Premier League table was underlining United's improvidence in consistently drawing away games, and was seemingly set to erode the team's capacity to win trophies, while some World Cup hangovers and Wayne Rooney's ankle injury were further dark clouds looming over United's early-season travails.

Though the away-day duck was broken in September, with wins at Scunthorpe and Valencia, the Reds' procession of Premier League draws away from home was a source of huge irritation at Carrington. The next trip, a visit to Steve Bruce's fired-up Sunderland, promised another stern test of United's winning credentials.

Wariness was perhaps magnified because of United's midweek exertions in Spain. After all, the Reds' record in post-Champions League fixtures warranted serious consideration. In 2009–10, such games accounted for five of seven Premier League defeats. Four-fifths of that quintet came after European away trips.

Nevertheless, John O'Shea was at ease with juggling domestic and European duties. 'It isn't easy, but we have done it enough down the years to know how to handle it,' he said. 'You have to respond positively, otherwise you don't get the right result and it can end up costing you in the league. We must have the right attitude and the right physical approach. If we don't, Sunderland will come out on top.

'We should definitely have a couple of away wins on the board by now. I can't really explain why it's gone wrong. Teams haven't been tearing us apart. It has literally been the drop of a ball that has gone against us. We aren't under any illusions about how difficult the task is going to be. We have had very tough games at Sunderland down the years.'

United's preparations were dealt a bizarre setback shortly after arriving at the Stadium of Light. Having changed and vacated the away dressing room, the players began their warm-up blissfully unaware that a ceiling had collapsed and a sewage pipe had emptied its contents across the room.

'We went back in from the warm-up and we were told we weren't allowed back in to the dressing room,' recalls Chris Smalling. 'Obviously, we needed to get ready for the game and we heard the roof had collapsed. We went in there really briefly to salvage what we could, and there was literally me, Chicha and a few others – maybe six of us altogether – who managed to avoid having our stuff ruined. The smell was horrific. They managed to delay the game to cope with that drama, but it was the last thing we needed. Albert Morgan and the kitmen had plenty more kit, thankfully. You can look back and laugh now, but at the time it was a nightmare. There are better ways to prepare for games!'

Barclays Premier League

**Stadium of Light | Saturday 2 October 2010 | KO 3.00pm |
Attendance: 41,709 | Referee: Chris Foy**

**Sunderland 0
Manchester United 0**

Another away trip, another draw, but once again there was solace to be taken from a share of the spoils after locking horns with a steely Sunderland side at the Stadium of Light.

Steve Bruce's Black Cats dominated the first period and ought to have been ahead by half time, but a marked improvement in United's display after the interval yielded close calls for Nani and substitute Dimitar Berbatov, rendering a draw the fairest result.

Sir Alex Ferguson shuffled his pack after the draining midweek win in Valencia. With Wayne Rooney sidelined by ankle trouble and Berbatov showing after-effects of a lone-striker stint in Spain, Michael Owen and Kiko Macheda started. Ji-sung Park and Michael Carrick both missed out entirely, as Paul Scholes returned ahead of schedule from injury. John O'Shea replaced Patrice Evra at left-back, with the Frenchman held in reserve on the bench.

Sunderland should have been ahead by the break. On 15 minutes, Lee Cattermole skipped away from a Scholes challenge, advanced on goal and slipped a perfect pass through a shoal of bodies for Steed Malbranque. The Frenchman's first touch took him clean through on van der Sar, but the United goalkeeper brilliantly turned away Malbranque's shot with his knee.

Shortly before half time, Bolo Zenden came closer than anybody to breaking the deadlock. The Dutchman had little to aim for when he picked up possession, but his 20-yard shot arrowed through Rio Ferdinand's legs and slapped against the base of van der Sar's right-hand post.

In an immediate response, Nani curled a 20-yard free-kick just wide (although Black Cats goalkeeper Simon Mignolet watched on with a nonchalance that belied the near miss). Berbatov was introduced for Owen at half time, and within two minutes had a goal correctly chalked off for offside.

With the game on a far more even keel, the sides traded efforts. Malbranque's long-range shot deflected up and onto the roof of the net via Ferdinand's shin, before Nani stung Mignolet's palms with a 30-yard drive. Then substitute Chicharito, on for Macheda, spun and fed Berbatov, only for the Bulgarian to send a low shot skidding past the same upright Zenden had tattooed in the first period.

Despite their best intentions, however, neither side could prise all three points from the other. Sunderland bossed the first period, while a resurgent United could only rue Berbatov's close call in the late stages.

The Teams

Sunderland: Mignolet, Onuoha, Bramble, Turner, Bardsley, El-Mohamady, Henderson, Cattermole, Malbranque (Gyan 83), Zenden (Reid 82), Bent
Subs not used: Gordon, Mensah, Da Silva, Riveros, Ferdinand
Booked: Turner

Manchester United: van der Sar, Rafael, Ferdinand, Vidic, O'Shea, Nani (Bébé 80), Fletcher, Scholes, Anderson, Owen (Berbatov 46), Macheda (Hernandez 65)
Sub not used: Kuszczak, Evra, Smalling, Gibson
Booked: Rafael, Vidic

'I don't think we put enough in our offensive game to really claim the three points,' admitted Edwin van der Sar. 'I don't think the service was sufficient to get the goal. We were happy to go in at half time at 0–0. In the last fifteen minutes, we had one or two chances, but not enough to get the winner. We can be happy we had a clean sheet, but I think it was two dropped points because we've dropped too many already in away games.'

Sir Alex Ferguson preferred to focus on the positives – namely, a vastly improved defensive display in the team's final outing before another international break. 'The pleasing thing for me is that the back four were fantastic,' he said. 'The consistency of not losing is something we can take. I am not pleased, but I am satisfied. We were fantastic defensively. That's the area in which we have been leaking goals and throwing games away this season, so I'm pleased with that.'

Less content was Ji-sung Park, for more personal reasons. The South Korean had, at times, looked off the pace in the opening weeks of the campaign, but vowed to improve upon returning from South Korea duty. 'I know some people haven't been satisfied with my recent performances,' he said. 'It is not a hangover from the World Cup, but perhaps I was not fully mentally prepared for the new season. You have many ups and downs as a player and I'm sure I will get better. This international break will be the turning point for me and my performances will improve when I return to United.'

International breaks seldom spawn controversy at Carrington, but rumours were growing of a rift between Sir Alex and Wayne Rooney when, after featuring for England against Montenegro at Wembley, the striker contradicted the manager by denying having suffered from any injury problems. The boss moved quickly to quell talk of any unrest, saying: 'It's water off a duck's back to me.'

He also had to address talk that Owen Hargreaves would be making a long-awaited return to action, following suggestions from the midfielder's knee surgeon, Dr Richard Steadman, that Hargreaves could face West Brom at Old Trafford in the Reds' next fixture.

'Owen is not ready,' countered Sir Alex. 'He is injured. He has missed training for the last few days. We are having difficulty with the doctor coming out with statements that are not accurate. It is not fair to the player for him to say Owen is going to be playing tomorrow. It is ridiculous. I pick the team and I have been doing it for quite a while. We have this small interference, which is causing some confusion. He is out with a calf injury.'

Roberto di Matteo's Baggies were due at Old Trafford on the back of an eye-catching start to the season, which included a famous 3–2 win at Arsenal, and the United manager was well aware his side would be posed questions by the free-flowing visitors. 'You have to recognise that performance at the Emirates Stadium,' he said. 'To score three goals there tells you something. This will be a tough game, make no mistake.'

Barclays Premier League

Old Trafford | Saturday 16 October 2010 | KO 3.00pm |
Attendance: 75,272 | Referee: Mike Jones

Manchester United 2 (Hernandez 5, Nani 25)
West Bromwich Albion 2 (Evra o.g. 50, Tchoyi 55)

A pair of freakish concessions in five madcap second-half minutes heralded another uncharacteristic slip from United, who were held to a bizarre draw by the promoted Baggies.

Early goals from Chicharito and Nani had the Reds cruising, but the loss of Ryan Giggs to a hamstring injury sapped the hosts' momentum, allowing the visitors to hit back. Patrice Evra deflected Chris Brunt's free-kick past Edwin van der Sar, before the Dutchman fumbled a simple cross to gift Somen Tchoyi a close-range tap-in.

Despite the introduction of Wayne Rooney from the bench, United couldn't find a way to overturn the quickfire collapse, and a run of frustrating results was extended. The Reds' form had moved from worrying to damaging.

Pre-match speculation over the relationship between Rooney and his manager was fuelled when the striker was named on the bench. But the decision was swiftly validated, as Chicharito pounced to convert the rebound after Scott Carson had parried Nani's powerful free-kick. With five minutes played, the Mexican notched his first Old Trafford goal.

Working in perfect harmony with Dimitar Berbatov, who continued his fine run of form with another exceptional display, the Mexican terrorised the Baggies early on. Berbatov curled just wide and scuffed another effort off-target before playing the support role in a one-two with Nani, who drilled home a superb second goal after pouncing on Nicky Shorey's slip.

Nemanja Vidic then thumped a header against the base of Carson's post as United threatened to run riot, but instead the first half petered out until the regrettable removal of Giggs. Within ten minutes of the restart, West Brom drew level in jaw-dropping circumstances.

First, Chris Brunt fired in a right-wing free-kick from a tight angle that nicked Evra and eluded van der Sar before trickling over the Dutchman's line. Then, with United retreating and rattled, van der Sar dropped a routine catch from Brunt's cross straight at the feet of Tchoyi. The Cameroon forward couldn't believe his luck and poked his side level from all of two yards.

Cue Rooney and Paul Scholes, introduced at the expense of Anderson and Michael Carrick, although little changed as West Brom remained resilient. Gabriel Tamas denied Rooney a late winner by clearing the striker's indirect free-kick off the line, but United were also left relieved when an injury-time break from Graham Dorrans fizzled into nothingness, despite the visitors' greater supporting numbers.

The Teams

Manchester United: van der Sar, Rafael, Ferdinand, Vidic, Evra, Nani, Carrick (Scholes 71), Anderson (Rooney 71), Giggs (Gibson 42), Hernandez, Berbatov
Subs not used: Kuszczak, Smalling, O'Shea, Macheda
Booked: Gibson

West Bromwich Albion: Carson, Jara, Tamas, Olsson, Shorey, Tchoyi (Thomas 69), Morrison (Dorrans 86), Mulumbu, Scharner, Brunt, Fortune (Bednar 78)
Subs not used: Myhill, Pablo, Reid, Cox
Booked: Carson, Shorey

'We need to be more angry,' fumed Patrice Evra afterwards. 'For this to happen once at Everton is okay. Then I did the same interview after the Liverpool match and said I hope we never do it again. But we have done. We have two choices: either we accept it or we don't. We have to show the correct face of Manchester United. We have to show character and personality.'

Sir Alex again sought to extract positives, particularly from an impressive first 45 minutes, but his mood simmered close to boiling. 'It's very frustrating,' he said. 'The only criticism of the first-half performance is that we didn't finish them off. It's not a defining result, but we can't keep doing that. We were frustrated with that. I thought it was going very well; there are no complaints about the first-half performance. But if they're 2–0 down and you give them a goal, you're giving the other team a lifeline.

'Edwin's mistake was uncanny. Here is a player with one hundred and thirty caps for Netherlands and the most fantastic career you could imagine and he makes a mistake like that. You cannot even criticise him, because he doesn't deserve that. He is allowed to make one horrendous mistake in his life. It was at a time when we didn't need it, of course, but it happens. You just have to wash it away.'

The boss cited the departure of the injured Ryan Giggs as a turning point, and conceded the veteran's comeback would have to be carefully monitored in order to avoid a repeat breakdown. 'The loss of Ryan as a wide player was a big one for us,' he said. 'He has done his hamstring again. He got it against Bolton, but he had trained all week and had been doing very well. But it has gone again and maybe we need to give him a longer recovery.'

While United supporters steered clear of the Sunday papers for fear of reading more damning accounts of the Reds' spectacular setback against the Baggies, it transpired that an altogether bigger story had broken: news of Wayne Rooney's desire to leave Old Trafford was out, and the press speculated that the striker would leave United in the January transfer window. The most scrutinised club and player in the country were seemingly on a very public collision course. It all made for a surreal atmosphere within the private confines of Carrington.

'You're reading and hearing all these stories, but you're just thinking: "I know how much he likes it here,"' reveals John O'Shea. 'You're running through every scenario in your head, thinking that he can't be going but then wondering if the club are going to sell. But behind it all you're just thinking: "He loves it here so much." We were just wondering what was going on, because something obviously wasn't right.'

'There were no signs it was coming,' adds Jonny Evans. 'We see Wazza every day in training and it was all a bit surreal. Wazza was just getting on normally. We were all having breakfast together, training together, but we were seeing everything in the papers. There was just this huge commotion outside, but at Carrington it was calm and normal, which made it really strange. You try not to pay attention to it. You go home and you get fans stopping you and asking you what's going on, because it's major stuff, obviously, but we couldn't really see much going on. It's a strange situation. When things are being said in the press, it's almost like they're not coming from those people.'

The press wouldn't have to feed on faceless conjecture for long, as Sir Alex Ferguson held his pre-match press conference at Old Trafford ahead of the Champions League visit of Bursaspor. As the nominated player to join the manager, O'Shea had a ringside seat for one of Sir Alex's most notable hours as Manchester United manager.

'Oh my God,' smiles the defender. 'I'd gone along to Old Trafford and I was told the press conference would be split in two: the manager was going to do Bursaspor and then he was making a statement about Wayne. So the Bursaspor press conference was a total non-event – the Turkish press had been delayed at the airport and the British press asked three or four questions before they said: "Can we talk about Wayne now?" I got off the stage sharpish. How's your luck, getting involved in a press conference when all this is kicking off! I stayed to listen, because I didn't know what the manager was going to say, and then he went out, read the statement on Wayne and firmly put the ball back in his court.'

Sat in Old Trafford's Europa Suite, carefully holding a prepared sheet of bullet points, Sir Alex answered questions to confirm Rooney had been injured, and that he had indeed indicated a desire to leave United in August. He then went on to add: 'We've never had any argument, not a bit. I think you have to understand the mechanics of these situations when people want to leave the club. It's an easy one to say he's fallen out with the manager, a very easy one to say. I think there are traces of that, too.

'What we're seeing now in the media is disappointing, because we've done everything we can for Wayne Rooney, since the minute he's come to the club. We've always been there as a harbour for him. Any time he's been in trouble, the advice we've given him ... I've even been prepared to give him financial advice, many times. But you do that for your players, not just Wayne Rooney. That's Manchester United. This is a club that bases all its history and its tradition on the loyalty and trust between managers and players and the club. That goes back to the days of Sir Matt [Busby]. That's what it's founded on. Wayne's been a beneficiary of this help, just as Ryan Giggs, Paul Scholes and all the players have been. That's what we're there for.

'There's been no falling out. That's why we need to clarify the situation now for our fans. Because what we saw on Saturday was unacceptable. When we were at 2–2 and the fans were chanting for Wayne Rooney [to be introduced into the game], it put pressure on the players and it didn't do any good for the team. So we've got to clarify the situation and try to do it right. There's no offer on the table for Wayne because they're not prepared to listen to an offer. But there's always an offer there for Manchester United to negotiate with a player. That's still there.'

The stunned media quickly sought to relay the news to the world: Wayne Rooney was leaving Manchester United. Or so it seemed. In the meantime, the striker would miss the visit of Bursaspor because he had accidentally suffered – with no small dose of irony – an ankle injury after a challenge from Paul Scholes in training. But though he wasn't playing, the day of the Bursaspor game was inevitably dominated by Rooney, especially after the striker released the following statement shortly before kick-off:

'I met with David Gill last week and he did not give me any of the assurances I was seeking about the future squad. I then told him that I would not be signing a new contract. I was interested to hear what Sir Alex had to say yesterday and surprised by some of it. It is absolutely true, as he said, that my agent and I have had a number of meetings with the club about a new contract. During those meetings in August I asked for assurances about the continued ability of the club to attract the top players in the world.

'I have never had anything but complete respect for Manchester United Football Club. How could I not have done given its fantastic history and especially the last six years in which I have been lucky to play a part? For me, it's all about winning trophies – as the club has always done under Sir Alex. Because of that, I think the questions I was asking were justified.

'Despite recent difficulties, I know I will always owe Sir Alex Ferguson a huge debt. He is a great manager and mentor who has helped and supported me from the day he signed me from Everton when I was only eighteen. For Manchester United's sake I wish he could go on forever, because he's a one-off and a genius.'

The genius could address that issue later. Firstly, he and his side had to negotiate the first part of a double-header with the Turkish champions that promised to make or break hopes of escaping Group C.

Champions League Group C

**Old Trafford | Wednesday 20 October 2010 | KO 7.45pm |
Attendance: 72,610 | Referee: Gianluca Rocchi**

Manchester United 1 (Nani 7)
Bursaspor 0

Nani's blistering early strike took the Reds closer to the knockout stages with a routine single-goal win at a subdued Old Trafford.

The effects of a whirlwind few days had clearly taken their toll on players and supporters alike, as Sir Alex's men never looked – nor needed to be – at their best to overcome the Turkish champions and build a two-point lead over Rangers and Valencia, who drew at Ibrox.

Sir Alex had intimated he would make changes to the side that had imploded against West Brom, and he duly brought in Tomasz Kuszczak, Chris Smalling, Darren Fletcher, Ji-sung Park and Kiko Macheda. Mercifully, the reshuffled side forged ahead inside seven minutes. And in some style.

Nani collected Darren Fletcher's pass on the right flank, cut inside and made a beeline for the Bursaspor penalty area. As alarmed defenders back-pedalled, the Portuguese winger took full advantage and arrowed a left-footed drive into the far corner.

In a largely drab first period, neither side created clear openings. With United firmly ensconced in the visitors' half, it took a superb last-ditch saving tackle from Rafael to deny Ozan Ipek as he bore down on goal in a rare attack by the visitors. At the opposite end, lone striker Macheda also toiled thanklessly, despite putting in a sweat-soaked shift and making some superb runs.

Patrice Evra's cross-shot after an hour forced a save out of Dimitar Ivankov at his near post, before the Bursaspor stopper emerged triumphant from the second instalment of his battle with Nani, clutching the winger's powerful effort from the edge of the box. Gabriel Obertan looked impressive in a substitute cameo on the right flank and almost capped his outing with a header that inched wide of the post.

The final opening of the match – and, really, the only glaring chance – fell to another substitute, Chicharito. The Mexican latched on to Nemanja Vidic's perfect pass, but could only slide a finish just wide of the upright. No matter, the job had been done and the Reds had taken maximum points on a difficult day.

The Teams

Manchester United: Kuszczak, Rafael, Smalling, Vidic, Evra, Nani, Fletcher, Carrick, Anderson (Hernandez 77), Park (Obertan 71), Macheda
Subs not used: Amos, Neville, Berbatov, O'Shea, Bébé
Booked: Nani

Bursaspor: Ivankov, Stepanov (Ozturk 46), Erdogan, Insua, Wederson, Sen, Svensson, Ipek, Tandogan (Keceli 71), Ergic, Yildirim (Bahadir 46)
Subs not used: Ozkan, Cimsir, Batalla, Nunez
Booked: Ipek, Keceli

Sir Alex had already had his pre-match say on Wayne Rooney's situation and, in a crammed Old Trafford tunnel, the press heaved for insight into the United dressing room. What did Rooney's teammates make of the situation?

'It's happened before with players negotiating with clubs about their contract and a lot of talk in the papers,' said skipper Nemanja Vidic. 'We are just trying to train and not speak too much with each other, because we don't want to take the focus from the games on the pitch.'

Patrice Evra admitted: 'If one player in the team does not trust the others, he should not play in the team. Me, I trust everyone. I know we can win.' When asked if he hoped Rooney would remain, he said: 'I hope so, but I'm not Sir Alex Ferguson … I'm only Patrice Evra.'

'There have been a few instances of big players leaving Manchester United, but Manchester United goes on,' shrugged Darren Fletcher. 'It's such a big club, the biggest in the world. You have to keep going, you have to respond. The fans don't let you settle for anything other than winning.'

After learning of the content of Rooney's statement, Sir Alex quickly leapt to the defence of his club and its future. 'There's not a thing wrong with Manchester United, not a thing wrong with it. I've only won twenty-seven trophies,' he wryly observed. 'We realised a few years ago that Giggs, Scholes and Neville were never going to last forever, so our policy is to develop footballers in their place.

'I had a player once who said to me that Rooney and Cristiano Ronaldo weren't good enough and he was not prepared to wait until they were. But that's the trouble with potential. People don't identify potential. They're very poor at it. I've identified all my life the potential in young people. I know potential. I know how to develop and have faith in it. And young people surprise you when given the opportunity. That's what this club is all about.

'We have a structure at the club that's good. We've the right staff, the right manager and the right chief executive, who is a brilliant man.

'It's difficult to maintain a cycle of more than four years at a time. At the end of the day, we lost a fourth successive title by a point. It would have been a record. We don't like that and we'll try to do something about that. But we'll be there. We'll be okay. I have every confidence in that.'

And of dealing with the Rooney situation? 'We will have a view of it tomorrow and see where we go from there. We will probably put it to bed tomorrow. The door is open, we are that kind of club. We want to keep good players, particularly when they are as young as Wayne.'

The following morning brought meetings and phone calls aplenty. Sir Alex, David Gill and the club's owners, the Glazer family, mulled over the matter at length. Wayne Rooney and his agent, Paul Stretford, also joined the discussions. As the day wore on and talks continued, there was a softening of stances in private. Publicly there was still no news. Late on Thursday evening, 24 hours after United's win over Bursaspor, a small crowd gathered outside Rooney's house and urged him not to leave and join Manchester City (his most likely destination, according to various media reports). Police cleared the crowd and the following morning Rooney headed to Carrington with the benefit of a night to digest the events of the day. Then, incredibly, he agreed to sign a new contract. In less than a week, Rooney's future had gone from unquestioned to uncertain to concrete.

'In the last couple of days, I've talked to the manager and the owners and they've convinced me this is where I belong,' the striker revealed in a statement. 'I said on Wednesday the manager's a genius and it's his belief and support that have convinced me to stay. I'm signing a new deal in the absolute belief that the management, coaching staff, board and owners are totally committed to making sure United maintains its proud winning history – which is the reason I joined the club in the first place.

'I'm sure the fans over the last week have felt let down by what they've read and seen. But my position was from concern over the future. The fans have been brilliant with me since I arrived and it's up to me through my performances to win them over again.'

Rooney immediately gave an interview to MUTV, in which he addressed the matter in greater depth. 'I had some concerns, and I made them aware to David Gill and the manager, and it went from there,' he said. 'It didn't really move forward in terms of contract talks. Obviously, over the last couple of days that's all been made public knowledge, which made it a bit more difficult, and we felt – myself and the club – we had to move quickly to sort it out.

'I have spoken to the manager, David Gill, the Glazers and all of them have confirmed to me that this is the right club for me to be at and the club is going to continue being successful and winning things. I had other things I wanted to air as well, and I was happy to move forward and sign the deal at the club.

'I am sure it has been difficult for the manager as well. He has to look after the club and was trying to convince me to sign a new deal at the club. He is a great manager. I have said many times that one of the big reasons I joined this club was to work under him, with his experience, passion and will to win. I wanted to be successful working with him. I have managed to do that. I am hoping in the next few years we can do that again.'

'It's been a difficult week, but the intensity of the coverage is what we expect at Manchester United,' said a weary Sir Alex Ferguson. 'I said to the boy that the door is always open and I'm delighted Wayne has agreed to stay. Sometimes, when you're in a club, it can be hard to realise just how big it is and it takes something like the events of the last few days to make you understand. I think Wayne now understands what a great club Manchester United is.

'I'm pleased he has accepted the challenge to guide the younger players and establish himself as one of United's great players. It shows character and belief in what we stand for. I'm sure everyone involved with the club will now get behind Wayne and show him the support he needs to produce the performances we know he is capable of.'

Soon after penning his new deal, Rooney made his way to the Carrington dressing room and addressed his team-mates. 'A few of the lads thought he would stay anyway, and once he signed it was just a case of getting on with it,' says Jonny Evans. 'He just sat us down and said he was staying. I think he wanted to apologise in case he'd caused any disturbances among us, but he hadn't. I think the lads were more laughing at him and having a bit of banter with him than anything.'

'It transpired it was just an interesting technique of getting a new deal,' laughs John O'Shea. 'I think Wayne, if he could turn back time, he might do things a bit differently, but both parties were happy in the end. It was just one of those things that escalated because the media, like ourselves, were just wondering what was going on. Thankfully, it all worked out in the end. He came and apologised to everyone, so there was no problem there. He said he'd done what he had to do, basically, and he was sorry if he'd offended anybody. Obviously, there were a few comments that will stay in the dressing room – they were quite smart and funny but all friendly.'

And so, after one of the most turbulent weeks in the club's recent history, a nice, gentle home fixture was required. Unfortunately, United had Stoke away. Hardly the circumstances in which to expect a first away win of the Premier League season, surely?

Barclays Premier League

**Britannia Stadium | Sunday 24 October 2010 | KO 1.30pm |
Attendance: 27,372 | Referee: Andre Marriner**

Stoke City 1 (Tuncay 81)
Manchester United 2 (Hernandez 27, 85)

United stormed Stoke's Britannia Stadium fortress for the third time in as many seasons, posting a maiden away league win of the campaign thanks to Chicharito's clinical brace.

The Mexican struck in either half, powering in a wonderful backheader and then tapping home a late winner after Tuncay had levelled for the hosts with a superb shot.

As is increasingly customary at the home of the Potters, Sir Alex favoured an experienced starting line-up; he named Gary Neville and Paul Scholes in his side, with John O'Shea at left-back and Patrice Evra shunted forward to a left-wing role. Chicharito partnered Dimitar Berbatov in attack.

After an opening 27 minutes of keenly contested posturing, the first meaningful attack of the game yielded the first goal, although it was barely even creditable as a half-chance. Nani played a one-two with Patrice Evra and crossed to the far post, Nemanja Vidic nodded the ball back into the mixer, and Chicharito – the smallest man on the park – leapt and contorted to beat Sorensen with a sweet backheader.

As United dominated, with Chicharito's energetic approach at the fore, referee Andre Marriner rose to prominence. He harshly booked Gary Neville for a foul on Matthew Etherington and then failed to caution the defender for a second time when he scythed down the same player moments later.

Neville made way at the interval for Wes Brown and still United dominated matters. Evra should have had a penalty when he was crudely shoved inside the area by Rory Delap, while Chicharito could only stretch to steer Berbatov's superb cross narrowly past the far post.

With every spurned opening, nerves frayed a little more, as memories flooded back of United's growing penchant to blow leads. Sure enough, with nine minutes left, Scholes lost possession and the ball found its way to Tuncay, who fired a stunning left-footed shot beyond van der Sar's grasp and into the top left-hand corner.

Under Sir Alex, however, United had shown on countless occasions – including in Rooney's contract negotiations – that there is no such thing as a lost cause. With five minutes remaining, a patient move culminated in Evra slashing a cross-shot across the box for Chicharito to stab home from close range.

A handful of ecstatic United fans spilled onto the pitch to celebrate with the players and their exuberance was understandable: the Reds had won away for the first time this season, in classic last-gasp fashion, to provide an immaculate finish to a turbulent week.

The Teams

Stoke City: Sorensen, Huth, Shawcross, Faye, Collins (Higginbotham 57), Pennant (Gudjohnsen 79), Wilson, Delap, Etherington, Walters (Tuncay 66), Jones
Subs not used: Begovic, Pugh, Wilkinson, Whelan
Booked: Collins, Wilson

Manchester United: van der Sar, Neville (Brown 46), Ferdinand, Vidic, O'Shea (Carrick 70), Nani, Fletcher, Scholes (Obertan 87), Evra, Berbatov, Hernandez
Subs not used: Kuszczak, Smalling, Macheda, Gibson
Booked: Neville, Scholes

'I'm working a lot because I want to stay here a long time and win a lot of tournaments,' beamed Chicharito, before going on to describe his incredible opening goal. 'I jumped and saw the ball behind me and tried to head it towards the goal. I don't remember ever doing it in training. It's a good goal but the most important thing is the result. Here there are no heroes, it is about the team.'

Like it or not, though, the Mexican was fast becoming a hero. 'He's a good person,' conceded Gary Neville. 'He works very hard and has all the attributes. He'll score lots of goals for United. When he scored that second, everyone was massively relieved. It's a great three points for us and can hopefully kick-start our away season.'

But just as the Reds had rediscovered the winning groove away from home, they were back at Old Trafford in defence of the Carling Cup. Mick McCarthy's Wolves rolled into M16 and Sir Alex, despite the top-flight opposition, planned to shuffle his pack.

'We have a big complement of players here, and Fabio, Gibson, Kiko, Obertan, Bébé, Evans and Smalling will all be involved against Wolves,' he said. 'I thought our young players did very well at Scunthorpe. We had seven chances and scored five goals. It's a great ratio – I wish I could say that every week!

'There's been a slight change this season in that we feel we should be giving some experience to the younger players in European games, too, as another stage in their progress. So it'll be a young but very capable team tonight. We've been doing that in the League Cup for quite a few years now and we've had good success in it.'

One of the youngsters promised involvement was Chris Smalling, who had an eye on playing a part in a third straight tournament success for United, especially after the exit of some major rivals in the third round. 'There's definitely a sense of the cup being there for the taking when you look at the teams that have gone out,' said the hulking defender. 'When we got back on the coach at Scunthorpe, we couldn't believe City and Chelsea had gone out and we watched Liverpool lose to Northampton. We all sense there's a good opportunity to win the trophy and that's our aim.'

Carling Cup fourth round

Old Trafford | Tuesday 26 October 2010 | KO 8.00pm |
Attendance: 46,083 | Referee: Mike Jones

Manchester United 3 (Bébé 56, Park 70, Hernandez 90)
Wolverhampton Wanderers 2 (Elokobi 60, Foley 76)

Javier Hernandez's growing stock took another huge leap when the striker clambered off the bench to nab another dramatic late winner for the Reds.

Thrown into an absorbing cup tie with ten minutes remaining, Chicharito settled matters with a beautiful shimmy and clipped finish in the final minute of normal time. Wolves, who had twice hit back to level, were shattered.

The visitors had played their part in an enthralling second half that contained almost all of the game's talking points. Indeed, the first period was notable for two efforts only: one from Kiko Macheda that thudded into Wayne Hennessey's palms, and a free-kick in a threatening position from ex-Red David Jones that cannoned against the United wall.

After the break, however, the Reds unleashed a flurry of efforts through Michael Carrick, Darron Gibson and Ji-sung Park, all of which narrowly missed the target or forced work from Hennessey. Soon, the deadlock was broken as Bébé fortuitously bagged his first United goal, watching as his cross clipped George Elokobi, looped over Hennessey and crossed the line despite the efforts of Kevin Foley.

The lead lasted all of four minutes. Wolves levelled through left-back Elokobi, who rose highest to head home a corner from the right side. Young goalkeeper Ben Amos, making only his second senior appearance, complained he had been blocked in his attempt to reach the cross, but his appeal fell on deaf ears.

As the game swung from end to end, Park atoned for his earlier miss by finishing a move he'd started outside the area with a sweeping left-footed shot into the corner of the net. But, in keeping with the to-and-fro nature of the match, Wolves soon drew level when Foley swept a low shot past Amos. The visitors then seized the initiative and Sylvan Ebanks-Blake fizzed a shot fractionally past the post.

That miss seemingly paved the way for extra time, until Chicharito, on as a substitute for Bébé, latched on to Gibson's through-ball, eluded the challenge of Steven Mouyokolo and lifted a cool finish over Hennessey to ensure the Carling Cup holders marched on.

The Teams

Manchester United: Amos, Brown, Smalling, J.Evans, Fabio (Neville 74), Bébé (Hernandez 81), Carrick, Gibson, Park (Morrison 90), Obertan, Macheda
Subs not used: Kuszczak, Rafael, Brady, Eikrem
Booked: Gibson

Wolverhampton Wanderers: Hennessey, Foley, Berra, Mouyokolo, Elokobi, Hunt, Mancienne, Jones, Jarvis (Doyle 85), Fletcher, Ebanks-Blake (Bent 80)
Subs not used: Hahnemann, van Damme, Stearman, Edwards, Milijas

'We always believe we can score,' smiled Ji-sung Park. 'When we conceded the second goal, I thought we still had time and knew we'd have great chances to score again. Everybody expected Chicha to score when he came on, and we all know he has the ability. It's important for him to keep scoring goals and we believe he can.

'We played well in the first half but couldn't finish anything. At half time we said we needed to concentrate more in the last third of the pitch. In the second half we did that and we made some great chances and scored some great goals.'

Chicharito, meanwhile, had already scored in every competition in which he'd played – Community Shield, Champions League, Premier League and now Carling Cup – and his rapid assimilation to life at United had caught everybody's eye. Tellingly, among the most impressed was a fellow predator: Michael Owen.

'It's obviously early days for him but he's made a really good impression at the club,' said the veteran marksman. 'Players will obviously score goals in teams, but I don't think there are many goalscorers around. Chicharito is one. You can see it in his eyes. It is more instinctive. You are born with it. He reminds me of myself, more so than the other strikers. You just see it in his mannerisms. There are loads of people who can score, who might even score twenty a season, but they're not goalscorers. They might be good finishers, but he's different.

'Look at my goals and his goals and you'll rarely see us curl one into the top corner from outside the box. We can do it, but it's just not a natural position for a goalscorer. You play by percentages and you score your goals inside the box. His movement suggests he knows where the ball is going to drop – you cannot teach that. He knows how to score, how to get in positions. He's a cracking lad, everyone likes him and he's great around the dressing room, which is important. The signs are great.'

Unfortunately for Owen, his own chances of making an impression were dashed by a hamstring injury that threatened to rule him out for several weeks. Fellow striker Wayne Rooney had jetted to Dubai to rest his ankle completely, Owen Hargreaves' recovery had 'stalled', according to Sir Alex, but the manager did concede Ryan Giggs should be back in training at the start of November. Giggs would be missing for the visit of high-flying Tottenham but another golden oldie, Edwin van der Sar, prepared for the game by celebrating his 40th birthday – a milestone rather than a millstone for a player who, West Brom blip aside, continued to operate at the top of his game.

'It's a great achievement,' said Michael Carrick. 'There are goalkeepers down the years who have played a lot later into their careers than outfield players, but to do it at this level and at this club is some going.'

'If he really wanted to, he could go on for another few years,' John O'Shea added. 'But obviously that's down to him and there won't be pressure from anybody at the club to make him continue. But he's in great condition, looks after himself well and trains very hard. He's incredible.'

Barclays Premier League

Old Trafford | Saturday 30 October 2010 | KO 5.30pm |
Attendance: 75,223 | Referee: Mark Clattenburg

Manchester United 2 (Vidic 31, Nani 84)
Tottenham Hotspur 0

With goals lurching from the sublime to the ridiculous, Nemanja Vidic and Nani combined to hand United a crucial victory over Tottenham Hotspur at Old Trafford.

Skipper Vidic flashed home a header from Nani's superb free-kick just after the half-hour mark, before the winger scored a bizarre second, tapping in after Heurelho Gomes had surrendered possession to take a free-kick that Mark Clattenburg and his officials had failed to award.

The goal and the farce that surrounded it detracted from an otherwise compelling game between two fine sides that started brightly and danced along at a thrilling tempo throughout.

Inside the first 90 seconds, Ji-sung Park latched on to Darren Fletcher's pass, bore down on goal and hit a low shot that slammed against Gomes' right-hand post. When Nani drew a low save from the Spurs goalkeeper moments later, Tottenham could easily have buckled under United's early pressure.

Instead they hit back. The impressive Rafael van der Vaart pounced on a Vidic slip, saw off the attentions of Michael Carrick and smashed a superb 25-yard effort against Edwin van der Sar's right-hand post.

When it came, the game's opening goal was far more simplistic, yet just as well executed. Younes Kaboul's foul on Chicharito drew a clear free-kick and a yellow card. Nani's superb delivery of the set-piece was met perfectly by Vidic who, having shed Benoit Assou-Ekotto, powered his header into the net.

The skipper's second goal of the season did little to dampen Tottenham's enthusiasm for the game, and the visitors could quickly have drawn level. Van der Vaart's chipped corner picked out Luca Modric on the edge of the United area, and the Croatian's half-volley was bound for the top corner until van der Sar superbly parried it away.

Chances began to dry up as the second half began and wore on, although Chicharito was narrowly off-target, and both Gareth Bale and Roman Pavlyuchenko sent efforts fizzing wide.

A second goal was required, but nobody could have foreseen the bizarre circumstances in which it arrived on 84 minutes. Nani was felled by Wilson Palacios inside the Spurs area, but referee Clattenburg waved play to continue, despite the winger clearly stopping the ball with his hand as he fell and began to claim a penalty. Gomes grounded the ball as if to take a free-kick, Nani noticed the ball – motionless but in open play – and looked to the referee, who gestured to play on. The winger duly did so, placing a finish under the scrambling dive of Gomes. Tottenham protested long, loud and in vain as an impromptu conference between Clattenburg and his linesman, Simon Beck, concluded the goal should stand.

They were bizarre scenes that tarnished an absorbing game, but one that had a positive outcome and, crucially, marked back-to-back Premier League wins for United for the first time in 2010–11.

The Teams

Manchester United: van der Sar, Rafael (Brown 64), Ferdinand, Vidic, Evra, Nani, Fletcher, Carrick, Park, Hernandez (Obertan 87), Berbatov (Scholes 64)
Subs not used: Kuszczak, Smalling, O'Shea, Bébé

Tottenham Hotspur: Gomes, Hutton, Gallas, Kaboul, Assou-Ekotto, Lennon, Jenas (Palacios 66), Modric, Bale, van der Vaart (Crouch 77), Keane (Pavlyuchenko 62)
Subs not used: Cudicini, Bassong, Kranjcar, Sandro
Booked: Gallas, Kaboul, Modric

'It was bizarre,' smiled Sir Alex, referencing Nani's controversial goal. 'No one knew at the time what was wrong. One minute the goalkeeper had the ball in his hands and next it's in his net. Nani looked back and looked at the referee and the referee said play on, so what can he do but put the ball in the net?

'You can look at the referee and look at the linesmen and blame them, but the goalkeeper should know better. He's an experienced goalkeeper. I thought he made a mess of it. I thought it was a penalty first of all and I think Nani felt he handled the ball. But the referee didn't blow for it. The referee played on because the goalkeeper took possession of the ball. He then went to take a free-kick thinking it was a foul. He made an error.'

For all the wild debate that circled one of the strangest goals ever witnessed at Old Trafford, the overriding issue could not be missed: United had just overcome extremely tricky, in-form opponents to string together successive wins. Though Chelsea's late win at Blackburn had started the day on a downer for the Reds, Darren Fletcher insisted the squad, as ever, would focus in-house rather than on rivals.

'We just want to take care of ourselves,' he said. 'We realised that Chelsea had scored a late goal to win, but all our focus and concentration was on the match. We can't control what Chelsea do, we can only control what Manchester United do. That's always been said by the manager and the players, so we were fully concentrated on the game and we wanted three points so we could keep going on the little run we've started.

'We've played well this season. I think the only time we haven't really played well was at Sunderland. Apart from that, in every game we've done well and if we can put a run of wins together then let's keep it going.'

With eight games on the horizon in November, United would have plenty of opportunities to build on their momentum.

5

November

A hectic month began with an arduous trek to the Champions League backwaters of Bursa in Turkey, where the Reds aimed to all but clinch qualification for the knockout stages of the competition with victory over Bursaspor.

They would have to do it without a host of major players, however. Rio Ferdinand was rested ahead of a string of vital Premier League games, Wayne Rooney continued to recover from his ankle injury in Dubai, Ryan Giggs and Michael Owen were never in contention to make the trip, and Jonny Evans and Federico Macheda had minor niggles. Meanwhile, Darron Gibson and Anderson were both struck down by a virus and stayed behind in Manchester.

The loss of both Evans and Ferdinand decreed Chris Smalling would start, but Sir Alex Ferguson had no issue with blooding the rookie defender after an impressive start to life at Old Trafford. 'Rio has come on very well in the last few weeks, but the form of Chris Smalling makes it very easy for me to play him,' he said.

'Some players come to Old Trafford and take time, but fortunately for the lad he has taken to it very quickly. He's adapted, he's receptive to training, he's intelligent. He has the physical part, he's tall, quick and a good passer of the ball. The stage we are at with him is to give him as much experience as we can.'

Champions League Group C

Ataturk Stadium | Tuesday 2 November 2010 | KO 7.45pm |
Attendance: 19,050 | Referee: Wolfgang Stark

Bursaspor 0
Manchester United 3 (Fletcher 48, Obertan 73, Bébé 77)

United edged to the brink of qualification for the Champions League knockout stages with a hard-fought 3–0 victory in Turkey, as Darren Fletcher's opener was followed by late goals for Gabriel Obertan and Bébé.

The Reds rode out a lacklustre first period before striking the all-important first blow shortly after the interval through Fletcher, and by the end were very worthy winners against the Group C underdogs.

Sir Alex, missing a host of players through injury and illness, made three changes to the side that started against Tottenham, with Chris Smalling replacing the rested Rio Ferdinand, Paul Scholes returning in central midfield and Obertan handed his second start of the campaign. Javier Hernandez and Ji-sung Park dropped to the bench, while Dimitar Berbatov led the line up front. Conversely, Bursaspor fielded a full-strength team, and they were backed to the hilt by typically fervent home support.

The Reds are well versed in playing such atmospheres, however, and a soothing start boded well, especially when Evra's impressive run and cross found Berbatov. But the Bulgarian was unable to generate enough power on his header to trouble fellow countryman Dimitar Ivankov in the Bursaspor goal.

United's gameplan was disrupted by the loss of Nani to a groin injury, while the hosts began to threaten as Volkan Sen stung the palms of van der Sar from 20 yards. Paul Scholes did beat Ivankov just before the break, only to have his goal chalked off for handball as he burst into the box en-route to slotting home.

The Reds needed only three minutes of the second period to forge ahead. As United surged forward, Carrick teed up Fletcher with a lovely, cushioned pass, which the Scot controlled and lashed low into the far corner.

Bursaspor rallied as van der Sar repelled efforts from Ivan Ergic and Federico Insua, while Ibrahim Ozturk headed wide from a corner. But United's killer goal arrived from the impressive Obertan with 17 minutes remaining. Substitute Park found the Frenchman on the left and Obertan cut inside before unleashing a devastating right-footed effort high into the net to register his first Reds goal.

The firsts kept coming. Four minutes later, Bébé latched on to a measured through-ball and the Portuguese winger raced through to toe-poke home a deflected finish for his maiden Champions League goal.

Though Nani's injury took some of the gloss off an otherwise textbook European performance, Sir Alex had much to savour as his side sat pretty in Group C. A point at Rangers on matchday five would ensure progress.

The Teams

Bursaspor: Ivankov, Tandogan, Erdogan, Ozturk, Vederson, Bahadir, Svensson, Insua (Nunez 74), Ergic, Sen (Odabasi 81), Yildirim (Ipek 74)
Subs not used: Ozkan, Has, Keceli, Stepanov

Manchester United: van der Sar, Rafael, Smalling, Vidic, Evra (Fabio 81), Obertan, Carrick, Fletcher (Bébé 63), Scholes, Nani (Park 29), Berbatov
Subs not used: Kuszczak, Brown, Hernandez, O'Shea

The importance of catching Bursaspor cold after the interval was not lost on Darren Fletcher, whose clinically taken strike calmed what could have been choppy waters for the Reds. 'I think the early goal helped,' said the Scot. 'We felt we'd created the better chances and had good possession of the ball and if we could get the first goal we could control possession and it would open up for us, and we did that. We're in a great position now with two games to go. The quicker we qualify the better.'

Though the Reds were delighted to have recorded another away victory and moved to ten points in Group C, the win had come at a price. Nani would certainly miss the visit of Wolves to Old Trafford, while Fletcher was also a doubt. Then, upon returning to Manchester, the virus that had initially affected only one or two players spread quickly through the squad, coaches and management.

'If someone picks up a cold or a virus then it spreads through the dressing room,' says John O'Shea. 'I'd seen one or two lads with this virus, then two or three days later we suddenly had ten players sat on the toilet! It was a strange scenario, but it does happen from time to time. Once, Carrington was closed for a few days and everything was fumigated. You'd think as athletes we should be more resistant to these things, but this was some kind of super-bug! The club handled it well, though. Anyone who showed signs of it was sent home and kept away, so it was managed quite well. It's scary, though, when one or two players with a bug turns into seven or eight missing. I was one of the lucky ones who avoided it.'

Michael Carrick wasn't so fortunate. The illness represented a galling setback for the midfielder, who was finally free of a trouble-some Achilles injury after visiting a specialist in September. 'I should have got something done about my Achilles sooner, because I was carrying it for a while,' he admitted. 'It's easier to say that now I've got rid of it because I feel great. But it is probably only because of how I feel now that I realise how bad it was. I feel good now and am happy with my game.'

The midfielder also rebutted claims he had a point to prove after struggling to hit top form in the early part of the season. 'I didn't think I had to answer any critics,' he declared. 'The only opinions that count are those of the manager and the staff. You just have to brush aside the rest of it and believe in yourself.

'I know when I'm not playing well. I wasn't hitting my best form so I couldn't argue about the teams the manager was picking. I'm not big enough to be saying I should be playing every game, so it was up to me to play well again. You have to stay positive. I knew things would come good and I'm enjoying my football again now.'

The virus ensured Carrick's ascent to form was put on hold, but the midfielder's absence from the squad to face Wolverhampton Wanderers opened the door for an unlikely returnee. Owen Hargreaves, whose contribution to the 2009–10 campaign amounted to an injury-time cameo at Sunderland in May 2010, had been training without side-effect for more than a week, was clear of illness and had thrust himself into contention for a start against Wolves.

Meanwhile, Wayne Rooney, now back from holiday in Dubai, would be clocking up further air miles with a week-long trip to America – specifically, Nike Town in Oregon – where the striker would undergo rigorous conditioning work to hasten his return to full fitness and see off his pressing ankle concerns.

Not that Sir Alex could share the news at his pre-match press conference. Even the manager had succumbed to the bug, leaving Mike Phelan to explain the situation to the media. '[Sir Alex] came down with a virus yesterday. He felt a little bit like that on the flight coming back from Turkey,' said the Reds' assistant manager. 'Yesterday he felt worse, so we've kept him away from the club for a little while. It's related to the virus that's been going around. It's one of those things that gets hold of you and is hard to shake off, but he will be at the game tomorrow.'

With players dropping in and out of contention to play, Sir Alex's was seemingly the only guaranteed presence.

Barclays Premier League

Old Trafford | Saturday 6 November 2010 | KO 3.00pm |
Attendance: 75,285 | Referee: Phil Dowd

Manchester United 2 (Park 45, 90)
Wolverhampton Wanderers 1 (Ebanks-Blake 66)

The sign of potential champions? Shorn of several key players through illness and injury, and facing a well-drilled Wolverhampton Wanderers side, the Reds negated a disjointed display to take the spoils thanks to Ji-sung Park's injury-time winner.

The South Korean, whose first-half opener had been cancelled out by ex-Red Sylvan Ebanks-Blake, slotted inside Marcus Hahnemann's near post in the third of four added minutes to send Old Trafford wild and extend United's winning run to six games in all competitions.

For long periods, it seemed the virus that had swept through Carrington would prove costly, while the mood inside Old Trafford was further dampened when surprise recall Owen Hargreaves was substituted with an early hamstring injury. The 29-year-old lasted barely four minutes on his return, pulling his left hamstring as he flicked a cross into the visitors' penalty area. He was soon replaced by Bébé, and received a warm ovation as he limped towards the home dressing room.

Given the patched-up nature of United's side, Wolves looked to seize on any weaknesses early and pressed aggressively. The Reds briefly sparked into life around the quarter-hour mark, as Bébé and Park both tried their luck, only to find visiting defenders hurtling towards their efforts. Far closer was Nenad Milijas' effort at the other end, which took a sizeable deflection off Nemanja Vidic and crept just wide.

The visitors were left to rue that close call as United took the lead in the final minute of the half. Gaining possession on the left,

Fletcher advanced infield and slipped a fine pass to Park, who steadied himself before finishing past the exposed Hahnemann.

Suitably buoyed, United bossed the majority of the second period, but were pegged back when substitute Ebanks-Blake latched onto Milijas' half-hit shot, turned away from Vidic and slotted a close-range shot between van der Sar's legs. Game on, and a hush gripped Old Trafford when another substitute, Steven Fletcher, slashed an effort hopelessly over the bar from ten yards in the dying stages.

Time remained, however, for United to snatch victory. In the 93rd minute, Park declined the invitation to sling a cross into a packed penalty area and instead meandered into it, outfoxed a pack of defenders and slipped a low shot inside Hahnemann's near post. Old Trafford turned feral in response, bellowing its delight at the latest example of the indefatigable spirit that defines United.

The Teams

Manchester United: van der Sar, Brown, Ferdinand, Vidic, Evra, Hargreaves (Bébé 9 (Macheda 74)), Fletcher, O'Shea (Scholes 74), Park, Obertan, Hernandez
Subs not used: Kuszczak, Smalling, Fabio, J.Evans
Booked: Hernandez

Wolverhampton Wanderers: Hahnemann, Foley, Berra, Stearman, Ward, Hunt (Ebanks-Blake 64), Edwards (Fletcher 64), Milijas (Mancienne 77), Henry, Jarvis, Doyle
Subs not used: Hennessey, van Damme, Elokobi, Mouyokolo

'We've done it so many times and you have to admire the perseverance of the team, the never-say-die spirit,' marvelled Sir Alex Ferguson. 'It was a long struggle. Given the changes I had to make, trying to get the continuity of performance was difficult today. I thought Wolves were the better team in the first half, but we got a great goal right on half time and I thought that would settle us. In the second half, we lost a bad goal but went on to get a late winner.

'Some players played with touches of flu and others with diarrhoea, so we've done really well to get a result. This morning we had to check on Patrice Evra, Paul Scholes and Nemanja Vidic, who were all under the weather. Nemanja, in particular, did well to play. Patrice battled on and I was only going to use Paul if I needed to. I did need to and he did well.'

With Owen Hargreaves once again consigned to the treatment room, the rest of the squad were devastated to see him trudge away from his comeback game. 'We were gutted for Owen,' says John O'Shea. 'He was looking good in training. His involvement had to be managed, of course – he wasn't just going to go straight back into full-blown training every day, and when he was training he looked great. That's why the manager put him back in. On the day, given the occasion, the adrenaline was pumping so much for him that he went out and did his hamstring. It was incredible, just so unlucky.

'I worked with Owen a lot last season when I was out for a few months, and I know the work he had put in, and has continued to put in, to get back to full fitness. We were all absolutely buzzing for him to get the start and he'd looked ready to kick on again. It was just so frustrating for him. It's not as if he's done anything wrong to keep having setbacks; his rehab work has been incredible. He travelled everywhere to get the best advice, and with the advice he got he put everything in. It's just so frustrating for the lad because you think back to what a player he was for us when he was fully fit. Fingers crossed he can get back to playing football.'

With just four days until the looming Manchester derby at Eastlands, Hargreaves was among a mass of players set to miss out on the short trip across the city. Still the virus affected the squad, and Sir Alex could only hold his breath, cross his fingers and hope the majority of his players recovered in time to face Roberto Mancini's Blues. 'We've no idea at all on a side,' he confessed. 'We've

United's huge travelling party prepares to jet off for an epic pre-season trip to America, Mexico and Ireland.

Texas' Reliant Stadium is packed as United hammer the MLS All-Stars to round off the US tour in style.

Goalkeepers Edwin van der Sar, Ben Amos and Tomasz Kuszczak unwind at NASA headquarters in Houston.

The Reds delight in snapping up the first silverware of the season, as Chelsea are deservedly beaten in the Community Shield.

Darren Fletcher celebrates hitting the killer second goal as United's Premier League assault begins with a win over Newcastle.

Nani curses his missed penalty as Brede Hangeland is mobbed for heading Fulham's late equaliser at Craven Cottage.

A stunned Old Trafford watches on as Dimitar Berbatov hits a wonderful overhead kick against Liverpool, en route to a hat-trick.

Against Rangers, Antonio Valencia lies stricken with an horrific ankle injury that sidelined him until March.

After a surreal week, Wayne Rooney poses with Sir Alex Ferguson to celebrate signing a new United contract.

Chicharito contorts to head a brilliant opener at Stoke, as United finally register an away league win.

Tottenham's irate players mob the officials at Old Trafford, after Nani's highly contentious clincher for United.

Ji-sung Park cannot escape his jubilant colleagues after snatching a last-gasp winner against Wolves.

Rafael da Silva squares up to ex-Red Carlos Tevez at Eastlands, in an otherwise drab derby encounter.

Skipper Nemanja Vidic goes wild after levelling matters at Aston Villa, where United had looked destined for defeat.

A five-fingered salute from Dimitar Berbatov marks the striker's quintet against Blackburn Rovers at Old Trafford.

Sir Alex Ferguson watches on as United's grip on the Carling Cup finally slips at a snow-swept Upton Park.

Ji-sung Park again proves the man for the big occasion, heading home the only goal of the game against Arsenal.

still got some players out with 'flu and we've sent some players home. We're not in a good position at the moment. Ryan Giggs is out. Nani is doubtful. It's not a great position for us to be in. We are counting heads at the moment, but we have a strong squad. We just carry on.'

United had successfully reminded their near neighbours of the local pecking order with a league double and a Carling Cup semi-final success in 2009–10, and Sir Alex conceded the fixture had undergone an escalation from neighbourhood spat to international spectacle since City's establishment as a financially mighty rival.

'The Liverpool game is one of honour in terms of trophies won,' he said, assessing the comparative status of United's rivalries. 'We are undoubtedly the two most successful clubs in British football. Now the meetings with City are ones of great intensity, which is built up by the media explosion around what they are doing and what they are trying to achieve. The fact we are both in the same city means there is an incredible intensity in this derby game now, which was not there ten or fifteen years ago.'

For once, the manager's words would not prove prophetic.

Barclays Premier League

**Eastlands | Wednesday 10 November 2010 | KO 8.00pm |
Attendance: 47,679 | Referee: Chris Foy**

Manchester City 0
Manchester United 0

It's fair to say a drab Manchester derby was due, given the oodles of entertainment and drama served up across four helpings in 2009–10.

With City hamstrung by cautious tactics, and injury-hit United equally averse to the concept of heading back across the city without a point, a draw looked likely from the first whistle.

Mercifully, Sir Alex was able to call upon the majority of those players struck by the Carrington virus. Just 48 hours earlier, he had been pondering whether or not he would have enough fit players to put together a full match-day squad. Sadly, Ryan Giggs failed to overcome his hamstring strain and missed his first derby since 1991, curtailing a run of 33 successive derby appearances.

He picked the right one to miss. Neither side could create a telling opening in the first period, with Ji-sung Park, Nani and Patrice Evra hitting the target without ever stretching Joe Hart, while Carlos Tevez's curling free-kick extended Edwin van der Sar into his only save of the half.

A dead leg for Rafael prompted the introduction of Wes Brown shortly after half time, and the substitute's cross was met spectacularly by Dimitar Berbatov, only for his scissor-kick to hurtle straight at Hart. In riposte, Tevez scuffed a shot straight at van der Sar in the first end-to-end exchange of the game. Sadly, it was also the last.

Evra made way for John O'Shea on 69 minutes after succumbing to an ankle injury suffered in the first period, while Roberto Mancini introduced Adam Johnson for James Milner down the same flank. Sir Alex then traded Berbatov for Chicharito, after the Bulgarian began to tire in a thankless lone-striker role.

Neither side committed enough numbers forward to launch a true assault on victory, but Eastlands was nevertheless gripped by a hushed dread as the game entered injury time. United, sensing the inevitability in the home side's mood, did press on in search of yet another last-gasp winner, only for time to run out.

And so both sides were left with the bare minimum they had coveted pre-match: a point.

The Teams

Manchester City: Hart, Boateng (Kolarov 80), K.Toure, Kompany, Zabaleta, Milner (Johnson 72), Y.Toure, de Jong, Barry, Silva, Tevez (Adebayor 90)
Subs not used: Given, Richards, Lescott, Vieira

Manchester United: van der Sar, Rafael (Brown 48), Ferdinand, Vidic, Evra (O'Shea 67), Nani, Fletcher, Carrick, Scholes, Park, Berbatov (Hernandez 77)
Subs not used: Amos, Smalling, Obertan, Gibson
Booked: Brown, Scholes

'I think today was a real derby game,' admitted Nemanja Vidic. 'We saw two teams who were defending very well and I think it was a fair result. There was a big pressure for City to win and for us this is always a difficult place to come. We came here to win the game, but City were good today – they played well and we didn't have too many chances. Our target is always to win the game and even this time we are disappointed not to. At times we played some good football, but we didn't create many chances.'

'The game was quite one-sided and City didn't really come forward and leave their defensive position,' added Edwin van der Sar. 'They were clearly aiming for a point, whereas we really wanted to win and we played like that. They were more defensive and I didn't have much to do apart from a free-kick. If the game had lasted longer, we might have got more from it and I don't think it was a good point for us.'

Seldom are stalemates savoured at Carrington. While United were attracting headlines for remaining unbeaten well into the season, Darren Fletcher conceded the squad would rather have traded those draws for a mixture of wins and losses. 'People are talking about us not losing, but we have drawn too many, especially away from home,' said the Scot. 'We have to start winning our away games if we want to push up this league. Overall, you would be better winning two games out of three and losing the other one, rather than winning one and drawing two. That's why we were disappointed on Wednesday. We could have got the win and felt we produced a performance good enough to get us one.'

For all United's away-day travails, the prospect of visiting Villa Park, the setting for so many famous memories for the Reds, carried no foreboding. Not since August 1995 had Sir Alex Ferguson's side tasted defeat there. 'It's a really good ground to play at,' said Fletcher. 'It's a fantastic setting that has a good feel to it. The pitch is always good and every match seems like a big occasion. You can't explain why you have a good record at some grounds and not others, but the important thing is not to take it for granted. We can't just expect to win because it's Villa Park.'

Barclays Premier League

Villa Park | Saturday 13 November 2010 | KO 12.45pm |
Attendance: 40,073 | Referee: Mike Dean

Aston Villa 2 (A.Young (pen) 72, Albrighton 76)
Manchester United 2 (Macheda 81, Vidic 85)

Despite toiling in vain and looking second best against a youthful Villa side for the majority of the game, United's innate failure to accept defeat yielded an unlikely late surge and a share of the spoils in Birmingham.

The Reds had somehow maintained parity for 72 minutes, despite being ravaged by the plucky young hosts, then conceded twice in four minutes before roaring back to level quickly and, incredibly, almost pinch victory late on.

The pulsating clash was in complete contrast to the dreariness of Eastlands, as two injury-hit sides went toe to toe. Alas, for United, the outcome was the same: another away draw and two dropped points.

While Sir Alex's men were dominant in possession early on, Villa's young team, laced with familiar faces from recent Reserve team meetings with the Reds, did their utmost to match United's endeavours during a somewhat scrappy first half. As both sides traded effort at the expense of quality, the only glaring chance of the first period fell to Dimitar Berbatov, who fired wide after being released by Chicharito.

Villa finished the half strongly and began the second period on top, with Marc Albrighton lashing into the side netting and then guiding a header wastefully wide of Edwin van der Sar's far post. Then, in a matter of seconds, James Collins headed an Ashley Young corner against the bar and Gabriel Agbonlahor thumped a shot against the upright.

United were reeling and it was no surprise when the hosts moved ahead. Chasing a cross from Agbonlahor, Young was sent tumbling in the area under a challenge from Wes Brown. Penalty. Young dusted himself down to send van der Sar the wrong way.

Sir Alex responded by introducing Kiko Macheda and Gabriel Obertan for Berbatov and Javier Hernandez, but the situation soon worsened as Stewart Downing crossed to the back post for Albrighton to slot home from five yards.

Somehow, the double deficit galvanised United and sent Villa into panic. Macheda provided a lifeline nine minutes from time when he fired a stunning effort into the top corner after a neat lay-off from Darren Fletcher.

Five minutes from time the Reds drew level, as Nani meandered down the left, cut back and whipped over a peach of a cross that Nemanja Vidic stooped to head into the far corner. Now Villa were reeling. Obertan almost nicked victory soon afterwards, as his shot rebounded to safety off Brad Friedel's chest, but time ran out on the unlikeliest of comebacks. Instead, United could reflect on a hard-earned point with a blend of elation and frustration.

The Teams

Aston Villa: Friedel, L.Young, Dunne, Collins, Warnock, Albrighton (Lichaj 88), Bannan, Hogg (Herd 89), Downing, Agbonlahor (Delfouneso 78), A.Young
Subs not used: Guzan, Osbourne, Lowry, Johnson
Booked: Bannan, A.Young, L.Young

Manchester United: van der Sar, Brown, Ferdinand, Vidic, Evra, Nani, Carrick, Fletcher, Park (Smalling 86), Berbatov (Obertan 73), Hernandez (Macheda 73)
Subs not used: Amos, Fabio, O'Shea, Gibson
Booked: Brown, Hernandez, Nani, Vidic

'We could have lost six goals in the second half,' admitted a bewildered Sir Alex Ferguson at full time. 'They hit the woodwork three times and Albrighton missed two great chances. We were all over the place. I think the way Villa played kept them at a high boiling point. Some of the tackling was fair, some of it wasn't, but the referee allowed things to go and sometimes that makes a great game.

'I think we've seen a great game today. Great credit to Aston Villa. They got stuck in, tackled, fought and the crowd kept them going. To be 2–0 down with ten minutes to go and get a point, we have to be pleased with that. With another five minutes we would have won the match, there was no doubt about that, but we waited too long to get there.'

Despite the rousing manner of the fightback, there was no escaping the fact that six wins and seven draws from the opening 13 league games did not constitute an impressive record. Hopes that the Reds would soon return to more conventional, clinical form were boosted by the return of Wayne Rooney from Nike Town.

'It was exactly what I needed,' said the striker. 'I needed to get away and get my fitness up. I got injured at the club and the medical team took the decision to send me off to Dubai and then to America. I had time off because the club gave me time off. There was no training for me to do back home.

'The media made a big thing about it. They said I shouldn't have gone away. It's happened to other players in the past. I went out there with a guy from the Manchester United medical team and we worked very hard. It was really intense fitness training.

'We'd start at nine a.m. and not get back until either six or seven o'clock. It was just what I needed because I wanted to make sure I was ready to come straight back into the team. I didn't want to take four, five or six games to get my fitness back.'

'Hopefully Wazza will come back and be the Wazza we remember. That is what everyone is hoping,' admitted Rio Ferdinand. 'We all hope he comes back in great shape and ready to play for Manchester United and England. A fit Rooney is one of the best players in the world.'

The return was hardly news to warm the cockles of anybody affiliated with United's next opponents, Wigan Athletic. But the prospect of Rooney running out at Old Trafford again threw up an intriguing sub-plot: just how would the home support react to the striker's public questioning of the club's ambition?

'I think the evidence will be on the football pitch,' speculated Sir Alex. 'We want to get Wayne to his best. When that happens, everything will be okay.'

Barclays Premier League

**Old Trafford | Saturday 20 November 2010 | KO 3.00pm |
Attendance: 74,181 | Referee: Martin Atkinson**

Manchester United 2 (Evra 45, Hernandez 77)
Wigan Athletic 0

United moved level on points with champions Chelsea at the top of the table after a routine victory over stubborn Wigan Athletic, who were reduced to nine men in the second period.

A rare goal from Patrice Evra enriched a dreary first period, then Antolin Alcaraz and Hugo Rodallega were needlessly sent off before substitute Javier Hernandez added a second with little more than ten minutes to go.

Defeats for Arsenal and Chelsea provided a timely double boost, while the sight of Wayne Rooney back on the bench after a month on the sidelines also gave cause for optimism. From the off, however, Gabriel Obertan supported Kiko Macheda in attack, after the duo had inspired United's turnaround at Villa Park a week earlier.

Wigan's gameplan was one of containment, allowing United plenty of possession in wide or deep areas, but seldom vacating the penalty area. Ali Al Habsi was forced into a decent save by Nani's dipping drive, but the Portuguese was at his most threatening from set-pieces, which posed questions aplenty of the resolute visitors. Sadly for United, Wigan had the answers and seemed far from troubled for the majority of the first period. Then, on the stroke of half time, came an unlikely breakthrough.

Just as murmurs of discontent were emanating from a home support well aware of the need to exploit slips from the other title challengers, Ji-sung Park swung a deep cross to the back post where Evra hung in the air and directed a clinical diving header back towards the far corner to register his third United goal.

Still Wigan would not open up in search of a comeback. Rooney was introduced just before the hour mark as part of a double substitution – he and Paul Scholes replaced Macheda and Park – but it was a double setback of a different kind that cost the visitors any slim hopes of a point, as Alcaraz received his second yellow card for a late challenge on Fletcher. Rodallega soon followed with a straight red for a two-footed lunge on Rafael.

Sir Alex's response was swift, throwing on Hernandez for Michael Carrick. Just 13 minutes after his introduction, the Mexican sealed victory by latching on to Rafael's cross and steering home an unstoppable diving header at the Stretford End.

Nani and Chicharito both narrowly missed another Rafael cross, Rooney missed a sitter and Evra fired wide as the Reds racked up and missed chances aplenty in the dying stages. By then, though, a potentially pivotal win had already been secured.

The Teams

Manchester United: van der Sar, Rafael, Ferdinand, Vidic, Evra, Nani, Fletcher, Carrick (Hernandez 64), Park (Scholes 56), Obertan, Macheda (Rooney 56)
Subs not used: Kuszczak, Giggs, O'Shea, J.Evans

Wigan Athletic: Al Habsi, Gohouri, Caldwell, Alcaraz, Figueroa, Thomas, Diame, Stam (McArthur 80), Gomez (Moses 58), N'Zogbia (di Santo 80), Rodallega
Subs not used: Pollitt, Watson, Boselli, McManaman
Booked: Diame
Sent off: Alcaraz, Rodallega

'I don't think my son was even born the last time I scored a goal for United,' Patrice Evra joked after his unlikely goalscoring heroics. 'It was a good cross from my best friend Ji-sung Park. I think I'll get him a big present for Christmas – maybe a car!

'I said before the game that if we beat Wigan and Blackburn next week, we would be top of the league and I am still confident of that. But I think the team can give much more than we are giving right now. We are still at the top, but against Blackburn we need to play from the first minute, not just at the end of the game. We are Manchester United and we need to be more aggressive and score more goals.'

Sir Alex Ferguson was quick to agree with the Frenchman: there was still room for plenty of improvement. 'What I'm finding is that we seem to be playing a lot of our best football in the last twenty minutes of games,' said the manager. 'We need to get more quickness in our play in the first half of matches. I thought we were a bit slow in our build-up. We really could have done our goal difference a power of good in the last twenty minutes. We missed a lot of chances and we could have had five or six, easily. It was not a great performance – [it was] competent and nothing more. We know ourselves that come the second half of the season we will get better.'

The return of Wayne Rooney was met with a largely encouraging response from the home support. It was a promising positive in his first outing since signing a new deal, and both the striker and his manager declared themselves satisfied afterwards.

'It was brilliant,' said Rooney. 'I can understand fans' frustrations with the contract negotiations; obviously it happened in the public eye, which made it more difficult. But at the end of the day, the main thing for myself and the club is that we managed to agree that deal. I've signed a new deal to stay here and my long-term future is at United.'

'It was a good reception; it will be pleasing for him,' concurred Sir Alex. 'It will settle him down and make him realise he is at the right club. It was a quiet comeback. He got involved in a few bits of the interplay. He needed twenty-five minutes or so. He will play against Rangers on Wednesday – that's the perfect game for him to come back and get ninety minutes.'

Rooney could expect an altogether different welcome from the home support at an invariably raucous, effervescent Ibrox. From sampling the din at Celtic Park in previous Champions League trips north of the border, Ji-sung Park knew to pack his earplugs.

'The atmosphere in the stadium is totally different,' he said. 'You cannot compare it to a league game or others in the Champions League. It's more aggressive on the pitch and the atmosphere in the stadium is really high. There is a lot more media attention as well. Nobody has to say anything – it is just a natural feeling that this is a different game. And it doesn't only apply to the British players. It is equally special for the foreign ones as well.'

Champions League Group C

Ibrox Stadium | Wednesday 24 November 2010 | KO 7.45pm |
Attendance: 49,764 | Referee: Massimo Busacca

Rangers 0
Manchester United 1 (Rooney (pen) 87)

Wayne Rooney marked his first start in almost two months with a coolly converted late penalty to book United's passage to the Champions League knockout phase.

For long periods, the game seemed destined to end in a repeat of September's stalemate at Old Trafford – albeit slightly more entertaining than that fixture – before Steven Naismith felled Fabio inside the penalty area, handing Rooney the chance to crack home the spot-kick and spark wild celebrations with the away support.

Again, United had to withstand little attacking thrust from Walter Smith's Gers. An unfamiliar back four of John O'Shea, Jonny Evans, Chris Smalling and Fabio repelled the hosts all evening, and comfortably calmed the baying home support. The atmosphere was almost killed inside two minutes when Dimitar Berbatov was clearly tripped, only for no penalty to be awarded.

As United continued to make all the running, Berbatov then headed Fabio's cross straight at Allan McGregor in the Rangers goal, before Rooney glanced another cross from the Brazilian onto the hosts' crossbar. Despite dominating, the Reds were almost behind at the interval as Kenny Miller shot against Edwin van der Sar from a tight angle.

After the break, Rooney curled a free-kick wide of the target from 30 yards before teeing up Michael Carrick for an opening that the midfielder blasted straight at McGregor, who nevertheless saved impressively. The Scottish international then collected Berbatov's low shot as United upped the ante.

A mix-up between Evans and van der Sar almost let in Steven Naismith in a rare Rangers attack, but the Reds survived and continued to dictate the pace of the game, penning the hosts back for long periods and eventually making the breakthrough when Naismith clumsily kicked Fabio in the chest inside the area.

The stage was set for Rooney to wrap up the evening, which he duly did before embarking on a joyous bellowing celebration in front of the away fans. One supporter even vaulted the hoardings to personally welcome the striker back to the fold. After all, he had been missed.

The Teams

Rangers: McGregor, Davis, Foster, Broadfoot, Weir, Whittaker, Naismith, McCulloch, Hutton (Beattie 88), Weiss (Fleck 80), Miller
Subs not used: Alexander, Perry, Wylde, Loy
Booked: Hutton, Naismith, Whittaker

Manchester United: van der Sar, O'Shea, Smalling, J.Evans, Fabio, Nani (Obertan 76), Carrick, Scholes (Anderson 67), Giggs, Berbatov (Hernandez 76), Rooney
Subs not used: Amos, Evra, Brown, Macheda

'It took a lot of courage to take the penalty kick,' Sir Alex said of Wayne Rooney's nerve-shredding late winner. 'It was not an easy night and he missed a couple of chances, but that's what you expect with the rustiness in his game. He's got a bit to go. We are pleased for him.'

'Obviously it is a bit of a relief for me to score,' Rooney admitted. 'Hopefully I can build on this now. There were not many nerves. I knew what I was doing and where I was going. I can only do that. If the keeper guesses the right way and saves it, so be it. Thankfully it went in. I wanted to celebrate with our fans. Hopefully I can go on a goal-scoring run now, but I'm just delighted to be back playing again. I want to build on this performance and this goal.'

'Now we want to go and win the group,' added Sir Alex. 'We've got Valencia at home and we can look forward to that. We knew it was going to be tough here. Rangers were organised and disciplined and very difficult to break down. Our away form in Europe has been good over the years and I think we deserved to win it tonight.'

The boss also confirmed rumours, sparked by Scandinavian press reports, that the Reds were set to sign Danish goalkeeper Anders Lindegaard from Norwegian side Aalesunds, although he denied the deal was already tied up, saying: 'It's not completed at the moment but there hasn't been a hiccup, either. It will probably happen in the next two or three weeks, but the announcement was a bit premature.' Danish international Lindegaard, 26, would arrive at the start of December and be confined to the training ground for a month before he could formalise his transfer and be available to play in January.

In the meantime, the return to goalscoring form of Rooney seemed promising, especially after indications at Ibrox that the striker's on-field understanding with fellow striker Dimitar Berbatov remained sharp. Coaxing Rooney back towards top form and extending Berbatov's impressive early-season displays were uppermost on Sir Alex's agenda.

'In fairness to Dimitar, we've been changing the strike partners quite a lot this season,' he said. 'I have to accept responsibility for that. We've got a lot of good, young options who have played in a lot of games recently, players like Javier Hernandez, Federico Macheda and Gabriel Obertan. But Dimitar is suited to playing with Wayne. We hope we can get Wayne back to his best.'

The strike duo were likely to be paired again against Blackburn Rovers at Old Trafford, as the Reds resumed the quest for a 19th top-flight title. A spate of missed opportunities away from home had not proven too costly, with Chelsea and Arsenal dropping points with reckless abandon. Indeed, United remained the only unbeaten team in the division.

'It's important we have qualified for the knockout phase of the Champions League,' said Nemanja Vidic. 'We are very happy. Now we can focus more on the Premier League. We are on top, level on points with Chelsea, but we would like to have more points than we do. Still, it is not bad that we haven't lost a game. I'm surprised at where we are, although this year teams are better and are competing more against the top four or five. The top five have all lost so many points, but there is still a long way to go. If someone had told us we would have this many points at this stage of the season we would have been disappointed. Now we have a tough game against Blackburn, but we are not in a bad position.'

United completed the deal to sign Anders Lindegaard the day before Blackburn's visit, and the Danish international was an enthralled onlooker as his new club put on a show to remember against the visitors.

Barclays Premier League

**Old Trafford | Saturday 27 November 2010 | KO 3.00pm |
Attendance: 74,580 | Referee: Lee Probert**

Manchester United 7 (Berbatov 2, 27, 47, 62, 70, Park 23, Nani 48)
Blackburn Rovers 1 (Samba 83)

Dimitar Berbatov wrote himself into United folklore with a five-star display at Old Trafford as the Reds tore apart Sam Allardyce's Blackburn.

The Bulgarian netted an incredible five times, while Ji-sung Park and Nani were also on target as the Reds smashed seven goals to surge to the top of the Barclays Premier League table.

United's outstanding performance of the season, and biggest win since April 2007, stemmed from excellence in every position. The back five were imperious, while the midfield exuded energy and purpose, with Wayne Rooney steadily approaching his influential best. At the heart of everything good, however, was Berbatov.

He and Rooney took little more than a minute to combine for the Reds' first goal. Rooney outjumped his marker at the near post to meet Nani's cross and his glancing header fell to Berbatov, who volleyed home a simple finish from six yards to bag his first goal since completing a hat-trick against Liverpool in September.

Cheered by the early breakthrough, Sir Alex's men set about their visitors and a second goal duly arrived on 23 minutes. Park carried the ball forward from the left flank, exchanged passes with

Rooney and clipped an unerring finish over Paul Robinson. Five minutes later, Blackburn sealed their own demise as Pascal Chimbonda teed up Berbatov, who advanced on goal and blasted home a finish.

United were unstoppable. A procession of chances came and went in the remainder of the first half, but a pair were taken within three minutes of the restart. Berbatov wrapped up his hat-trick by side-footing the ball home from 12 yards to complete a stunning team move he'd started himself deep inside United's half. Nani then made it 5–0 when he twisted and turned inside the area before shooting into the far corner.

Clearly revelling in one of those rare occasions where everything falls into place, there was no easing off from United. Berbatov grabbed his fourth and fifth goals with a pair of close-range tap-ins inside 70 minutes, while substitute Gabriel Obertan came close to piling on more misery with a finish that inched wide. Chris Samba headed a goal back for the visitors before a fine save from Robinson denied Berbatov a sixth and the honour of becoming the first double-hat-trick scorer of the Premier League era.

Not that the Bulgarian cared a jot, of course. His face was tattooed with joy as he and his jubilant team-mates left the field at full time, savouring a truly special afternoon's work.

The Teams

Manchester United: van der Sar, Rafael, Ferdinand, Vidic (J.Evans 63), Evra, Nani, Carrick, Anderson, Park (Obertan 72), Berbatov, Rooney
Subs not used: Kuszczak, Giggs, Hernandez, O'Shea, Fletcher

Blackburn Rovers: Robinson, Salgado, Samba, Nelsen, Chimbonda, Jones, Emerton (Linganzi 51), Dunn, Goulon (Hoilett 28), Diouf (Morris 51), Roberts
Subs not used: Bunn, Givet, Hanley, Mwaruwari
Booked: Diouf, Salgado

'I can't believe it,' grinned Dimitar Berbatov, clutching the match ball signed by his team-mates. 'I scored five in a game . . . it happened! I have scored that many before, but it was a long time ago, back home in Bulgaria. Today I did it in the Premier League. To stand next to people like Andy Cole and Alan Shearer [in the record books] is a great honour. The first goal was the most important. It gives you the confidence to play. As a striker, people tend only to look at the goals you score. I am more concerned with how I play, but today it was all about goals for me.'

All the plaudits were directed at the Bulgarian. 'Dimitar's performance was great,' smiled Michael Carrick. 'His goals were of the highest order. The one just after half time when he played the one-twos is up there for the goal of the season. It was something special. We all know scoring five in a game doesn't happen very often, so I am really pleased for him.'

'It was a fantastic achievement,' echoed Sir Alex. 'He could have scored six, too, because Paul Robinson made a fantastic save near the end. When strikers are not scoring they don't think they are doing their job right. That has always been the case.'

With spirits soaring among the players, it was with excitement rather than trepidation that they met the news that Liverpool would be United's FA Cup third round opponents at Old Trafford. But Sir Alex's men scarcely had time to dwell on the news, as a trip to East London for another cup tie – a Carling Cup quarter-final clash with West Ham – beckoned.

The boss was again expected to use the match to blood youngsters and hand playing time to those in most need. One of them, Chris Smalling, was eager to take advantage of several high-profile teams exiting the competition early and march on to the semi-finals. 'When so many big teams went out, we knew we had a good chance to go all the way,' said the defender. 'For a lot of us new boys who don't play that often, it's great to be part of a cup run. It's great experience and we don't want it to end.'

Carling Cup fifth round

Upton Park | Tuesday 30 November 2010 | KO 7.45pm |
Attendance: 33,551 | Referee: Mark Clattenburg

West Ham United 4 (Spector 22, 36, Cole 55, 66)
Manchester United 0

All good things come to an end. United's first defeat in 29 games, the maiden loss for the season and a first Carling Cup reverse in more than three years were all brought about by a sound thrashing at Upton Park.

Following the heady brilliance of demolishing Blackburn, a much-changed United side were disjointed throughout a comprehensive 4–0 drubbing by a hungry, well-drilled Hammers team.

From the line-up that overcame Rovers, only Anderson survived the strategic cull. The Brazilian had been a model of busy brilliance three days earlier and Sir Alex sought to extend his fine form with another fitness-honing run-out on a snow-dusted Upton Park.

The evening began in promising fashion for United, who almost took the lead through Gabriel Obertan. John O'Shea picked out the Frenchman, who took two touches to create space for a shot that Rob Green brilliantly tipped on to the post. Javier Hernandez slid in at the far post for the rebound, but James Tomkins beat the Mexican to the ball.

United appeared in total control, with both midfield and defence confidently keeping possession. But on 17 minutes, ex-Red Jonathan Spector had a goal chalked off for offside and the tide turned. Almost immediately, the American nodded Victor Obinna's cross past a stranded Tomasz Kuszczak to nudge the hosts ahead.

Ryan Giggs planted a free header straight at Green as the Reds sought to rally, but instead it was the hosts who struck next. Bizarrely, Spector was again the scorer, breaking through midfield and capitalising on defensive uncertainty to turn home only his second goal in English football, hot on the heels of the first.

Sir Alex promptly changed both personnel and formation at half time, introducing Kiko Macheda for Bébé and moving to a 4–4–2 approach. While the Reds' mood and purpose seemed galvanised, the hosts were reluctant to surrender their lead. Instead, they built on it as Carlton Cole reached Obinna's cross before Evans and nodded the killer goal past Kuszczak.

However much United pressed forward, there was never a sense that a comeback was on the cards. West Ham, conversely, always looked like adding to the scoreline, which they duly did when Cole again got in front of Evans to beat Kuszczak with a left-footed strike into the far corner.

Chicharito clipped a shot off the top of Green's bar with United's outstanding effort of the second half but, sadly, the Reds' reign as holders went with a whimper rather than a bang.

The Teams

West Ham United: Green, Faubert, Tomkins (Reid 74), Upson, Ben-Haim, Barrera (Hines 76), Spector, Kovac, Boa Morte, Obinna, Cole (Stanislas 89)
Subs not used: Boffin, Parker, McCarthy, Piquionne
Booked: Reid

Manchester United: Kuszczak, O'Shea, Smalling, J.Evans (Brown 72), Fabio (Rafael 65), Obertan, Anderson, Giggs, Fletcher, Bébé (Macheda 46), Hernandez
Subs not used: Amos, Carrick, Park, Eikrem

'Things could have been different had that shot from Gabby Obertan gone in,' rued Ryan Giggs. 'We started the game pretty well, but that shot didn't fall for us – it hit the post. Then West Ham scored shortly afterwards and that knocked the stuffing out of us. Whenever you come to West Ham, no matter how they're doing, it's always a tough game and they always want to beat us. Even though they're not doing so well in the league, the crowd gets behind them.

'It was disappointing to lose 4–0, though. We came here confident we could win. West Ham played well – you have to give them credit – and they scored some good goals, but we feel we could have defended those goals a lot better. Disappointment can help you, though. It doesn't feel good at the moment, but hopefully the young players who have experienced this can learn from it. Next time they're playing, they'll be determined to improve their performance and get a better result. We're Manchester United and we have to rise above disappointment. You have to carry on, keep playing your football and not let your head drop.'

6

December

The Reds' defeat at West Ham took place against a backdrop of early winter snow. If the result wasn't a sign of things to come, the weather certainly was.

Heavy snowfall brought the UK to a standstill and some football fixtures inevitably fell foul of Mother Nature. United were due to open the month with a seaside jaunt to Blackpool, but the Tangerines' Bloomfield Road stadium was ill-equipped to handle the elements. Without undersoil heating, Blackpool hired a heated pitch cover to stave off the snow and freezing temperatures. Their efforts were in vain, however, as match official Peter Walton decided 24 hours in advance that the game would not go ahead.

In the Reds' absence, the remaining major protagonists jostling for the Premier League title all managed to complete fixtures. While Arsenal secured top spot with a late win over Fulham and Manchester City edged out Bolton, Chelsea's spectacular implosion continued with a home draw against Everton that left the Blues a point behind United, who now had a game in hand.

An unintentional mantra of winning at home and drawing away had put the Reds right in contention for a record-breaking 19th title.

'The league's been wide open so far and it's definitely possible that could still be the case at the turn of the year,' admitted Sir Alex. 'It's another indication that it's a different league now and we've certainly seen a lot of surprising results. We need to start kicking on and trying to close the door. We've given away a lot of silly goals and until we get that right we'll continue to be inconsistent in terms of our form away from home.'

The manager also revealed Owen Hargreaves had returned to Germany in order to see a specialist to treat his torn hamstring. 'It's a complete tear, so he could be out for six to eight weeks,' Sir Alex said. 'If players realise they've injured their hamstring early enough and come off before they do any more damage, you can get them back in three to four weeks. But this was a tear and it's unfortunate. He's going to Munich to see a specialist.

'Having this hamstring problem is a real kick in the teeth to Owen, because he'd been training so well prior to the Wolves game. His training had been absolutely superb. And although he'd been training with us for only about nine or ten days, we were confident enough to play him against Wolves when we had 'flu in the squad and one or two injuries. It was disappointing how it turned out.

'I think we're all concerned. Owen hasn't played for more than two years and we'd have to be super-optimists to think everything's rosy in terms of a comeback. What we're trying to do is help the lad. That in itself is our biggest challenge, to try and help him get back to a level where he can still play football.'

Hargreaves would jet to Germany after the Reds' next game, a Champions League Group C finale against Valencia. The undersoil heating at Old Trafford meant both sides would have an ideal surface on which to play, but it took a monumental effort from staff at the club to ensure the area surrounding the stadium would be gritted and free from ice.

The Reds' defence, meanwhile, had managed to freeze out all comers in their European exertions to date, and were on the brink of making competition history by becoming the first team to qualify for the knockout stages without conceding a goal. While goalkeeper Edwin van der Sar had previous in setting the standards for clean sheets (with a 1,311-minute goalless run in the Premier League), his sights were instead set on merely topping Group C.

'It is quite clear,' he said. 'We are through now, but we want to get top spot in order to avoid any of the bigger teams in the earlier rounds. That's what we need to do against Valencia. So far we haven't played against the biggest teams in the Champions League. Maybe that has something to do with not conceding. When you start playing a higher standard of opposition it's going to become more difficult.'

Not conceding against the Spaniards would provide a double fillip: a competition record and, theoretically, a weighted draw against group runners-up in the knockout stages.

Champions League Group C

Old Trafford | Tuesday 7 December 2010 | KO 7.45pm |
Attendance: 74,513 | Referee: Pedro Proenca

Manchester United 1 (Anderson 62)
Valencia CF 1 (Hernandez 32)

One out of two isn't bad. United's proud defensive record finally came to an end, but a rare strike from Anderson – his first at Old Trafford – sealed the Reds' passage to the knockout stages of the Champions League as group winners.

Already assured of qualification to the second round, both sides scuffled for victory in an end-to-end tussle. Pablo Hernandez fired the visitors into the lead after slack possession play from United, before Brazilian midfielder Anderson tucked away a rebound after Ji-sung Park's shot had been parried.

Sir Alex Ferguson gave rookie goalkeeper Ben Amos his

Champions League debut, and both he and his opposite number, Vicente Guaita, were given chances to shine in an entertaining encounter in which both sides signalled an early intention to attack.

Alejandro Dominguez came close in quick succession, firstly drawing a smart save from Amos with a cheeky effort from distance, then cracking a low drive against the outside of the youngster's post. Then Berbatov opted to try to round Guaita, only for the youngster to deny the Bulgarian by thrusting out an arm and halting his progress. Moments later he deflected Park's volley away with his legs.

It would prove a vital save, as Valencia took the lead in the same passage of play. Michael Carrick's errant pass was pounced upon by the alert Dominguez, who advanced and slipped a pass to Hernandez, who struck a powerful low shot between Amos' legs.

The Reds' riposte was brisk. Wayne Rooney curled a stunning effort from 25 yards that thudded against the underside of the crossbar and Nani's volleyed rebound skidded agonisingly wide of the far post. Soon after half time, Berbatov came close with a pair of headers. Guaita was under siege, repelling everything thrown at him. The youngster's preference for parrying had proven effective, but soon afterwards it played a major role in United's equaliser.

Cutting in from the left and using Rooney's run as a decoy, Park unleashed a superb shot that looked destined for the top corner. Guaita did well to keep the shot out, but his save landed only at the feet of Anderson, who tucked away the rebound and embarked on a rare goal celebration.

Valencia were stung into life. Hernandez somehow missed a gilt-edged chance from six yards, before Guaita frustrated Berbatov twice in a minute with a pair of fine saves to keep out the Bulgarian's header and shot.

Inevitably for a game conducted at such a breathless pace, the sides ran out of steam in the final 15 minutes. United could breathe a little easier, however, having secured top spot in Group C.

The Teams

Manchester United: Amos, Rafael, Ferdinand (Smalling 50), Vidic, Fabio, Nani (Giggs 81), Anderson (Fletcher 90), Carrick, Park, Berbatov, Rooney
Subs not used: Kuszczak, Hernandez, Obertan, Macheda
Booked: Anderson

Valencia: Guaita, Miguel, R.Costa, Dealbert, Mathieu, Hernandez (Feghouli 82), Banega, Albelda, Alba (Mata 68), Dominguez (Isco 54), Aduriz
Subs not used: Sanchez, Maduro, Soldado, T.Costa
Booked: Albelda, Miguel

'Valencia are a great team and they played some fantastic football – one or two touches, every player involved. It's difficult to play against a team like that, like Barcelona,' enthused Nani. 'But we did well and we should have won the game because we created a lot of opportunities to score. Still, it was a good result because we finished in first position. Now we are happy and we wait for the next team.'

It was the visit of another formidable opponent, Arsenal, that had prompted Sir Alex Ferguson's withdrawal of Rio Ferdinand in the second half, with the influential defender suffering from a minor hamstring injury. 'It's not a pull or anything like that, but we can't take any chances with the game next Monday,' Sir Alex conceded, before admitting some regret at his side's wastefulness in front of goal against the Spaniards.

'I think we made a lot of chances and played a lot of good football until five minutes after we scored,' he said. 'We should have been two up at that time. But then we just settled, we tried to see out the game and sometimes that can be dangerous. It's a psychological thing and of course you have young defenders there.'

Among their number was Chris Smalling, who continued to look the part in Ferdinand's absence. If the master was deemed unfit to face Arsenal, the apprentice was relishing the task, although the England Under-21 international did seek to play down talk that United could match the Gunners' feat of 2003–04 and go through an entire league campaign without defeat.

'I'm not sure we'll ever see a team go through a whole season unbeaten again,' he said. 'So many sides are losing matches unexpectedly now. You would have to applaud any team who did do it. For us, it is just about continuing the momentum. We didn't get into top gear during the first month of the season. Now it's time for us to kick on and send out a message because we are getting stronger as a team.

'I'm really happy with the way [my season] has gone so far. The manager has given a lot of the younger lads a chance and has shown faith in me. Rio and Vida are the first-choice central defenders, but I have to be ready if called upon. I have been watching from the sidelines and learning from them in training, so I'm confident I'll be ready to step in if required. When the fixtures first came out, everyone saw this as a pivotal period. Monday is a massive game, but we don't have any need to fear Arsenal. We'll have seventy thousand fans cheering us on. They should be intimidated more than we are.'

As the game drew closer, the chances of Smalling featuring looked increasingly remote as Ferdinand recovered speedily from his setback, while Patrice Evra was also on course to feature. The league leaders had climbed the table with a youthful verve, but Sir Alex insisted he could see signs of growing maturity in the Arsenal ranks.

'I think they'll still try to play the attractive football Arsene believes in, but there's definitely been a slight change,' he said. 'The general shape of the team has been far more mature and aggressive this year. They're top of the league and that's a sure indication they're better than last year. They were very difficult to beat in the days of Emmanuel Petit and Patrick Vieira and the three at the back – [Martin] Keown, [Tony] Adams and [Steve] Bould. That brought them great success and I think this team is showing that kind of maturity now.

'The games between us, particularly four or five years ago, were so important because both of us were challenging for league titles. Chelsea have now come in and it's been ourselves and Chelsea over the last five years. Nonetheless, it's Manchester United against Arsenal and the history of both teams guarantees a match of intensity and, a lot of the time, controversy. I think Monday night's game will be more or less the same because the pride and history of both clubs determine that.'

Ji-sung Park, conversely, still felt the gulf in experience between the two sides made it unlikely Arsene Wenger's side could match the Reds stride for stride across the course of a season.

'Arsenal have shown they are a good side,' said the South Korean. 'They have a lot of young players, but they have played very well this season and they have more experience than last season. But we have a lot of it and that is one of the most important things in the title race. Arsenal are doing well now, but maybe in March, when the pressure comes on, you will end up with different results.

'Our good performances against Arsenal will continue. It's good to have that winning mood. We have produced some good performances recently, against Blackburn and Valencia, and we can do that against Arsenal as well.'

As it often transpires in the biggest games, Park's contribution would prove key.

Barclays Premier League

Old Trafford | Monday 13 December 2010 | KO 8.00pm | Attendance: 75,227 | Referee: Howard Webb

Manchester United 1 (Park 41)
Arsenal 0

United once again overcame Arsenal with a display of discipline and substance, plus a measure of style, to go two points clear at the top of the Barclays Premier League with a game in hand.

Ji-sung Park contorted brilliantly to head home Nani's deflected shot shortly before half time and, as the Gunners toiled in vain to draw level, Wayne Rooney passed up the chance to secure victory by missing a second-half penalty.

As had become the norm in games between United and Arsenal, the visitors enjoyed the majority of the ball, yet the hosts always looked far more likely to do something with it. Indeed, the Gunners scarcely mustered a noteworthy attempt in the first half, although, in their defence, both Cesc Fabregas and Robin van Persie were deemed fit enough only for the bench.

With 20-year-old Polish goalkeeper Wojciech Szczesny making his Premier League debut, the Gunners were hardly in ideal shape going into their biggest game of the season. United certainly set about the visitors with the intention of making a quick break-through. Both Rooney and Nani tested Szczesny's handling with early efforts, before the Portuguese drilled fractionally wide after a poor header from Sebastien Squillaci.

As the half wore on, United's composed tactic of drawing Arsenal on, then hitting swiftly and decisively on the break came to the fore. One such counter brought the opening goal shortly before half time, as Michael Carrick and Rooney combined to feed Nani wide on the right. The winger cut inside and shot and, although it deflected up and away off Gael Clichy, Park showed superb reactions to twist and loop a header over Szczesny and in off the post.

United's menace on the break continued after the interval. One foray forward engineered an opening for Anderson after good work from Rooney, but Szczesny sprinted from his line and smothered the ball to deny the Brazilian. Immediately, Arsenal's best chance fol-lowed. Samir Nasri's low shot was parried by Edwin van der Sar to Marouane Chamakh, but Nemanja Vidic slid in heroically to block what seemed a simple tap-in for the Arsenal striker.

Arsene Wenger introduced both Fabregas and van Persie from the bench, but the Gunners would muster no more opportunities. United, meanwhile, could have put the game to bed. Nani wastefully blazed over after an epic run and Anderson also chanced his luck from distance, but clearest of all was a penalty awarded for handball against Clichy. Rooney stepped up to take it, but hammered his shot high over the bar.

Fortunately, the miss didn't prove costly, and league leaders United could look ahead to meeting Chelsea, with the champions – and the entire division – struggling to keep pace.

The Teams

Manchester United: van der Sar, Rafael, Ferdinand, Vidic, Evra, Nani, Fletcher, Carrick, Anderson (Giggs 85), Park, Rooney
Subs not used: Kuszczak, Brown, Smalling, Obertan, Berbatov, Hernandez

Arsenal: Szczesny, Sagna, Squillaci, Koscielny, Clichy, Song, Wilshere (van Persie 64), Rosicky (Fabregas 64), Nasri, Arshavin (Walcott 77), Chamakh
Subs not used: Fabianski, Djourou, Denilson, Bendtner
Booked: Arshavin, Chamakh, Nasri, Song

'Three points are three points,' admitted Rio Ferdinand, justifying the resilient nature of United's victory. 'In these games, sometimes you don't play well but you've got to go out and play as well as you can. We got the three points and that's the main thing. Arsenal test you in different ways – they are a very talented side with great players – but I thought we contained them very well and we had the best chances.'

'We defended very well and the back four were fantastic tonight, absolutely magnificent,' gushed Sir Alex. 'With that foundation, it always gives us a great chance. I think we're starting to get there. I think our form is improving. And, as I say, with the back four playing like that, if they play like that from now on and give us the consistency, then we're in with a good chance.

'We had to play well. In these major games you want to perform and I think we did perform tonight, particularly in the first half. In the second half, Arsenal came into it a bit; they didn't make any real chances in the game but they pegged us back a little. Now we've got a difficult game against Chelsea next Sunday. That's going to be a very important game.'

The fortunes of the two sides could hardly have been in starker contrast. United had stormed to the top of the league, while Carlo Ancelotti's champions had taken three points from five games and looked woefully out of sorts. Nevertheless, United were dealt a blow in the build-up with news that Paul Scholes' groin injury would rule him out until January.

One of Scholes' younger midfield peers, however, had cause for celebration. After a string of impressive performances, Anderson was handed a new four-and-a-half year contract extension. 'He's been absolutely brilliant, tremendous,' said Sir Alex. 'He offers something different from the other midfield players we've got. He's got tremendous pace and he can beat a man and he's always decisive in his passing, in terms of penetration.'

While the 22-year-old had committed his future to United for the foreseeable future, one of Old Trafford's favourite sons was departing the club after an 11-year stint in Manchester. Ole Gunnar Solskjaer had risen to managerial prominence with a trophy-laden stint in charge of the Reds' Reserves and had caught the eye of his former club, FK Molde of Norway. Solskjaer, forever embedded in folklore for his Treble-clinching strike against Bayern Munich in 1999, was given a rousing ovation by a packed Old Trafford ahead of the victory over Arsenal. As he prepared to depart Carrington for his homeland the following day, Ole admitted his sadness at leaving.

'I should have done a Cantona and retired without warning,' he smiled. 'I'm not a goodbye person, really. It feels like that makes it even sadder. The club has been amazing with me and I'm really proud that the supporters have liked what I've done. I take it as a compliment, of course. I've been privileged to play with the best players. Beckham, Scholesy, Giggsy, Keane, Cantona, Gary

Neville . . . I've played with the best players in the history of the club, so I'm really proud. And I've said exactly the same as anyone else who has played here and wants to go into management: if you do well enough and you get the chance to manage United, of course you'd take it. So I'd like to come back.'

Another ex-Red would be back at Old Trafford sooner rather than later. Gabriel Heinze had left United under something of a cloud in 2007, amid attempts to force a move to Liverpool before eventually joining Real Madrid, but his return was ensured when his current club, Marseille, were drawn to face Sir Alex Ferguson's side in the second round of the Champions League.

'We got Marseille in the draw rehearsal and it proved right,' the Reds boss revealed. 'Marseille are a handful at their own ground – a fantastic atmosphere and incredible support guarantees that. They've had a good change in fortunes in the last two or three years, after a dry spell, and I think it'll be a difficult tie. Didier Deschamps is the coach there and they've got one of our old players in Gabriel Heinze, so it'll be nice to see him.'

Attentions quickly turned back to domestic matters and the visit to Stamford Bridge. Continued heavy snow cast doubts over the fixture once again, however, and Chelsea announced a postponement 27 hours before the match was due to kick off. 'The decision to postpone the game was taken on safety grounds after comprehensive consultations between the club, local authorities and the police,' said a Blues spokesman. 'A high-profile event of this scale affects an area much wider than Stamford Bridge, and considering the icy conditions forecast, an early decision was taken to ensure the safety of both fans and those staffing the event.'

The postponement carried positives and negatives. On the one hand, there was an overriding frustration in the dressing room at being unable to face Carlo Ancelotti's side when they looked most vulnerable. On the other hand, the postponement afforded the Reds extra time to prepare for a hectic run of games post-Christmas. Sights were now set on the Boxing Day visit of Sunderland and assistant manager Mike Phelan was confident the players were equipped to cope with the festive fixture list. 'You go onto auto pilot in some ways,' he explained. 'We've been through this period so many times and we know how to get the balance right. If the squad is fully fit and everybody's raring to go, then we'll plan over the Christmas period as we always have done.

'There will be training days, recovery days and the odd day off if we can squeeze it in. But the games come thick and fast. Christmas is not a period that is a fitness issue – it's about recovery, making sure players get the rest they need to recuperate and get over any injuries. We have a big enough squad to cope with most eventualities. There's a game every two or three days – not too dissimilar to what it's like in the season, to be fair – but it can be a hectic period.'

There was certainly no slowing of breaking news as Christmas approached. Nemanja Vidic, Nani, Anderson and Michael Carrick were all laid low with a virus and were doubts to face Sunderland. Sir Alex heralded the resumption of his press conferences with a warning about how his quotes were treated in the media, and the manager also confirmed he expected Edwin van der Sar to announce his retirement at the end of the season. Coincidentally, Anders Lindegaard, the man aiming to succeed the veteran Dutchman as United's first-choice stopper, was in full training at Carrington, since his season with Aalesunds in Norway had already finished.

'In terms of the physical fundament of my game, it was very beneficial to come to Carrington before I could actually play,' says the Dane. 'I was training very hard – twice a day, every day – and I don't believe I had a day off in December until I was able to go on Christmas vacation. But it was definitely like a pre-season for me, and it's very hard to come here after a month of vacation, with the best players in the world on top of their game, fit and going into the Christmas programme. They were all in great shape and I came in like the fat kid and had to do my own pre-season programme, get my fitness level right and get my game going again.

'Also, when you come in from a little club like I have, many things have to change to bring your game up to the right level, not just on the pitch but off it, too. At this level it's a lifestyle – it's about eating right, sleeping right and training right. It's been hard sometimes along the way to say no to sweet stuff, like candy in the evening, but that's what you have to do. It's much better to stand around in five years with gold medals around your neck than a couple of extra per cent of body fat!'

Sacrifice is part and parcel of life as a footballer, but comes especially to the fore at Christmas. Once again, the Reds trained on Christmas Day, but there were few complaints within the squad. 'It's something I've done every year since I was sixteen and I left school,' Michael Carrick said. 'I moved to London to be at West Ham and that's just how it's been. It feels normal.'

'Luckily, now I have kids who get up very early,' added Rio Ferdinand. 'They open their presents before I go in to training. We go back home and have Christmas dinner, but you can't have as much as you would like. You have to chill out. We go to a hotel in the evening. Christmas isn't the same when you play football, but I have many more years to look forward to. I enjoy playing football too much to worry about it.'

Barclays Premier League

Old Trafford | Sunday 26 December 2010 | KO 3.00pm |
Attendance: 75,269 | Referee: Phil Dowd

Manchester United 2 (Berbatov 5, Ferdinand o.g. 57)
Sunderland 0

Back in action at last. United's hectic festive schedule began with a comfortable home victory over Sunderland, as Dimitar Berbatov headed an early opener, then had his second-half strike deflected in by Anton Ferdinand as the Premier League leaders continued to set the pace.

Restricted to only two matches in December prior to the Black Cats' visit, United's appetite for action was quickly apparent. Berbatov headed home the opener inside five minutes, then he and Anderson both struck the woodwork and several other chances were spurned inside the opening half-hour.

The killer goal arrived shortly after the interval, as Berbatov's shot deflected tellingly off Anton Ferdinand. But in truth, there were few signs of nerves at the Reds' profligacy, so infrequent were Sunderland's forward forays. Sir Alex Ferguson was even able to replace Ryan Giggs and Anderson midway through the second period as he planned ahead for a tricky trip to Birmingham.

Deprived of Nani and Darren Fletcher through injury and illness respectively, Sir Alex made two enforced changes to the side that beat Arsenal. Giggs replaced the Portuguese winger on the left flank, while the return of Berbatov prompted a reprise of his strike partnership with Wayne Rooney.

Within five minutes, the duo combined to devastating effect. Giggs latched on to Anderson's pass and exploited woeful positioning by the visitors by meandering towards goal and feeding Rooney, whose measured chip was emphatically nodded home at the back post by Berbatov.

Buoyed by such an early advantage, United's play continued with vim and vigour. Rooney's impish chip drifted fractionally past Craig Gordon's far post before Berbatov went even closer, thumping a low shot against the upright. Anderson continued the assault on the woodwork five minutes later, curling a superb effort against the underside of the crossbar as Gordon watched on, helpless.

The Scottish stopper made his first save of the game soon afterwards, plunging smartly to his right to hold a low shot from Rooney after marvellous approach play from Berbatov and Park. The Bulgarian then shot powerfully into the side netting before Giggs drew a brilliant save with an effort from just inside the area.

Remarkably, Sunderland reached the 20-minute mark only one

goal behind, then readjusted to shore up a criminally vacant midfield. The plan stymied United's flow, and had Asamoah Gyan kept his head in the opening minute of the second half rather than blaze over, the visitors could have been level.

Any lingering hopes of a comeback were dashed when Anderson swept a pass to Berbatov, whose stabbed shot for the far corner deviated off Ferdinand and looped over the left shoulder of the toppling Gordon.

With a comfortable win assured and an imposing run of games approaching, Sir Alex replaced Giggs, Anderson and Berbatov with Kiko Macheda, Darron Gibson and Chicharito. United's work had long since been done, and thoughts could quickly turn to the invariably taxing trip to St Andrew's.

The Teams

Manchester United: van der Sar, Rafael, Ferdinand, Vidic, Evra, Park, Carrick, Anderson (Gibson 63), Giggs (Macheda 63), Berbatov (Hernandez 82), Rooney
Subs not used: Kuszczak, Neville, Smalling, Bébé

Sunderland: Gordon, Elmohamady, Ferdinand, Onuoha, Bardsley, Zenden (Angeleri 88), Malbranque (Cook 82), Henderson, Riveros, Gyan, Bent (Meyler 69)
Subs not used: Mignolet, da Silva, Adams, Reed
Booked: Bardsley, Meyler

'I think we did a great job in the first half-hour,' said Patrice Evra. 'We pressed the ball very well and there was some nice play. We scored the early goal, which is always the target. We need to score the early goal to kill the game, because after that they can have no confidence and can cause you no trouble. The football was great, but it was a dangerous game. At half time everyone kept saying we needed to keep focus, because when you play like this and don't score, sometimes you can concede silly goals. But we defended well again.'

With a trip to Birmingham City looming two days later, Sir Alex was far from displeased at the way his side eased off in the second period, especially as the Midlanders' fixture at Everton had been postponed due to ongoing weather troubles. 'It was a comfortable performance,' said the manager. 'I think in the first half we were absolutely fantastic – it could have been any score. Second half, I thought we put our tools away a bit and saved our legs. We knew the Birmingham game was off and we were very economical in the second half. You have to be. I took Anderson and Ryan off. We've got a game in two days' time, of course, and with Birmingham not having played they'll be nice and fresh.'

United's cause would be hampered by the absence of Ji-sung Park, who had been called up by South Korea for Asia Cup duty and would be missing until late January, much to the chagrin of his team-mates. 'We're disappointed Ji is going away at this time because he's been playing so well,' admitted Ryan Giggs. 'The lads would have Ji in the team every time because of his work-rate and what he puts into the game. But this is what the squad is for. We have players who aren't getting games but will be ready to come in and do a job.'

United had dropped two points at St Andrew's in early 2010 and looked to wrap up the year with a victory to send out a message to the chasing pack. The importance of seeing off Alex McLeish's side was apparent, but the Reds were wary of the task at hand. 'I remember last year's game well – I've never felt so cold in my life,' said Patrice Evra. 'I've played in Moscow, but I never felt that cold. Honestly, in the warm-up I couldn't breathe. It was so difficult. We drew there last season, but it was so difficult and the pitch was hard. That's why we must make sure we recover very well and make sure we are ready for this game because it will be very tough. It's one of the most dangerous and important games of the season.'

Barclays Premier League

St Andrew's | Tuesday 28 December 2010 | KO 7.45pm |
Attendance: 28,242 | Referee: Lee Mason

Birmingham City 1 (Bowyer 89)
Manchester United 1 (Berbatov 58)

When your luck's out, your luck's out. United appeared certain to take all three points at St Andrew's until, with a minute to play, Lee Bowyer popped up to nab a controversial leveller for the hosts.

The midfielder's goal might have been ruled out on three counts: a foul by Nikola Zigic in the build-up, a handball from the hulking Serb and an offside against the lurking Bowyer. United, who had led through Dimitar Berbatov's fine opener, deserved more.

The Reds ended 2010 on top of the Premier League and with games in hand on title rivals. But the concession of two late points at Birmingham City, in such controversial fashion, sullied an impressive evening's work. Darron Gibson was the sole alteration to United's line-up, coming in for Ji-sung Park, who had departed for Asia Cup duty with South Korea.

Both sides opted for lone strikers, with Berbatov occupying the role for the Reds. Wayne Rooney was deployed on the left side of a five-man midfield and had the game's first effort when he shifted infield and fired a shot wide of Ben Foster's post.

The former United keeper produced a wonderful save soon after to divert Ryan Giggs' errant cross on to the inside of the post, but such goalmouth excitement was a rarity in a game conducted almost exclusively in midfield.

Amid all the steel on show, it was a flash of silk that allowed the deadlock to be broken, and predictably it was provided by Berbatov. The Bulgarian neatly flicked a pass to Gibson, accepted the return and fired a low shot inside Foster's near post. A minute later,

Berbatov evaded two defenders before his low effort bounced away off the outside of the other upright.

United looked increasingly dangerous going forward. Gibson came close with a shot from the edge of the box that seared just wide, but Birmingham continued to plug away and introduced target man Zigic with eight minutes remaining.

Soon after Nemanja Vidic had forced Foster into action with a powerful header, Zigic came to the fore with a major supporting role in Bowyer's goal. It was a frustrating end to the evening, and the year, but a glance at the Premier League table gave the Reds plenty of hope for what lay ahead.

The Teams

Birmingham City: Foster, Carr, Johnson, Dann, Ridgewell, Larsson (Hleb 70), Ferguson, Bowyer, Beausejour (Zigic 82), Gardner, Jerome (Phillips 85)
Subs not used: Taylor, Jiranek, Fahey, Derbyshire
Booked: Bowyer, Dann, Gardner

Manchester United: van der Sar, Rafael, Ferdinand, Vidic, Evra, Giggs, Gibson (Hernandez 90), Carrick, Anderson (Fletcher 73), Rooney, Berbatov
Subs not used: Kuszczak, Neville, J.Evans, Obertan, Macheda
Booked: Anderson, Giggs, Vidic

'Handball, a foul on the centre-half, he went right through him,' fumed Sir Alex, listing the illegalities of Bowyer's leveller. 'If the referee can't see that, what chance have you got? At this level, in a game of that importance, what you hope you're going to get is a referee that can see that. If he can't, what chance have you got? I've got no complaints with my team today – they fought hard, they worked hard and had only two days' rest. They have run their socks off to get a result and it's hard on them.

'I think we outplayed them in the second half and we didn't deserve that. But football is a funny game. It's a tight league and every team that comes here has a difficult game. I think we deserved to win. We were the better team, but maybe we should have finished them off after we went 1–0 up. There were a number of times we counter-attacked, but we needed more care in our final pass and shot. It was just one of those days.'

'It's easy to get carried away with that result and we were certainly down when we came off the pitch,' added Michael Carrick. 'Late goals are always hard to take but given how it happened we feel hard done by. There was a push in the back and then obviously the hand-ball. But it's done now, so we have to dust ourselves down and move on. We're still in a good position when you look at the bigger picture. We haven't lost, we're in good form – we played well tonight, controlling the game – so we go into the next match looking to keep the momentum up.'

The Reds' bid to keep the ball rolling would begin with another Midlands trip, this time to West Bromwich Albion. Thereafter, January would hold six more games – including the rearranged visit to Blackpool – as United's season began to shift from engaging to compelling.

7

January

New Year, new start. United's frustratingly patchy away form had been married to a near flawless home record during the first half of the 2010–11 season, but an early-afternoon trip to West Brom on New Year's Day provided the perfect opportunity to showcase the Reds' strength of character away from Old Trafford and underline the side's title-winning credentials.

'We've got an opportunity to bounce back from drawing at Birmingham and we're looking to win this game and get our away form going,' promised Darren Fletcher. 'It's a big game and they got a point against us at Old Trafford, so they'll be confident. West Brom started the season well, but have gone through a rough patch recently that they'll be looking to improve upon. Meanwhile, we need to start winning away from home.

'Our performance levels have been good. We've been to some hard places and played well, but we've conceded late goals, which is disappointing. That's tainted what have been good per-formances. But we need to turn these performances into victories and go on a run of wins away from home if we want to win the league. And after dropping points at Birmingham we're desperate to get back out there, put things right and get back on track.'

Sir Alex confirmed United would have to take on the Baggies without Nani, who was in line to return against Stoke three days later, while Paul Scholes had suffered a recurrence of his groin injury and had been prescribed complete rest.

'We expect a tough game on Saturday,' Sir Alex told his pre-match press conference. 'West Brom have been a refreshing team this season – they play the right way and have a good threat. Their goal tally has been very good this season, particularly away from home. So we know it won't be easy.' Although fresh from turning 69 on New Year's Eve, Sir Alex would be in the party spirit only if his side returned from the Midlands with all three points.

Barclays Premier League

**The Hawthorns | Saturday 1 January 2011 | KO 12.45pm |
Attendance: 25,499 | Referee: Chris Foy**

West Bromwich Albion 1 (Morrison 14)
Manchester United 2 (Rooney 3, Hernandez 75)

United began 2011 in winning fashion, but were far from vintage as headers from Wayne Rooney and Chicharito bookended a largely out-of-sorts performance at the Hawthorns.

Rooney nodded the Reds ahead inside three minutes with his first goal from open play since March 2010, only for James Morrison to haul the Baggies level with a scorching volley. Peter Odemwingie then missed a penalty for the hosts before Reds substitute Chicharito headed the winner with 15 minutes remaining.

The Mexican's strike was assisted by a magnificent cross from Rooney, who later demonstrated commendable commitment to the cause by playing on through the pain barrier, despite suffering an ankle injury in a challenge with Chris Brunt.

The bizarre late chapter capped an eventful game for the England striker, who put the Reds ahead with the first goal of the New Year. Gabriel Obertan rolled the ball back for Patrice Evra to whip in a first-time cross, which Rooney met with a well-placed header that skidded beyond Scott Carson's dive.

West Brom played on undeterred, however, and drew level when Morrison returned Nemanja Vidic's headed clearance with interest and the midfielder's vicious volley arced past the helpless Tomasz Kuszczak. The hosts bossed the remainder of the first period and should have had a penalty when Gary Neville hauled down Graham Dorrans inside the box. Concerned by his side's openness, Sir Alex withdrew Rooney to a wide role and pushed Darren Fletcher into central midfield to boost numbers.

Still the hosts posed problems. Dorrans lashed into Kuszczak's side netting and Brunt's deflected free-kick was just off-target. After the interval, Brunt again came close before Paul Scharner headed marginally wide. But the clearest opening for West Brom came when Rio Ferdinand tripped Jerome Thomas as the winger entered the box. Odemwingie took the penalty, but spurned it with a horrible miss, scuffing the ball wide left.

United soon took advantage, as substitute Javier Hernandez – on the field for 15 minutes – reacted quickest to Rooney's fizzing left-wing corner to twist and nod home from close range. Tails up, the Reds almost pulled further away when Rooney headed over from Fletcher's cross in the next attack, before Jerome Thomas escaped punishment for clearly handling Fabio's cross.

As United saw the game out, Brunt was booked for a crude foul on Rooney in the 88th minute. The England striker limped from the field without replacement, as United's three substitutions had already been used. As soon as the announcement was made that there would be five added minutes, however, Rooney gamely charged back on to the field to play his part in running down the clock on a crucial victory.

The Teams

West Bromwich Albion: Carson, Reid (Zuiverloon 64), Ibanez (Tchoyi 71), Scharner, Cech, Morrison, Mulumbu (Fortune 90), Brunt, Dorrans, Thomas, Odemwingie
Subs not used: Myhill, Shorey, Cox, Miller
Booked: Brunt

Manchester United: Kuszczak, Neville (Fabio 71), Ferdinand, Vidic, Evra, Fletcher, Carrick, Anderson, Obertan (Gibson 61), Rooney, Berbatov (Hernandez 61)
Subs not used: Amos, Owen, J.Evans, Bébé
Booked: Vidic, Fabio, Hernandez

'In these situations, when you're not playing at your best – and we didn't today – the three points is all that counts,' conceded Rio Ferdinand. 'Ideally, you'd like to play well but you've got to win games – it's as simple as that. I don't care how we win. Both the players and the fans go back to Manchester happy today.'

The defender, a veteran of four title-winning sides at Old Trafford, succinctly summed up the need to, on occasion, win ugly. Sir Alex, meanwhile, was bursting with admiration for Wayne Rooney, who had found the net from open play, teed up the winning goal and played through the pain barrier in a performance reminiscent of his usual self.

'People talk about world-class players. That was a world-class performance by Wayne today,' enthused the manager. 'He was absolutely magnificent; he drove us the whole way. It was a really good corner from him to set up the winner – he doesn't normally take the corners but it was a good one. Wayne was a bit unlucky not to score an extra couple of goals. But the goal he did score today will give him unbelievable confidence and hopefully he kicks on from here.

'He had an ankle injury but he came back on and that shows his courage. Our doctor thought, "That's him – he'll be out for a couple of weeks." But he came back on and he should be okay for Tuesday.'

The Reds would have to wait just three days before the next challenge: an invariably taxing fixture against Stoke City. Nevertheless, Sir Alex still found time to reflect on the perennial dilemma that has dogged him throughout his latter years: when to call it a day.

'I'm sixty-nine now,' he said, 'but you say to yourself, what happens when you retire? What do you do? I said to my wife some time ago that we could always travel, but at our age, you can't just jump on a plane. That's why I have no plans. There are no plans for me to retire. I hope my health stays as it is so I can carry on. I made a mistake some years ago because I thought my sixtieth birthday was a good time to retire. I changed my mind!'

For the visit of Stoke, the manager would be able to count on the returning Nani, who had shrugged off a groin injury that had ruled him out of the Reds' opening three festive games. It would be all hands to the pump against Tony Pulis' well-drilled, physical side.

'We know what to expect from Stoke,' said Darren Fletcher. 'They've really consolidated themselves as a Premier League side and Tony Pulis has done a great job. You know you're in for a battle when you play Stoke and you have to win that battle and earn the right to play. It's going to be a difficult game. They have some players who like to attack and Tony Pulis doesn't like his side to sit back. They can go direct if they want to, but they also have some good footballers up front. We know they'll be a danger from set-pieces – they're a big, strong, physical side – so we'll have to match them and make sure we're on our toes.'

Barclays Premier League

Old Trafford | Tuesday 4 January 2011 | KO 8.00pm | Attendance: 73,401 | Referee: Mark Clattenburg

Manchester United 2 (Hernandez 27, Nani 62)
Stoke City 1 (Whitehead 50)

Prior to Christmas, Sir Alex Ferguson had outlined his chief desire for the festive period: still to be perched atop the Premier League table after Stoke's visit to Old Trafford. Thanks to Chicharito and Nani, the manager once again got his wish.

The attacking pair struck goals of sublime quality in either half to ensure Tony Pulis' side, who offered robust resistance throughout and briefly levelled through Dean Whitehead, were again vanquished, taking United's haul to ten points from four games in 11 days.

Mindful of the jaded way in which his side pilfered victory at the Hawthorns – and with the FA Cup visit of Liverpool to consider – Sir Alex made six changes to the starting line-up that had overcome the Baggies. Galvanised by a collective freshness, United began brightly, popping passes around and dominating possession. Darron Gibson twice went close from distance, Ryan Shawcross survived a strong shout for handball on the edge of his own box and Dimitar Berbatov poked just wide from deep inside the area.

It took a move of intricate precision to open the scoring. Berbatov's pass released Nani on the right wing, the Portuguese advanced into the box, slid a perfect cross through Danny Collins' legs and the onrushing Chicharito back-heeled a finish beautifully inside Asmir Begovic's near post.

The slender nature of United's half-time lead was exposed shortly after the interval as Stoke peppered the hosts with crosses. Soon after Tuncay had headed wastefully wide, the Turk provided a perfect cross for the unmarked Whitehead to nod past Tomasz Kuszczak.

Sobered, the league leaders set about exerting pressure once more and regained the lead 12 minutes later. Nani slipped a pass inside for Chicharito, who shimmied to shoot before returning the ball whence it came. Nani needed only two touches: one with the right foot to fashion space, another to curl an unstoppable left-footed effort inside Begovic's far post from the edge of the area.

Thereafter the game descended into a stand-off, with neither side able to commit fully to nabbing another goal to emphasise or alter the scoreline. The spectacle meandered towards a narrow, vital victory for United. It maintained the momentum of the Reds' bid to reclaim the Premier League title and ensured Sir Alex a satisfactory outcome to a hectic festive programme.

The Teams

Manchester United: Kuszczak, Rafael, Smalling, Vidic, Evra, Nani, Gibson (Carrick 78), Fletcher, Giggs, Hernandez (Owen 78), Berbatov
Subs not used: Amos, Anderson, Fabio, J.Evans, Obertan

Stoke City: Begovic, Wilkinson, Huth, Shawcross, Collins, Tuncay, Whitehead, Wilson, Delap (Walters 69), Etherington (Pennant 69), Jones (Fuller 76)
Subs not used: Sorensen, Higginbotham, Whelan, Pugh

Having utterly shone during his personal duel with Kenwyne Jones – one of the most physically imposing opponents in the Premier League – young Chris Smalling was walking on air after the Reds' hard-fought win.

'We looked at the footage beforehand and Stoke are a real handful, especially Kenwyne Jones,' smiled the defender. 'He's been tormenting centre-halves this season. I knew it was going to be a really difficult battle, but I enjoyed it out there. He's got a great standing jump, so you really have to get about him and tussle with him. I've played a lot of Champions League games, so now I've got into different competitions I feel like I'm playing my part. I'm really knocking on that door and hopefully the manager can see that I can play well.'

Having snuffed out the visitors' chief threat so comprehensively, Smalling also paid tribute to United's match-winners, Chicharito and Nani. 'Chicha is dangerous,' he said. 'When we play little six versus five games in training he can be a nightmare to mark. You need your wits about you because he can come from the left or the right. He

really deserved his goal. And Nani's been a real loss. He's so important in terms of our goal threat going forward and he's a real threat
down that wing. He scores so many goals with his left foot. Everyone
thinks he's right-footed, but it's great for him to pop up and get
another wonder goal.'

After watching his table-toppers come in for widespread criticism
after the scarcely deserved victory at West Brom, Sir Alex was swift
to extol his side's virtues after another key win. 'You can look at as
many stats as you like – shots at goal, number of passes . . . But when
you look at our home record, some of our performances at home
have been fantastic,' he stated.

'We've had two bad performances away from home, against
Sunderland [in October] and on Saturday against West Brom. It was
a battling performance against Birmingham and we maybe should
have won the game. Otherwise, we've had some good performances
away from home. Okay we've thrown a few points away, but that
doesn't mean to say we didn't play well. We're an easy target for that
kind of talk. We've just got to dismiss it and focus on what our ambition is and that's to win the league.

'I think we're going to be in the shake-up. I think if you're in
there when it comes to New Year, it's a good guide as to where you're
going to be at the end of the season. Our history tells us we play
better in the second half of the season and big games are not an issue
for us because we relish that.'

Though Sir Alex was not expected to reinforce his squad in the
January transfer window – other than with the long-since-agreed cap-
ture of Anders Lindegaard – there was a flurry of loan activity
throughout the month. Tom Cleverley was potentially due to be
recalled from Wigan until he suffered a hamstring tear and was told
to remain at the DW Stadium for the rest of the season. Another
injured midfielder, Matty James, was recalled from Preston, while
Danny Drinkwater's stint with Cardiff was curtailed in favour of a
new deal with Watford.

Magnus Eikrem became Ole Gunnar Solskjaer's first signing for

Molde, James Chester and Cameron Stewart both joined Hull City in permanent deals and Corry Evans joined the Tigers on loan. Ritchie De Laet and Joe Dudgeon agreed to spend the remainder of the season with Portsmouth and Carlisle respectively. Most prominently, Italian striker Kiko Macheda returned to his homeland until the end of the season, joining Sampdoria and admitting: 'I need to play. It will pain me to be away from Sir Alex, who is the best manager in the world, but this will be good for me.'

'Federico feels he has been neglected on the international front,' added the United manager. 'This has given him an opportunity to play in Italy, where they can see him every week. We would have preferred him to play in the Premier League and he had opportunities to do that with several clubs. But he has made a good case and every player should always want to play for his international team.'

Macheda's departure ruled him out of the Reds' mouth-watering FA Cup clash with Liverpool, for which Sir Alex already had doubts over Edwin van der Sar (illness) and Wayne Rooney (injury). Nevertheless, the manager was intent on picking as strong a team as he could, despite coming off the back of a flurry of Premier League games.

'The FA Cup is a tournament you can never be sure about,' he warned. 'We made a mistake last year of picking a team we thought would be good enough to beat Leeds. We had a reminder that the FA Cup has shocks in it. We had one last year and we hope we don't get it this year. In hindsight, I could have picked a stronger team. It was the first time I'd lost a third-round tie since I came to the club and it didn't sit well with me. I was sick for a few days; I didn't enjoy it.'

Sir Alex had expected to do battle with his close friend, Roy Hodgson, only to discover soon after his press conference that the former Fulham boss – and reigning LMA Manager of the Year – had lost his job 192 days into his role as Liverpool manager. In bizarre circumstances, Kenny Dalglish, who had quit the post two decades earlier, cut short a family holiday to return to Liverpool and take the reins for the trip to Old Trafford.

FA Cup third round

Old Trafford | Sunday 9 January 2011 | KO 1.30pm | Attendance: 74,727 | Referee: Howard Webb

Manchester United 1 (Giggs (pen) 2)
Liverpool 0

United ensured a nightmare start to Kenny Dalglish's second stint at the Liverpool helm, winning a penalty inside a minute that was clinically converted by Ryan Giggs.

Visiting captain Steven Gerrard was dismissed for a wild lunge on Michael Carrick just after the half-hour but, despite a numerical advantage, Sir Alex's men couldn't run up the handsome scoreline their dominance deserved. Instead, Liverpool kept a foothold in the game and almost earned a replay when Fabio Aurelio's free-kick forced an impressive save from Tomasz Kuszczak.

The Pole was deputising for virus victim Edwin van der Sar, while United's pre-match plans were also disrupted when Wayne Rooney failed a fitness test on his ankle and Nemanja Vidic dropped out of the squad after picking up a knock in training.

Nevertheless, Old Trafford buzzed with expectancy prior to kick-off, with the 9,000 visiting supporters paying warm tribute to their returning hero. It took less than a minute for their optimism to be crushed. Almost straight from kick-off, Dimitar Berbatov controlled Darren Fletcher's long pass and motored away from Daniel Agger, who sent the off-balance Bulgarian tumbling with a stray leg. Despite the Dane's protestations, Howard Webb deemed the challenge clumsy enough to point to the penalty spot. Giggs fired the ball confidently past Pepe Reina to spark an outpouring of joy from the home supporters.

'You're getting sacked in the morning,' they chorused to Dalglish, who, to his credit, saw the funny side of the good-natured ribbing. His side also responded positively. Maxi Rodriguez tested Kuszczak

On another freezing trip to St Andrew's, goalscorer Dimitar Berbatov helps line up United's defensive wall.

Wayne Rooney grimaces after suffering an ankle knock at West Brom, but gallantly completes the game as United bag a vital win.

Sir Alex Ferguson gets one over a familiar foe, dumping Kenny Dalglish's Liverpool out of the FA Cup.

Birmingham's Ben Foster consoles Wayne Rooney after a near miss – one of few errant efforts as the ex-Red concedes five at Old Trafford.

Dimitar Berbatov is mobbed by jubilant colleagues after capping another famous comeback at Blackpool.

A shocked Ryan Giggs heralds Nemanja Vidic's clinical curled finish against Aston Villa.

United's unbeaten league record comes unstuck at Molineux, despite Nani opening the scoring against Wolves.

Wayne Rooney swings the derby United's way with the most spectacular strike of his career.

Chicharito demonstrates his prowess once again with a neatly poked opener – the first of a pair – at Wigan.

Frank Lampard hammers home a controversial late penalty at Stamford Bridge to keep the champions in the title race.

As United surrender limply at Anfield, Nani lies stricken after a shocking lunge from Jamie Carragher.

Rafael and Fabio celebrate symmetrically after the latter opens the scoring in a morale-boosting FA Cup win over Arsenal.

Chicharito milks the acclaim after his tie-winning brace against Marseille books a
Champions League quarter-final berth.

Against all odds, Dimitar Berbatov pinches the points for ten-man United against
stubborn Bolton at Old Trafford.

Wayne Rooney heralds another pivotal moment after putting United ahead at Upton Park, but his celebration costs him a two-game ban.

United's wonderful travelling support prepare to put in a strident performance as the Reds finally win again at Stamford Bridge.

Sir Alex works away from his usual office, watching his side beat Fulham from the Directors' Box as he serves a five-game touchline ban.

Goalscorers Chicharito and Ji-sung Park celebrate the latter's quickfire tie-killer against Chelsea as United march into the last four in Europe.

with a fierce drive, while Rio Ferdinand cleared Martin Kelly's cross as Fernando Torres lurked for a leveller. The visitors were dealt another setback, however, when Gerrard inexplicably launched himself into a two-footed challenge on Carrick and was duly dismissed by Webb.

Nani toe-poked straight at Reina before Jonny Evans powered a header against the Spaniard's upright as United sought a killer second goal. After the interval, Fletcher's cross was headed narrowly off-target by Chicharito, but Liverpool remained largely compact and their menace grew with the introduction of substitutes Ryan Babel and Jonjo Shelvey. Sir Alex replaced Fletcher with Anderson, but the Brazilian instantly earned a yellow card for a foul on Torres on the edge of the area. Fabio Aurelio forced Kuszczak into an outstanding save from the resulting free-kick.

United's response was swift and Reina was inundated with action in the final minutes. The Spaniard flung himself to stop Berbatov poking home a loose ball, then performed a staggering quadruple save, denying Rafael twice, Berbatov and Patrice Evra. His heroics would be in vain, however, as United ran down time to book a spot in the fourth round against Southampton.

The Teams

Manchester United: Kuszczak, Rafael, Ferdinand, J.Evans (Smalling 84), Evra, Nani, Fletcher (Anderson 63), Carrick, Giggs, Berbatov, Hernandez (Owen 75)
Subs not used: Lindegaard, Fabio, Gibson, Obertan
Booked: Anderson, Fletcher

Liverpool: Reina, Kelly, Skrtel, Agger, Aurelio, Meireles (Shelvey 61), Lucas, Kuyt, Gerrard, Maxi (Babel 61), Torres (Ngog 77)
Subs not used: Gulasci, Kyrgiakos, Wilson, Poulsen
Sent off: Gerrard

'Of course it was a penalty,' scoffed Dimitar Berbatov after the final whistle. 'There was enough contact for me to lose my balance and people know I don't go to ground easily. I thought Liverpool put in a good performance and I thought Jose Reina was their best player and made some good saves, but we were the better side.'

On the game's other controversial moment, Steven Gerrard's red card, Ryan Giggs said: 'I couldn't see it myself, but the players' reactions tend to tell you a lot and the players around the ball were not too happy. That early goal helped us, as did the sending-off, but we had chances to finish off the game and you are a bit nervous when you don't take them.'

The victory marked a personal watershed for Jonny Evans, who put in a shift to reaffirm his brimming potential after an inconsistent start to the season. 'It's been difficult in terms of dealing with the mental side of it,' admitted the defender. 'But I've always had confidence in my ability and great support from my family and the manager. I just had to step back and look at what things I needed to be doing, and that's just doing the basic things well, like defending and keeping clean sheets.'

Evans' chances of featuring in the Reds' next outing – the daunting trip to Tottenham – appeared remote when Sir Alex confirmed skipper Nemanja Vidic was likely to be fit, along with Wayne Rooney. But doubts persisted over 'flu victim Edwin van der Sar. Nevertheless, Serbian powerhouse Vidic lifted the lid on the mood inside the Carrington camp, admitting confidence was building with each passing week.

'We definitely have a positive feeling,' he said. 'We know that up until the win over Blackburn we hadn't performed as well as we could. But from my experience, this sort of time is when we usually come into good form. We all want to win the league. Last season was very disappointing and the quality of the league has improved. Sides such as Tottenham and Manchester City have raised their games, while other teams understand they have to improve if they want to stay in the league because it is so competitive.'

Speaking at his pre-match press conference, Sir Alex agreed with Tottenham manager Harry Redknapp's assertion that United's unbeaten league record would fall before the season finished. But the Reds boss was determined Spurs wouldn't be the side to end it.

Barclays Premier League

White Hart Lane | Sunday 16 January 2011 | KO 4.00pm |
Attendance: 35,828 | Referee: Mike Dean

Tottenham Hotspur 0
Manchester United 0

Having temporarily surrendered top spot to Manchester City, United returned to the Barclays Premier League summit by virtue of a hard-earned point at White Hart Lane, surviving the controversial dismissal of Rafael with a masterful defensive performance.

In a tense game between two sides brimming with attacking talent and intent, mutual respect won out as both sides harried and hassled each other into submission, although United had to surrender any notion of nicking victory when, with 16 minutes remaining, Rafael was dismissed for two bookings.

Few clear-cut opportunities arose for either side. Wayne Rooney forced three smart saves from Heurelho Gomes, but Tottenham enjoyed the lion's share of the play and both Peter Crouch and Rafael van der Vaart spurned presentable first-half chances.

Sir Alex Ferguson was able to call upon all his experienced players who had been rated as doubts to make the match. Edwin van der Sar, Nemanja Vidic, Michael Carrick and Wayne Rooney all started, while Paul Scholes returned to the bench.

The game began in breathless fashion. Less than ten seconds had passed when Gareth Bale's dangerous cross was plucked from the air by van der Sar, with van der Vaart lurking. A minute later, Rooney latched on to Dimitar Berbatov's pass, evaded a risky challenge from William Gallas and fired wide of Gomes' post.

That quickfire exchange set the tone for a frantic opening. Van der Sar comfortably clutched a van der Vaart free-kick, Gomes fielded Rooney's 20-yard snapshot and Crouch contrived to volley wide after a superb cross from Alan Hutton.

Van der Vaart could only power a header into the side-netting from Bale's chipped cross as Spurs ended the first half in the ascendancy, but United edged the early exchanges of the second period. First Michael Carrick's flicked header from a Ryan Giggs corner drifted wide, then Rooney was thwarted by the save of the match from Gomes, who plunged to his right to tip away the striker's fizzing low shot.

The hosts pushed back and United's cause was dealt a damaging blow with just over a quarter of an hour remaining. Rafael, booked for an earlier foul on Wilson Palacios, crossed paths with the onrushing Benoit Assou-Ekotto. The Cameroonian tumbled under the Brazilian's presence and referee Mike Dean duly dismissed the United defender, who clearly felt he'd shown no intent to clip his opponent.

Chicharito was introduced to offer a counter-attacking threat, but his first contribution was almost disastrous. He carelessly laid off a ball inside his own area, which van der Vaart pounced on and curled fractionally past van der Sar's far upright. With it went the hosts' final chance. United had earned that reprieve with a sweat-soaked shift, displaying all the hallmarks of a side steadfastly stalking the Premier League title.

The Teams

Tottenham Hotspur: Gomes, Hutton, Gallas, Dawson, Assou-Ekotto, Lennon, Modric, Palacios (Defoe 78), Bale, van der Vaart, Crouch
Subs not used: Cudicini, Jenas, Pavlyuchenko, Bassong, Kranjcar, Corluka
Booked: Palacios, van der Vaart

Manchester United: van der Sar, Rafael, Vidic, Ferdinand, Evra, Nani (Anderson 60), Carrick, Fletcher, Giggs, Rooney, Berbatov (Hernandez 78)
Subs not used: Kuszczak, Owen, Smalling, Scholes, J.Evans
Booked: Evra, Fletcher, Rooney
Sent off: Rafael

'You need to be honest. It was a good point because Tottenham played very well,' admitted Patrice Evra. 'It's not easy to come to Tottenham and win, so I think this is a good point. We came here to win but you need to give Tottenham credit.

'Nobody in the squad is talking about that challenge [of going unbeaten all season]. We're only talking about winning the league. That's the most important thing. Today, all the country was against Manchester United – everybody wanted us to lose. But we didn't lose. It is a great challenge for us.'

Evra also backed Rafael after his contentious dismissal, saying: 'I don't know about the referee's decision. We saw it again in the dressing room and it's a difficult one. For me, I don't think it's a yellow card, but I'm not a referee. Rafael did a great job for us and he's a strong right-back. When you play against a player like Gareth Bale you need a strong right-back and Rafael showed he's good enough.'

The Brazilian was soon counting the cost of his raging reaction to being sent off, as the Football Association quickly charged him with improper conduct for ranting in the face of referee Mike Dean. Rafael accepted the charge and was handed an £8,000 fine and warned over his future behaviour.

Sir Alex joked he might evade the Brazilian's one-match ban by playing him against Birmingham, disguised as his twin brother Fabio. 'I might put Rafael in there,' he smiled. 'They wouldn't know [the difference]. Their DNA is probably the same.

'But it was a bad decision to send him off. In a big game it can have an impact, especially with twenty minutes left. Having to replace Rafael has given us something to consider, plus one or two other changes. Fabio could replace him. O'Shea and Brown also played for the Reserves, so they are a consideration.

'Birmingham will play five across the middle of the pitch and try to keep possession and make it difficult for us, but that's where we'll have to find solutions. That's what you have to do at Manchester United when you play against a team who have a certain way of playing. Most teams come to Old Trafford with that tactic in mind and we have to find that solution.'

Barclays Premier League

Old Trafford | Saturday 22 January 2011 | KO 3.00pm |
Attendance: 75,326 | Referee: Mike Jones

Manchester United 5 (Berbatov 2, 31, 53, Giggs 45, Nani 76)
Birmingham City 0

Dimitar Berbatov plundered his third hat-trick of an increasingly prolific season as Birmingham City were mercilessly dismantled amid another rampant Old Trafford performance from United.

Ryan Giggs and Nani were also on target with eye-catching goals and a string of other opportunities went begging as Alex McLeish's side capitulated, most likely with one eye on their looming Carling Cup semi-final decider against West Ham. Craig Gardner, Sebastian Larsson and Cameron Jerome were all among their substitutes.

A minor groin strain ruled out Rio Ferdinand for the Reds, while Rafael also missed the game through suspension, with Chris Smalling and John O'Shea deputising. They would both enjoy quiet afternoons.

The tone was set early on as, for the second home game in succession, the hosts were ahead inside two minutes. O'Shea flicked on Giggs' right-wing corner, and the criminally unmarked Berbatov nodded home from virtually on the line.

Birmingham were pinned in their own half thereafter. As their frustration grew, Aleksandr Hleb caught Michael Carrick on the ankle and the United midfielder was replaced by Darron Gibson soon afterwards. Even a change in a key position failed to stem United's flow. A swift counter-attack culminated in Berbatov advancing into the area and firing an unstoppable shot through Roger Johnson's legs and past an unsighted Ben Foster.

The Bulgarian then poked narrowly wide, Foster fielded Gibson's powerful effort and Giggs saw his shot deflected wide, but the Reds killed the game off in first-half stoppage time as Berbatov won possession and beautifully exchanged passes with Wayne Rooney, who slid a perfect ball across the area for Giggs to fire into the roof of the net.

Little changed after the break. On 47 minutes, Nani tormented the visiting defence with a series of shimmies before eventually crossing to Rooney, who inexplicably headed wide of a gaping goal from inside the six-yard box. He atoned soon afterwards, though, brilliantly controlling Edwin van der Sar's long punt and releasing Giggs, who squared for Berbatov to stab in a finish off the underside of Foster's crossbar.

Another home game, another match ball for the Premier League's top goalscorer, but the final say would belong to Nani, who dazzled for long periods with his trickery, even if the end product didn't always match the approach. In the 74th minute, though, the two components were in perfect harmony as he meandered inside from the right flank before unleashing an unstoppable low drive inside Foster's far post to cap a five-star display from the league leaders.

The Teams

Manchester United: van der Sar, O'Shea, Smalling, Vidic, Evra (Fabio 45), Nani, Carrick (Gibson 25), Anderson, Giggs (Owen 55), Berbatov, Rooney
Subs not used: Kuszczak, Scholes, J.Evans, Obertan

Birmingham City: Foster, Carr, Johnson, Ridgewell, Murphy, Bentley (Gardner 85), Ferguson, Mutch, Fahey (Larsson 65), Hleb (Jerome 46), Derbyshire
Subs not used: Doyle, Bowyer, Zigic, Jiranek

'Berba was brilliant,' marvelled Chris Smalling. 'The ball is played up to him and it just sticks. He turns and runs at defenders and it's really causing a threat. He's got the runners around him, with Nani and Wazza [Rooney] running off him. It gives defenders a nightmare and makes it easier for us at the back. The link-up play with Wazza is brilliant and I think they're enjoying playing together. Hopefully there's more of that to come.'

Sir Alex was similarly delighted with his strike pairing's shift, beaming: 'They were very good together. We hope Wayne scores again soon; he deserves it because he's working his socks off. He played some great football today. He was also involved in the fourth goal just after half time, with some fantastic control from van der Sar's ball coming out of the clouds.

'It helps when you score an early goal. Getting one after a minute forces the opposition to open up. They have to face the game from a different perspective and we capitalised on that. It was a good score at half time, and I was able to take Patrice Evra off and bring young Fabio on. Then I was able to take Ryan Giggs off because we've got a big game on Tuesday at Blackpool.'

The manager also took time to pay tribute to Giggs. Fresh from making his 600th league appearance at Spurs, the winger shone against Birmingham, scoring one and making another before being withdrawn. 'He could easily play for another year, he's as fresh as a daisy,' grinned the boss. 'We manage him in the right way and he looks after himself correctly.'

Having seen and done most things in football, Giggs was relishing the chance to savour Bloomfield Road for the first time in his epic career. 'It is a good thing for us, going to a new ground,' he said. 'It's a new experience. It'll be a tight, compact ground and it'll be loud. United are coming to town, so everyone will be up for it. It'll be a battle and it'll be tough. As a player, you want challenges like that. It makes it all the more satisfying if you come out on top.

'It's a fantastic achievement for Blackpool to be in the Premier League and, not only that, to see them play such good football. They've been a breath of fresh air because they go out and attack teams. They have the mindset that they're going to score goals. There have been so many exciting games involving Blackpool this season. Hopefully, we go there and get three points.'

The pre-match remit was simple: beat the struggling Seasiders to move five points clear at the head of the Premier League table. But then, things are rarely simple with United.

Barclays Premier League

Bloomfield Road | Tuesday 25 January 2011 | KO 7.30pm | Attendance: 15,574 | Referee: Peter Walton

Blackpool 2 (Cathcart 15, Campbell 43)
Manchester United 3 (Berbatov 72, 88, Hernandez 74)

United posted a sensational come-from-behind victory at Bloomfield Road, toiling fruitlessly for 70 minutes before accelerating in the dying stages of the game.

In the last 18 minutes of normal time and a hefty ten-minute hit of stoppage time, the Reds bagged three goals – two for Dimitar Berbatov, one for Chicharito – to overturn the hosts' two-goal lead, earned through first-half headers from Craig Cathcart and D.J.Campbell.

Blackpool burst out of the traps and offered United no breathing room, but that breathless approach was ultimately their undoing, as the visitors' greater energy levels prevailed in an absorbing second half.

Bloomfield Road rocked during the early exchanges. United's

small but vocally immense 1,500-strong following made themselves heard, but only barely as the capacity home crowd urged their side on. After 16 minutes, Charlie Adam fizzed in a perfect corner that Cathcart headed emphatically past Edwin van der Sar for his first goal since leaving the Reds back in August.

As United toiled, the hosts grew in confidence. Van der Sar had to make a fine reaction save from Nemanja Vidic's errant header, then plunged to his left to keep out David Vaughan's low effort. The Dutchman was helpless, though, when Campbell headed home another Adam corner at the far post on the brink of half time.

Matters could have worsened for the Reds shortly after the interval. Rafael did brilliantly to clear Gary Taylor-Fletcher's cross, but then might have been penalised for a hefty shoulder barge on Luke Varney inside the United area. As Blackpool visibly began to tire, however, a pair of Reds substitutes started to turn the game. Ryan Giggs, on for Darron Gibson at half time, and Chicharito, on for Wayne Rooney on 66 minutes, were almost unplayable.

Soon, United's growing pressure told and yielded two goals in three minutes. Nani's clever reverse pass played in Darren Fletcher and the Scot squared for Berbatov to tap home from close range. Then the Reds levelled as Javier Hernandez beat the offside trap to meet Giggs' measured through-ball and finish coolly.

The visitors' dander was up, but the momentum was checked when Rafael clashed heads with Marlon Harewood and required lengthy treatment before being stretchered off and taken straight to hospital. Despite that distressing delay, United forged ahead in the 88th minute. Paul Scholes released Berbatov to advance and steer a left-footed shot past Richard Kingson, prompting ecstatic scenes among players and travelling supporters alike.

United safely rode out ten minutes of stoppage time to post a stunning victory that once again left supporters elated but exhausted. Blackpool Pleasure Beach is noted for its rollercoasters: following United is a more knuckle-whitening, stomach-churning experience than any of them.

The Teams

Blackpool: Kingson, Eardley, Cathcart, Evatt, Baptiste, Taylor-Fletcher
(Harewood 74), Vaughan, Adam, Grandin, Varney (Phillips 68), Campbell
Subs not used: Rachubka, Edwards, Ormerod, Southern, Sylvestre
Booked: Adam

Manchester United: van der Sar, Rafael (Anderson 80), Smalling, Vidic,
Evra, Fletcher, Gibson (Giggs 46), Scholes, Nani, Berbatov, Rooney
(Hernandez 66)
Subs not used: Lindegaard, Owen, Fabio, J.Evans
Booked: Gibson, Scholes

'We are a team that believes no matter how bad the game might
be for us – whether it's 1–0 or 2–0 – we are always confident that
if we can score one then we can score more,' said a defiant
Dimitar Berbatov, fresh from another match-winning contribution.
'That was the case today. We fought like a team, especially in the
second half. The first half was not so good for us and Blackpool
played a good game, but in the second half we showed spirit and
we won.

'You come here and it's not such a friendly ground and the pitch
is not as good as back home at Old Trafford, so it's a bit difficult
sometimes because the ball is jumping around. Lucky for us, it was
only 2–0 at half time. In the dressing room we told ourselves, "We
can do it, we can do it." And we did.'

Berbatov heaped praise on Sir Alex's substitutions, claiming they
changed the game, while Darren Fletcher paid tribute to the manager's rousing half-time team-talk.

'He inspires us and gets us going and he made us believe that
we could still do it,' said the midfielder. 'He said it was important
we got that first goal as early as we could so we'd have time to get
a second and hopefully a third. As a team we were desperate to get
out there and put things right. We were really disappointed to go

in 2–0 down, having lost two goals from set pieces. We had to regroup and respond and we did that, and it was a fantastic second-half performance. We knew if we could win, it would send out a massive statement and keep us kicking on in our challenge to win the league.'

Two days after the win at Bloomfield Road, Edwin van der Sar formally announced he would be retiring from football at the end of the season. That the Dutchman had been among the Reds' best players all season, despite turning 40, intimated the inevitable impact of his departure. It also prompted a glowing reference from Sir Alex Ferguson, who added Paul Scholes was yet to decide whether or not 2010–11 would be his final season.

'Fantastic – a magnificent person, professional goalkeeper, an absolute marvellous career he's had,' said the manager of van der Sar. 'He's an example to anyone who wants to become a goalkeeper. Edwin sails through life without any changes in it, he has a consistent nature. He's unflappable. He's calm, he doesn't look to search for press for himself, he's happy with what he's achieved in life and he's not searching for anything. He's such a good man.'

The Dutchman was given the weekend off as United prepared to take on League One Southampton, meaning a pencilled-in debut for Anders Lindegaard. The manager also confirmed his squad was carrying 'a couple of bruises' after the hard-fought win at Blackpool, but he was also determined to march on towards Wembley.

'Sir Alex has already had a little word with us over the last couple of days in training, telling us how frustrated he is that he has not been able to get his hands on the FA Cup [recently],' revealed Chris Smalling. 'We will be going all out for him and ourselves, and hopefully we can impose our presence on the game nice and early. Some people make changes in the FA Cup and view it in different ways, but it's an important competition to us and one we want to win.'

FA Cup fourth round

St Mary's Stadium | Saturday 29 January 2011 | KO 5.30pm |
Attendance: 28,792 | Referee: Martin Atkinson

Southampton 1 (Chaplow 45)
Manchester United 2 (Owen 65, Hernandez 76)

United moved into the fifth round of the FA Cup after a gritty victory at St Mary's, as second-half goals from Michael Owen and Javier Hernandez overturned Richard Chaplow's opener for Southampton.

The Saints midfielder had powered his side into the lead in the dying stages of the first half, but a second-half revision of personnel and tactics prompted an improved Reds display, capped by clinical finishes from a pair of arch poachers.

Hot on the heels of last week's epic turnaround at Blackpool, the Reds once again demonstrated the moxie that has become a hallmark of Sir Alex Ferguson's teams, even when the manager shuffles his pack dramatically.

Eight changes were made to the side that started at Bloomfield Road, most notably the introduction of goalkeeper Anders Lindegaard. With Edwin van der Sar's imminent retirement confirmed, the Danish international was given his chance to make his debut and stake an early claim to replace the veteran Dutchman.

Southampton certainly endeavoured to test his suitability. Rickie Lambert twice missed narrowly with free-kicks before drilling straight at the Dane, as the hosts bossed the early exchanges. The closest United came to forging ahead was when Owen curled just wide from the edge of the area; the striker also hit the frame of the goal with a shanked cross.

Just before the interval, Southampton made the breakthrough. Lambert's flick for Chaplow ricocheted into the midfielder's path and he drilled a finish high into Lindegaard's goal.

Sir Alex made a trio of substitutions in the opening 15 minutes of the second period, introducing Wes Brown, Nani and Ryan Giggs, and once again results soon followed. Gabriel Obertan jinked into the area and, although his cross was deflected, Owen reacted superbly to direct a header inside Barotsz Bialkowski's post.

Though Southampton hit back with a crisp strike from Dan Harding that inched wide, it seemed inevitable United would strike again. With 14 minutes remaining, Owen pounced on a sloppy Ryan Dickson pass to feed Giggs and the substitute threaded an inch-perfect pass to Chicharito. The Mexican lost his footing but was still able to slide a clinical finish just inside the far post to send the Reds' vocal travelling army wild.

As Wayne Rooney and Dimitar Berbatov watched on approvingly from the bench, both goalscorers had demonstrated the predatory prowess running throughout United's striking ranks. More of the same would be required in the final months of the season, as the Reds pressed on in search of three major honours.

The Teams

Southampton: Bialkowski, Butterfield, Seaborne, Fonte, Harding, Chaplow (Gobern 84), Schneiderlin, Guly (N'Guessan 79), Oxlade-Chamberlain, Barnard (Dickson 73), Lambert
Subs not used: Davis, Richardson, Martin, Doble
Booked: Butterfield

Manchester United: Lindegaard, O'Shea, Smalling, J.Evans, Fabio (Brown 46), Gibson (Giggs 58), Scholes, Anderson (Nani 58), Owen, Hernandez, Obertan
Subs not used: Kuszczak, Berbatov, Rooney, Bébé

'It was one of the most enjoyable days of my life so far,' beamed Anders Lindegaard. 'When you've dreamed of representing a club since you were four years old and finally the dream comes true, obviously it's a very big thing. I enjoyed it a lot. It was a good debut.

Everybody wants to play at this club and I'm no different. I'm not here just to sit and pick my nose. I'm here to play.'

Michael Owen, scorer of the all-important leveller, was similarly bullish about his desire for regular involvement, saying: 'It is frustrating, obviously, because you always want to play a bit more. But I am old enough and wise enough to know the manager's problems and the amount of players he has to keep happy. The hard bit is when you get asked – and your opportunities have been few and far between – the pressure is really on to play well. If you don't, you will get criticism and all the rest of it, but you will probably have to wait another three months for a chance. I did all right and it takes the pressure off a little bit.'

The Reds' reward for ousting the League One high-flyers was a winnable home tie against non-league Crawley Town in the fifth round of the FA Cup. But while the Conference side were soon captivated by the dream tie, United's attentions switched to the Premier League visit of Aston Villa, against whom a win or a draw would mark a club-record equalling 29 league games without defeat.

8

February

Fresh from back-to-back comeback victories at Blackpool and Southampton, and on the verge of a record-equalling unbeaten run, United entered February in impressive shape. Atop the Premier League, preparing for a navigable Champions League encounter with Marseille and marching through the FA Cup, the squad was brimming with confidence, a mood Rio Ferdinand attributed to the indefatigable spirit of Sir Alex Ferguson.

'You never lose faith when you play for Manchester United,' he said. 'It's in our make-up to think the game's not over until the final whistle has blown. Until then, you try your hardest. If you do that week in, week out, you get a bit of luck and you get your rewards. It comes from the manager: he's got that desire and will to win. He's been here twenty-five years and if he's still got it, then why haven't players who have been here for only a year, two years or ten years got it?'

A veteran of the majority of Sir Alex's United reign, Ryan Giggs embodied the manager's mantra. With Aston Villa due at Old Trafford on the opening day of February, the winger was well aware of the youthful verve Gerard Houllier's side would bring. 'I was really impressed with them when we played at Villa Park,' said Giggs.

'Young players can come into a team sometimes and freeze, but they really got about us and made it a high-tempo game. They came here last season and beat us. With the players they've got and the pace they have, they've got the ability to cause any team problems. We have to be ready for that.'

Barclays Premier League

Old Trafford | Tuesday 1 February 2011 | KO 8.00pm |
Attendance: 75,256 | Referee: Chris Foy

Manchester United 3 (Rooney 1, 45, Vidic 62)
Aston Villa 1 (Bent 57)

Wayne Rooney marked a return to goalscoring form in spectacular fashion, bagging a fine brace, as United overcame Aston Villa to equal a club-record 29 league games without defeat.

Nemanja Vidic also curled home a clinical finish to assure the Reds of victory, shortly after Darren Bent had reduced the arrears with a tap-in for the visitors, who never scaled the heights of their breathless November display against United.

In fairness, the Midlanders were fighting a losing battle from the first minute. Edwin van der Sar displayed all his experience and expertise to launch a quick free-kick 70 yards into the path of Rooney, who had raced into space behind Richard Dunne. The striker brought the ball under control with one touch before lashing it beyond Brad Friedel with another.

The American stopper had no chance of repelling the first shot of the game, but he performed heroics as United dominated the early play, with one especially excellent save to somehow turn Nani's left-footed snapshot past the upright. Ryan Giggs and Patrice Evra were also denied in more routine fashion before Dimitar Berbatov headed over from close range.

A deserved second goal arrived on the stroke of half time as

Rooney doubled his tally, and again he owed much to a colleague. After demonstrating his strength on the right wing, Nani curled in a sumptuous cross that bypassed the visiting defenders and provided Rooney with a simple half-volley conversion.

Villa improved in the second period, with Ashley Young central to their resurgence. Shortly after clearing van der Sar's crossbar with a free-kick, the tricky winger outfoxed three defenders to play in Stewart Downing, who crossed for Bent to side-foot home and give the visitors hope.

The next goal would prove crucial, and fortunately it fell United's way, as Vidic bagged the 17th goal of his Reds career. It was arguably his most technically accomplished. Amid a melee following a United corner, Rooney teed up the Serbian, who steered an unstoppable finish high past Friedel.

Although Young cracked a shot against the top of the United bar, Dunne denied Rooney a hat-trick with an outstanding last-ditch tackle and Berbatov fired off-target when well placed, the scoring was over and Sir Alex's current side had matched their heralded 1999 forebears in avoiding defeat for 29 league games.

The Teams

Manchester United: van der Sar, O'Shea, Ferdinand, Vidic, Evra, Nani, Carrick, Fletcher (Anderson 34), Giggs, Rooney, Berbatov
Subs not used: Lindegaard, Owen, Smalling, Hernandez, Scholes, Fabio

Aston Villa: Friedel, Walker, Collins, Dunne, Clark, Albrighton (Heskey 70), Makoun, A.Young, Petrov (Agbonlahor 75), Downing (Reo-Coker 80), Bent
Subs not used: Marshall, Delfouneso, Cuellar, Pires

'I've been happy with my play,' smiled Wayne Rooney, 'apart from the Blackpool game where I just couldn't get in the game. But I'm delighted today to score and hopefully I can go on a good run and help the team win games.

'It was a great start. We've done that the last few home games – scored early and taken it from there – but we knew tonight was going to be a difficult game. Villa passed the ball well at times and it was quite an open game in the second half. The most important thing was getting three points, which we're delighted to have done.'

The England striker also paid tribute to his skipper, Nemanja Vidic, for belting home a finish Rooney himself would have treasured. 'It was a great strike by Vida,' he says. 'To be honest, he's a great striker of the ball. Sometimes after training when the forwards are staying behind and doing finishing, he comes over and does a little bit. He's got a great strike on him, so it's a shame he's not that far up the pitch all the time.'

As Rooney resembled himself more with every performance, so he buoyed those around him. 'The man's got a great appetite to play and everyone should remember that,' beamed Sir Alex. 'He gets his rewards eventually.' Nani, meanwhile, was moved to bold forecasting. 'Wayne will go on a run now,' said the winger. 'Sometimes the games haven't gone the way he wanted, but this was his best performance of the season so far. He'll be more confident now and I'm sure he'll score more goals in the next few games.'

While it was potentially the start of a new chapter for Rooney, the following day marked the end of an epic tome for Gary Neville. United's club captain, a youth product and veteran of 602 appearances, announced his immediate retirement from the game. Though he caught some off-guard with his mid-season timing, the defender had been mulling his decision for a while.

'It's been a combination of events over the last few months and I've known for the last few weeks,' he said. 'You don't go and do something like this quickly. I went away for a week and still came to the same conclusion. It just felt like the right thing to do and that my time was up.

'I played my last game against West Brom and came to the

conclusion pretty quickly after that. I didn't want to delay it for four months. In my mind, it just wouldn't have felt right for me. I felt that, for the manager and the club and everything they have done for me, they should know that as well. They accepted it and supported me in my decision.

'I was picking up those little injuries, and your mentality at this club is just to come back and go again. But you get a feeling in your mind that you can't go again. That time had come for me. There was also the fact of being useful to the team and the squad. In the last two seasons, I think I played twenty-five or thirty games in each season. There were games, or periods of games, where I felt I was con-tributing to the squad. Once you've lost that, you get to know in your own mind that it's not quite right. You don't want to be a passenger.'

Neville's decision, which came as a surprise to the majority of his team-mates, provoked a typically sharp response in the dressing room: a 'To Let' sign was hung on the defender's locker almost immediately.

But even without the services of a man who had been a club fix-ture for two decades, the show had to go on. United's unbeaten run was the media's hot topic, after it reached record status, yet Darren Fletcher spoke for the entire squad when he admitted the feat would be meaningless if it didn't help contribute to silverware.

'It has been a rollercoaster,' said the Scot. 'There have been times when we've thought it was gone and then we've come back late in games. Everyone keeps talking about the unbeaten run. It's fantastic and gives you confidence knowing you're on this run and looking to set a new club record. But the most important thing – the thing all the players are focused on – is winning the league. We'd rather have that than maintain an unbeaten run.'

Fletcher was also well aware of the danger to United's momentum posed by bottom-of-the-league Wolves. 'People might not expect us to lose at Wolves, but we've got to be very cautious,' he said. 'The per-formances they have produced haven't really got them the points they deserve. I think they've been mighty unlucky in a lot of games. They've had some good results against the bigger teams, like Liverpool and Chelsea. We know it's going to be a very difficult match. Five or six years ago we experienced a loss at Wolves when we were sitting top of the league, so it just goes to show that you have to be wary.'

The omens were good. The table-propping Midlanders would welcome table-topping United, who boasted the new Barclays Manager of the Month and Player of the Month in Sir Alex Ferguson and Dimitar Berbatov. The former was comfortable enough with his side's state to start forecasting the points required to reclaim the title, even if he did expect a battle for three of them at Molineux.

'I think eighty-four points would definitely win the title,' he said, with his side on 54 points with 14 games remaining. 'I'm almost sure of that, so we've got another thirty points to find. Whether it's winning home or away, it's about getting enough points to get over that line. Consistency is the key and over the last two months it's been very good. Consistency is the thing that gives you the extra yard or extra belief.

'The players trust each other. They can look around the dressing room and we have some battle-hardened professionals who have been through this many, many times. We are going to find that in the run-in there are going to be some interesting games for Manchester United. We have a little lead but that can vanish overnight. Our job is to retain that consistency and relish what we are going to experience. This is a great time to play football, knowing you have an opportunity to win the league. But [Wolves manager] Mick McCarthy is a fighter and his team are fighters, so we expect a tough game.'

Barclays Premier League

Molineux | Saturday 5 February 2011 | KO 5.30pm | Attendance: 28,811 | Referee: Michael Oliver

Wolverhampton Wanderers 2 (Elokobi 10, Doyle 40)
Manchester United 1 (Nani 3)

Goodbye, invincibility. United's long unbeaten Premier League run was halted in unexpected circumstances, as relegation-threatened Wolves came from behind to win at Molineux.

Nani gave the Reds a dream start, firing home the opening goal inside three minutes. But by half time the hosts had made their set-piece prowess tell, as headers from George Elokobi and Kevin Doyle turned the scoreline on its head.

A woefully out-of-sorts United never recovered from the confusion arising from Rio Ferdinand's withdrawal with an injury during the warm-up. Jonny Evans was hastily named as a starter and Chris Smalling catapulted from the stands to the bench. The centre-back had barely taken his new seat when United took the lead.

Darren Fletcher fed Nani with a raking pass and the Portuguese winger teased Elokobi on the right-hand side of the area, feinting to cross before checking back on his left foot and unleashing a rasping effort inside Wayne Hennessey's near post.

In a frenetic start to the game, both Wayne Rooney and Nani then fired straight at Hennessey before the hosts drew level on ten minutes. A quickly taken corner from Matt Jarvis caught United napping and the unmarked Elokobi was on hand to head past Edwin van der Sar.

The Reds' flow was affected, but still the better chances fell to the visitors. Dimitar Berbatov headed Nani's cross onto the roof of the net, then stabbed a shot straight at Hennessey, before Nani's free-kick cleared the crossbar by a matter of inches.

But, shortly before the break, a set-piece again proved United's undoing. Nenad Milijas fizzed in an in-swinging cross from the right-hand side of the area and Doyle diverted Elokobi's header past van der Sar to whip the home crowd into a frenzy.

Nani then planted a free header just over the bar to remind the hosts that, although United were way below par, they were still capable of creating opportunities. The Reds' next opening fell to half-time substitute Paul Scholes, on for Michael Carrick, who slid a finish off-target after racing onto Rafael's low cross.

But neither the introduction of Scholes nor Chicharito could undo the hosts' steadfast defending. Mick McCarthy's side produced a sterling second-half display of defensive resolve that rarely looked like letting United back into the game, and Wolves comfortably held on to register a huge upset.

Talk of the unbeaten record rarely carried weight in the United dressing room, but now it could be forgotten altogether. The league leaders had received a timely reality check ahead of the most important stage of the season.

The Teams

Wolverhampton Wanderers: Hennessey, Zubar, Stearman, Berra, Elokobi, Hammill (S.Ward 65), Henry, O'Hara (Foley 59), Milijas (Ebanks-Blake 89), Jarvis, Doyle
Subs not used: Hahnemann, Craddock, Fletcher, Edwards
Booked: Henry, O'Hara

Manchester United: van der Sar, Rafael, J.Evans (Smalling 65), Vidic, Evra, Nani, Carrick (Scholes 46), Fletcher, Giggs, Berbatov (Hernandez 65), Rooney
Subs not used: Kuszczak, Owen, Anderson, O'Shea
Booked: Rooney, Scholes

'We're disappointed, particularly after going in front so early in the game,' sighed Sir Alex. 'The result was caused by bad play at set-pieces. We made a lot of chances, particularly in the first half. Nani had two great shots at the goalkeeper; Wayne Rooney had a good chance ... We played a lot of good football in the first half and made some great chances, but we were never at the races in the second half. We had an incredible amount of possession. The pitch wasn't very good, but nevertheless we never really created anything.'

A below-par performance may have been, in part, traceable to the last-ditch withdrawal of Rio Ferdinand through a calf injury. Not only did the blow threaten to rule the England skipper out of the following weekend's Manchester derby, it also proved unsettling in the immediacy.

'It was a strange one because Chris Smalling had been on the bench and I wasn't even expecting to be a sub,' recalls Jonny Evans. 'Then Mick Phelan told me I'd be on the bench. I was out warming up and then the next thing I knew Rio told me he had a calf injury so I was straight in.'

'I had a little niggle in my back, so I wasn't going to risk it,' adds Smalling. 'Then I saw Rio come in struggling with his calf and it was maybe around ten minutes before kick-off that the manager told me I'd need to get ready and I'd be on the bench to make up the numbers. It wasn't ideal preparation, but it was a mad day and it wasn't helped by the fact we lost the game.'

'As a footballer you've got to be prepared for being called up at any time,' continues Evans. 'So I don't think you can use it as an excuse. It's well known at this football club that you've got to be ready at any given time. We were in control and then they caught us unaware with two set-pieces. They got the lead and hung on really well, and we didn't pose a threat like we know we can do. There's no shame in losing the unbeaten record at Molineux, though. Wolves is a hard place to play. The pitch isn't great and they're a physically strong team, so I don't think losing at Wolves is that out of the ordinary. Any game in the Premier League is a tough one, especially in such a crazy season.'

Though collectively despondent to have slipped up – especially on the same day second-placed Arsenal blew a four-goal lead to drop two points at Newcastle – defeat always provokes a look to the future inside the United dressing room, and there could be few bigger fixtures to draw the gaze forward than the Manchester derby at Old Trafford.

'It's a massive game,' said Darren Fletcher. 'It provides the perfect opportunity to bounce back. It's a local derby, so all the players will be up for it, the fans will be up for it and we'll be ready for the game.'

'It's a terrific game for us now,' added Sir Alex, albeit with a caveat. 'It's a massive game we've got to look forward to. Unfortunately, we've got international matches in midweek, which, in my view, is crazy, but we have to get on with it. We've got plenty of players who will not be involved in internationals and will play next week. With the ones that do travel, we have to give consideration to that before they play at lunchtime on Saturday.'

The untimely break would further restrict the manager's options to face City. Rio Ferdinand's calf injury was sufficiently serious to rule him out of the derby and beyond, while Jonny Evans picked up a knock on Northern Ireland duty, meaning Chris Smalling would partner Nemanja Vidic at Old Trafford. Although there were no other injury concerns, despite the spate of internationals, the lack of cover in the centre of defence put pressure on Smalling's young shoulders.

'I found out I'd be playing a couple of days before the game,' recalls the England Under-21 international. 'The build-up was incredible. It was one of the biggest derby games for a while because of the money they've got and where they were in the league. It was time for me to step up to the plate. I'd played quite a few games up to that point, but this was the first time in terms of playing against good opposition in a key game. There were a few nerves leading up to it, but I got in a couple of days of good training. I watched a lot of videos of Carlos Tevez to make sure I was ready. I did a few bits in training, working on quick feet and making sure I wasn't sucked in because he's quick and he can turn you and take chances. It was a good test and I was relishing it.'

He wasn't alone. Paul Scholes, veteran of the fixture since the mid-1990s and scorer of the oh-so-sweet injury-time winner at Eastlands in April 2010, was similarly upbeat about doing battle with the Reds' local rivals on an ever-changing landscape. 'They are definitely getting closer,' said the midfielder. 'Whether they are alongside Chelsea and Arsenal yet, I am not sure. They would probably have to win something to become main rivals. But I'm sure this year they'll be fighting for it and the same will be true in years to come.

'It is more than local pride now. We are both going for trophies and we are both main rivals for trophies. Years ago, they were in the bottom half of the league, or not even in it, and we were always red-hot favourites. Even then it didn't necessarily mean we were going to win, as results proved. And they have better quality players now, which just makes matches against City even more interesting.'

Barclays Premier League

Old Trafford | Saturday 12 February 2011 | KO 12.45pm |
Attendance: 75,322 | Referee: Andre Marriner

Manchester United 2 (Nani 41, Rooney 78) ,
Manchester City 1 (Silva 65)

In just a shade over 100 years of existence, Old Trafford can't have staged many finer goals than Wayne Rooney's incredible overhead kick that swung the derby United's way.

It was another late winner that edged the increasingly influential fixture for the Reds, but quite apart from the circumstances, Rooney's stunning redirection of Nani's deflected cross into Joe Hart's top corner instantly achieved iconic status on technical merit alone.

Coming 12 minutes from time, it re-established United's lead after David Silva had unwittingly cancelled out Nani's opener, and ensured a vital return to winning ways after the shock of defeat at Wolves.

The match had been conducted on a knife-edge for long periods. City should have forged ahead inside five minutes when Silva was superbly played in behind the home defence, but the tricky Spaniard could only slide wastefully wide from inside the six-yard box.

For United, Nani quickly stood up as the most menacing

attacker, drilling a string of efforts narrowly off-target. Yaya Toure headed Silva's free-kick wide before Darren Fletcher hit the target, only to find it blocked by Hart's midriff. Just as the interval beckoned, with the contest hanging in the balance, United moved ahead.

Edwin van der Sar's long clearance was flicked on to Ryan Giggs, who brilliantly lofted a pass into Nani's path. The winger adroitly cushioned the ball with his right foot and moved away from Pablo Zabaleta before slotting home a left-footed finish to send the home support wild.

For the tenth consecutive home game, Sir Alex's men went into the break in front. Roberto Mancini's response was to replace Aleksander Kolarov with Shaun Wright-Phillips early in the second period and the sprightly little winger gave the visitors more attacking impetus, albeit without an end product.

In truth, neither side looked like scoring in the second half, yet both did. One goal was fortuitous, the other phenomenal. The former belonged to the visitors soon after the hour-mark, as substitute Edin Dzeko's errant shot thundered against Silva's back and looped past the helpless van der Sar.

United responded well and before long were ahead again amid unforgettable scenes. After an awkward touch from Rooney on the edge of the City area, Paul Scholes took charge, spreading the play to Nani, whose cross nicked Zabaleta and looped up towards the penalty spot. With the ball's flight deviated, Vincent Kompany slipped, allowing Rooney the space to twist and hurl himself into the air before unleashing a stunning overhead kick that tore through the air and thumped into Hart's top corner.

Old Trafford was gripped by a flash of stasis as every single onlooker and participant paused to comprehend what had actually unfolded: the goal of the season, to win the derby, that's what. Time to celebrate. And how the vast majority of the crowd revelled. The buzz of animated discussion continued long past the restart, beyond the final whistle and through the following days.

The Teams

Manchester United: van der Sar, O'Shea, Smalling, Vidic, Evra, Nani, Fletcher, Anderson (Berbatov 67), Scholes (Carrick 78), Giggs, Rooney
Subs not used: Lindegaard, Brown, Owen, Hernandez, Rafael
Booked: Giggs, Scholes

Manchester City: Hart, Richards, Kompany, Lescott, Zabaleta, Silva, Milner (Dzeko 61), Y.Toure, Barry, Kolarov (Wright-Phillips 52), Tevez
Subs not used: Given, K.Toure, Jo, Boateng, Vieira
Booked: Kompany, Milner

'I remember Nani's cross taking a deflection, the ball coming over and just hitting it,' says Rooney, recalling the strike. 'You're always working on your technique, but goals like that are instinctive. When I was in the air, I remember Berba shouting towards me as if to say "What are you doing?" Then I turned around and it was in the top corner. To score a goal like that in a derby was a great feeling and it's definitely one of the biggest buzzes I've felt after a goal. The celebration [a David Beckham-esque outstretching of the arms and arching of the back] ...? Rio asked me to do it before the game. I don't know why I remembered, but as I was running away to celebrate it came into my head to do it.'

'Wayne hit a volley against Newcastle some years ago that had the same ferocity and we've seen some excellent goals here, but in terms of execution you'll never see any better,' grinned Sir Alex afterwards. 'I have to say, it reminded me of Denis Law when it went in, but whether or not Denis hit them in with such ferocity I'm not so sure. It was unbelievable. I haven't seen anything like it before, that's for sure. It was absolutely stunning, unbelievable.'

Having sealed a quickfire return to winning ways, Rooney was well aware at the time of the importance of the three points, rather than the stylistic brilliance of their procurement. 'It was a massive game and we're glad we came out on top,' he said. 'We knew we had to win today to keep us top of the league and maintain the gap. I think this almost certainly rules City out of the title race now, unless a disaster happens. We felt we owed the fans a good performance and three points.'

The only negative to arise from the day was Sir Alex's revelation that Ji-sung Park would miss a month of action due to a hamstring injury. 'We got a blow on Saturday morning with the news that Ji-sung Park did his hamstring on Friday afternoon in training,' he said. 'It was unfortunate because it was his last kick of the ball in training. We were really looking forward to having him back after he'd been away for a month at the Asian Cup. He'll be out for up to a month, which is a blow to us.' That news was offset, however, by confirmation that Antonio Valencia was nearing the end of his road to recovery.

'I had an important talk with the club doctor at the start of the comeback period,' says the Ecuadorian. 'He was confident I would be back within five or six months. I kept that in my head; that was my focus. All I wanted was to get one hundred per cent fit, then I wanted to get back into training with the team, like I did before the injury. From there I would be able to get back into playing matches. That was my main focus. The club offered me a break in Spain to get some rest and sunshine, but I said: "No, I want to stay here." My main motivation was getting fit.

'The first two months were the most difficult, mainly because you are on your own. They had strapped my leg and I was able to move around, but for the most part of those two months I could do very little. I was in bed a lot, resting my leg. Eventually that gets really, really boring. Most of the time was spent reading books and watching DVDs, so you go out of your mind with boredom. When the injury began to improve, I was able to come back to Carrington. Then I started in the swimming pool and I was able to do some sprinting sessions. It was very important to get back and to get the support of your team-mates.'

The Ecuadorian trained with the Reds' Reserves before rejoining the main group. Ironically, a number of the Reserves would step up to senior duty before him, as Sir Alex looked to use the FA Cup visit of Crawley Town as a chance to give some of his promising youngsters a taste of a first-team match day, with Ryan Tunnicliffe, Joshua King and Paul Pogba all in contention. Nevertheless, the boss wasn't taking the non-leaguers lightly.

'We respect the fact that Crawley are the best non-league side for quite a while,' he said. 'There is always room for ambition and they could do well when they get into the Football League, given the kind of money they have behind them and the ambition they've got. We expect a tough game. They're very committed and aggressive.'

'I smiled when the draw came out,' added Michael Carrick. 'It's a classic draw and one a lot of people probably wanted to see. It's one of those great things the FA Cup is capable of throwing up. A lot of people are going to have a great day, but for us it's about getting through to the next round. We'll give Crawley the respect they deserve and we're certainly not taking the game lightly. But we do believe that if we play well we'll win.'

Ryan Giggs was omitted from the squad to face Crawley and was free to savour his weekend off, fresh from extending his rolling contract by another year, much to the delight of all parties. 'All I've ever wanted to do is play for United and I've been lucky enough to do that for twenty years,' said the winger, while Sir Alex added: 'You run out of words to describe Ryan Giggs. To have the desire and the ability to play at the top level in such a physically demanding position at his age requires a special person.'

But even without Giggs, surely United would have more than enough to plot a path past the unglamorous visitors and into the quarter-finals?

FA Cup fifth round

Old Trafford | Saturday 19 February 2011 | KO 5.15pm |
Attendance: 74,778 | Referee: Lee Probert

Manchester United 1 (Brown 28)
Crawley Town 0

United made heavy weather of it but managed to see off non-league Crawley Town by virtue of Wes Brown's first-half header at Old Trafford.

The Reds booked a quarter-final clash with Arsenal after a largely lethargic display, and only escaped the ignominy of a replay by a matter of inches as Richard Brodie headed against the hosts' bar in injury time.

Fronted with non-league opposition, between the draining duties of a huge Manchester derby and a Champions League trip to Marseille, Sir Alex Ferguson quite rightly rang the changes. Nine, to be precise, from the side that beat Manchester City. Wayne Rooney made the bench as insurance, but was joined by teen prodigies Joshua King, Ryan Tunnicliffe and Paul Pogba, who had shone in Warren Joyce's Reserves.

Some 9,000 Crawley fans – a notable increase on their average home gate of around 1,500 – made the trip to Old Trafford and were soon throwing their choral weight behind the underdogs. They were almost given plenty to crow about when midfielder Ben Smith's spectacular long-range effort arced just wide of Anders Lindegaard's post.

That effort was out of keeping with a first half in which United bossed possession and were always a final ball away from running up a handsome scoreline. The first – and only – goal of the game arrived when Darron Gibson's perfect curling cross was glanced home by stand-in skipper Brown.

Fabio might have doubled the lead five minutes later after a fine pass from Michael Carrick, but the Brazilian's stabbed shot went wide. Shortly afterwards, Gabriel Obertan cut inside from the left and drilled in a shot that Michael Kuipers palmed away. At the break, Anderson made way for Rooney because of a knee injury that would go on to disrupt the remainder of the Brazilian's season.

Both Rafael and Fabio would also succumb to injuries during the second half, depriving Sir Alex of all three of his starting Brazilians. In their place, Chris Smalling and Darren Fletcher joined a contest that was more even than many had predicted.

As the game wore on, Crawley's approach was less about coagulating United's play and more about asserting themselves as an attacking force. David Hunt volleyed wide from 12 yards, Matt Tubbs sent an overhead kick narrowly over the bar and the biggest scare of all was saved for injury time, when Brodie's looping header bounced to safety off the top of Lindegaard's bar.

The Teams

Manchester United: Lindegaard, Rafael (Smalling 54), Brown, O'Shea, Fabio (Fletcher 69), Bébé, Gibson, Anderson (Rooney 46), Carrick, Obertan, Hernandez
Subs not used: Kuszczak, King, Pogba, Tunnicliffe
Booked: Brown, Rooney

Crawley Town: Kuipers, Torres, Hunt, Mills, Howell, McFadzean, Bulman, Gibson (Cook 69), Smith (Rusk 81), McAllister (Brodie 63), Tubbs
Subs not used: Rents, Wilson, Napper, Shearer
Booked: Torres

'It didn't matter what the scoreline was today because it was their day, there's no question about that,' admitted Sir Alex. 'They deserved a draw, really, on the second half, with the effort they put in, the commitment. They made it very difficult for us and we were second to every ball. It's disappointing. Sometimes you get the breaks in the FA Cup and you struggle through one round. We've done that in the past and today was another example.'

'It was difficult,' admitted unlikely match-winner Wes Brown. 'They put everything into the game. We prepared right, we got the goal but they made it difficult for us and we couldn't really break them down. It was close. In the last fifteen minutes they started to throw everyone forward and get the ball in the box. I thought we handled it pretty well but, in all, we should've done better.'

There was no time to dwell on the performance, however, as the

Paul Scholes jostles with Manchester City's David Silva in the FA Cup semi-final at Wembley, as the Blues end United's hopes of repeating the 1999 Treble.

Skipper-for-the-day Rio Ferdinand contests a header with Everton's Diniyar Bilyaletdinov in a tight encounter decided by Chicharito's priceless late winner.

Ryan Giggs shows that Schalke goalkeeper Manuel Neuer can indeed be beaten, scoring the opening goal as United record a thrilling 2–0 win in Germany.

Referee Chris Foy and Michael Owen disagree at the end of United's defeat at Arsenal, with the Reds striker outlining his case for an earlier penalty.

Anderson slots home his second goal of the game as a much-changed Reds side romps through to the Champions League final at Schalke's expense.

D-day in the Premier League title race starts in unforgettable fashion, as Chicharito celebrates scoring against Chelsea within the first minute.

Edwin van der Sar and his defensive shield celebrate a season-defining victory after beating Carlo Ancelotti's champions 2–1 at Old Trafford.

Above: Needing just a point to confirm the title, Wayne Rooney and his team-mates go wild at Ewood Park after the striker's late penalty bags a draw against Blackburn.

Right: Patrice Evra and Nani revel in a dress rehearsal for the title celebrations by lifting an inflatable trophy thrown by the travelling Red Army.

Below: The champions, led by Edwin van der Sar in his final Old Trafford appearance, are afforded a final-day guard of honour by relegation-threatened Blackpool.

Champions! After an unforgettable season of twists and turns, Nemanja Vidic finally gets to lift the Premier League trophy.

Post-match, the champagne flows in Old Trafford's home dressing room, as the Reds toast a fourth crown in five seasons.

The silverware keeps coming, as Tom Thorpe lifts the FA Youth Cup for Paul McGuinness' Under-18s; a competition record tenth triumph for United.

Old Trafford – along with some of its favourite sons – bids a fond farewell to club captain Gary Neville, ahead of his testimonial against Juventus.

Wayne Rooney, United's goalscorer and star performer in the Champions League final, holds off a challenge from Barcelona's Sergio Busquets.

A disconsolate Ryan Giggs looks on as Barcelona's players jubilate after a deserved victory over the Reds at Wembley Stadium.

Despite the defeat at Wembley – and the teeming rain – United's
spirits cannot be dampened during a memorable trophy parade
through Manchester and Trafford.

United supporters turn up in their thousands at Old Trafford to salute their heroes,
who are now the most prolific champions in the history of English football.

Reds travelled to France for the resumption of Champions League duties. Before heading back to an inevitably hostile reaction in his homeland, following the previous summer's World Cup debacle, Patrice Evra committed his future to United until at least June 2014, and ominously warned: 'I've won a lot in the last five years, but I want to win more and I know that's the mentality of everyone here.

'Marseille are going to be confident of beating us, there's no doubt about that. It's a dangerous game for us, because we are favourites and Marseille have nothing to lose. I've watched some of their games this season and you can see they are a good team and they have a great manager in Didier Deschamps, who was my coach at Monaco. He's not afraid of any team and I know he'll get his players motivated before the game so they play with no fear. They will give one hundred per cent, but we are Manchester United and we need to show our qualities. It will be a tough game, but if we are professional and do our job we have a great chance of going through.'

Evra's positivity was mirrored throughout the United camp as the squad touched down in Marseille. 'This is when the Champions League really starts,' Paul Scholes said of the knockout phase. 'Hopefully this is the start of a good end to the season for us, and we can go all the way to the Champions League final and win it. But while we know [Marseille] won't be easy, we're looking forward to it. We're getting down to the latter stages now, so the results become even more important. It's time to really stand up and start playing.'

The Reds would have to take on the French champions without a raft of important players. Anderson had flown to Portugal to see a specialist about the knee injury he had suffered against Crawley, Ryan Giggs was rested as a precaution and joined Jonny Evans, Rio Ferdinand, Michael Owen, Ji-sung Park and Antonio Valencia in remaining in Manchester. Despite those absentees, Sir Alex was rubbing his hands with glee at what lay ahead.

'We have an important few weeks coming up,' he said. 'We are just starting four away games on the run, which is a great challenge for us. They are all fantastic matches, but it is a time we should enjoy. They are big games and, in that situation, the players don't let us down often. We are reaching that interesting stage of the season when everyone wants to beat Manchester United. I know my team is ready for what they face. Our attitude is simply to win them all. When games really mean something, big players respond. The experience comes out and then determination. You get the feeling when you reach this point of the Champions League that we are at the start of something proper, something exciting and grand.'

While those words would eventually prove prophetic, events at the Stade Velodrome were anything but exciting or grand.

Champions League second round, first leg

Stade Velodrome | Wednesday 23 February 2011 | KO 7.45pm | Attendance: 57,957 | Referee: Felix Brych

Marseille 0
Manchester United 0

A shared incentive of avoiding defeat and deferring judgement until the second leg at Old Trafford ensured the stalest of stalemates in Marseille, with the home side surprisingly coy in the face of United's customary European away counter-attacking.

Neither side made a glaring goalscoring opportunity on a night when both defences excelled themselves. Darren Fletcher's early, low drive was the closest either side came to a breakthrough. In boxing parlance, neither landed a telling blow because scarcely a punch was thrown.

Marseille made an aggressive start straight from the kick-off, however, with ex-Red Gabriel Heinze clattering Nani and Loic Remy firing wildly off-target inside the opening minute. Nani also chanced his arm from distance but missed the target. Still, the Portuguese winger was enjoying himself against Heinze, regularly surging beyond the Argentine. When the defender caught Nani outside the box, the resulting free-kick culminated in Fletcher driving a fierce low shot through a packed area. Marseille goalkeeper Steve Mandanda saw it late but pulled off a fine save.

Thereafter, both sides became sloppy in possession and presented each other countless opportunities to create chances. But each time a defender would rise to the challenge and either intercept, tackle or clear in the face of hesitant attacking.

The second period opened in similar fashion to the first. Brandao nodded a cross into the hands of Edwin van der Sar, while Heinze had to be alert to clear Rooney's cross as Mandanda flapped. Marseille enjoyed the better attacking moments, but John O'Shea and Nani combined to tee up Dimitar Berbatov, whose shot thundered against hulking defender Souleymane Diawara and rebounded to safety.

United grew as the half wore on, galvanised in part by the intro-duction of pass-master Paul Scholes, and only quick thinking from Mandanda prevented Nani finishing off some fine interplay with Berbatov late on. The game, uninspiring to say the least, finished goalless, although at least both teams would have everything to play for in the second leg.

The Teams

Marseille: Mandanda, Fanni, Diawara, Mbia, Heinze, Remy (Valbuena 79), Cisse (Cheyrou 70), Gonzalez, Kabore, A.Ayew, Brandao
Subs not used: Hilton, Taiwo, Andrade, Abriel, J.Ayew

Manchester United: van der Sar, O'Shea, Smalling, Vidic, Evra, Gibson (Scholes 73), Carrick, Fletcher, Nani, Rooney, Berbatov
Subs not used: Kuszczak, Brown, Hernandez, Fabio, Rafael, Obertan

'We're pretty disappointed with the performance,' said Michael Carrick, with no shortage of candour. 'Our passing wasn't great so we didn't give ourselves the chance of creating chances in the game. We defended well as a unit, as we've managed to do quite a few times in Europe, and the clean sheet gives us a good opportunity of winning the tie at home. We're confident we can do that, but we'll have to play better than tonight. The other side of our game – our attacking and possession as a team – has to be better.

'It's unfair on Marseille to say this was a winnable game. Any game away from home in Europe is difficult, but we didn't play anywhere near our best tonight and we know that. Hopefully we can put that right when we get them back to Old Trafford. It's a different game at home.'

Before the second leg, though, attentions switched to the ongoing pursuit of a 19th league title. Still criticism rained down on Sir Alex Ferguson's side in the media, with widespread suggestions that United had merely been the best of a bad bunch and had topped the table without playing well. They were assertions that rankled within the Reds camp.

'I think it helped us,' says Chris Smalling. 'People were saying we weren't playing well but we were still winning games. That got under our skin and every set of eleven players that plays together sticks together. There's a real togetherness that has dragged us through some difficult games this season as we ground out wins.'

'I am not surprised by where we are,' added Nemanja Vidic, with one eye firmly on a Premier League table that quickly pinpointed United's position. 'The table shows where we should be. In some games we scored a goal in the last minute, but there were others when we conceded them. We are where we are. We have the points we should have overall. We are just taking it game by game. We have important matches to play and the next one is against Wigan. We have to take the three points. I believe we can.'

Both Vidic and Smalling were pencilled in for the trip to the freshly relaid turf of the DW Stadium, as Sir Alex Ferguson continued to wait for the return of Rio Ferdinand and Jonny Evans. 'Nothing much has changed on the injury front,' the manager shrugged. 'We're trying to get Ryan Giggs fit for the Wigan game and Michael Owen is back training and could be available. Rio and Jonny Evans should both be back for Liverpool next weekend.'

Barclays Premier League

DW Stadium | Saturday 26 February 2011 | KO 3.00pm |
Attendance: 18,140 | Referee: Mark Clattenburg

Wigan Athletic 0
Manchester United 4 (Hernandez 18, 75, Rooney 83, Fabio 87)

Clinical goals either side of half time from Javier Hernandez and late strikes by Wayne Rooney and Fabio settled a see-saw encounter at the DW Stadium.

The victory certainly wasn't anywhere as comprehensive as the scoreline suggests. The hosts played their part in an entertaining game and were left irate by referee Mark Clattenburg's decision not to punish Wayne Rooney's clash with James McCarthy after eight minutes.

Chicharito struck a vital early goal to settle United's nerves, however, and then kick-started a late rush in which he, Rooney and Fabio turned in close-range finishes against a Latics side pushing on in vain.

Sir Alex made two changes from the side that drew away in Marseille, with Paul Scholes replacing Darron Gibson in the centre of midfield and Dimitar Berbatov making way for Hernandez.

The home side enjoyed plenty of possession in the opening quarter of an hour. After initially losing the ball, Nemanja Vidic was forced into a fine block tackle on the edge of his area to thwart Charles N'Zogbia, while Edwin van der Sar stood strong to block Victor Moses' effort after Scholes' pass had been charged down.

It proved a vital save. Two minutes later, United were in front as Nani sprinted down the left and slid a perfectly weighted pass across to Chicharito, who nipped in ahead of Ali Al-Habsi to poke a finish inside the near post.

Wigan hit back almost immediately and should have levelled when N'Zogbia flicked a perfect pass to Ben Watson, only for van der Sar to hurl himself at the midfielder's shot and block it to safety. Shortly before the break, Nani smashed a left-footed shot off the inside of the post to reiterate the visitors' threat on the break.

Still Wigan pressed. Maynor Figueroa stung van der Sar's palms with a thumping 30-yard drive, Moses fired over and substitute Franco di Santo had a goal correctly chalked off for offside. At the other end, Nani drilled into the side-netting and a cluster of defenders blocked Darren Fletcher's follow-up after Al-Habsi had spilled another Nani effort.

Chicharito wrapped up victory on 74 minutes after beautifully simple approach play with Rooney yielded an opening for the Mexican. The speedy striker raced through on goal before slotting home an unerring finish in front of the Reds' vocal travelling support.

Wigan's hopes sank, United's tails were up. Soon Darron Gibson released Dimitar Berbatov with a splendid long pass and the Bulgarian squared unselfishly for Rooney to tap into an open goal. Fabio then added a fourth from close range, converting at the back post after the hosts had failed to clear their lines.

On the short trip back to Manchester, United could reflect on a positive outing. Four goals, a fourth Premier League away win of the season and a four-point lead preserved. The Reds would go to Chelsea in good shape and with a chance to consign the champions essentially to also-ran status.

The Teams

Wigan Athletic: Al-Habsi, Gohouri, G.Caldwell, Alcaraz, Figueroa, McCarthy, Watson (Gomez 89), Diame, N'Zogbia (McArthur 90), Rodallega, Moses (di Santo 65)
Subs not used: Pollitt, Thomas, Piscu, S.Caldwell

Manchester United: van der Sar, O'Shea, Smalling, Vidic, Evra, Fletcher, Carrick, Scholes (Gibson 77), Nani (Fabio 85), Rooney, Hernandez (Berbatov 77)
Subs not used: Kuszczak, Brown, Rafael, King
Booked: Hernandez

'It was very important we got the three points,' admitted Chicharito. 'We're wanting to improve the away games because we know we've lost a lot of points. We wanted to improve that today and we played very well and scored goals. We are very happy because we are top of the league and the Champions League is there, too.'

The grinning Mexican may have provided a cheery perspective on a highly successful afternoon's work, but Sir Alex Ferguson was already buffing his defence in readiness for an inquest into Wayne Rooney's off-the-ball clash with James McCarthy. 'I have had a chance to see it,' confirmed the manager. 'There is nothing in it. But the question has been asked and because it is Wayne Rooney the press will raise a campaign to get him hung by Tuesday or electrocuted or something like that. It is unbelievable. Watch the press. It will be interesting to see it.'

A frenzy was indeed whipped up, but the striker escaped without punishment. Nevertheless, it did nothing to calm what had been a trying 2010–11 for Rooney. 'I have to say, it's been a difficult season for me, probably the worst I've ever had,' he said. 'The good thing is that I feel fresh at a time when most players are picking up injuries or feeling jaded. I really want to kick on from here and have a big impact on the most important matches of the season.'

The next two matches – trips to Stamford Bridge and Anfield – provided a perfect platform, both for Rooney to fulfil his personal wishes and for United to underline the team's title-winning credentials.

March

Springtime: when bums squeak and nails suffer. United entered March with a taxing, but exciting, double-header of trips to Chelsea and Liverpool in the space of five days. Patchy away form had been the difference between the Reds and an inexorable march to the title, but wins at two of the least hospitable away grounds in the Premier League would surely put title number 19 on the horizon.

Plus, surely United were due some luck at Stamford Bridge after controversial defeats in previous seasons – Martin Atkinson's award of John Terry's 2009–10 winner, which might have been chalked off for offside and a foul, continued to rankle, as did Michael Ballack's contentious late penalty in 2007–08. The Reds were also on a rare run of two successive defeats at Anfield; historically a happy hunting ground.

United's hopes were aided by news that Wayne Rooney would be available for selection. Calls for him to be banned for his clash with James McCarthy at Wigan had failed after referee Mark Clattenburg confirmed he had seen the incident and, in his view, dealt with it accordingly. Softening his initial stance slightly, Sir Alex said: 'Mark Clattenburg is the only person who comes out of this incident with any credit at all. Wayne Rooney is a bit fortunate – it was a clash and it was a silly thing to do, but it's finished now.'

At Carrington, the mood was upbeat. 'Going into March, everyone was pretty confident,' says Chris Smalling. 'We were coming off some good form and we thought we could extend that.' Rio Ferdinand was mindful of the Blues' big-money January signings, David Luiz and Fernando Torres, but doubted Torres' ability to fire the champions back into the title race. 'The Torres deal did make me think: "Wow, they've really gone for it." But will those transfers really improve Chelsea this season?' he wondered. 'I don't know. Next season, I would say, "Yes, they will." But it is hard to settle in quickly in January.'

The Reds' preparations were punctuated by a memorable landmark for Ryan Giggs, who had made his debut exactly 20 years earlier against Everton. 'There was an article in the paper about it and they had some stats in there that the lads were killing me about,' he says. 'Rafa and Fabio were only eight months old at the time! To be honest, though, it doesn't really feel like I'm thirty-seven. I have some great banter with the young players and still think of myself as just one of the lads.'

'Every cliché in the book has been used about the man already and I'm sure they will be said many times again. He's an absolute legend,' said John O'Shea. 'You've seen how the manager has built squads and teams over the years, and Giggsy has been a vital part of every single one of them. When you think of the greats, someone like Paolo Maldini springs to mind for his time with AC Milan, but I think you could say Giggsy has almost gone past him. The speed and the balance he still shows to go past people – whether it be an old, experienced defender or a new up-and-comer – is incredible. He's enjoying his football so much at the minute so I can't see why he couldn't continue until he's forty, but I'll let him decide on that.'

Giggs' legend would be further gilded by a record-extending 12th Premier League title, and the events of Stamford Bridge could go a long way to shaping that destiny.

Barclays Premier League

Stamford Bridge | Tuesday 1 March 2011 | KO 7.45pm |
Attendance: 41,825 | Referee: Martin Atkinson

Chelsea 2 (Luiz 53, Lampard 79 (pen))
Manchester United 1 (Rooney 29)

Déjà vu? United slipped to a controversial defeat at Stamford Bridge for the second season in a row, as Frank Lampard converted a late penalty to catapult Carlo Ancelotti's side back into the title race.

David Luiz had cancelled out Wayne Rooney's excellent opener before Chris Smalling was harshly adjudged to have fouled Yuri Zhirkov inside the United area with 11 minutes remaining. Referee Martin Atkinson, who allowed John Terry's controversial winner in the corresponding fixture last season, pointed to the spot and Lampard secured the points.

United's ire was heightened by a late red card for Nemanja Vidic, who was booked twice, while Luiz escaped censure for a crude block on Rooney when he was already on a yellow card.

The evening began in surprising fashion when, for the first time since May 2008 – 165 matches ago – Sir Alex Ferguson named an unchanged starting line-up. Eyebrows were also raised when Fernando Torres had the ball in the net after a minute, but Martin Atkinson's whistle had already been blown for a foul.

That set the tone for an absorbing 90 minutes. Florent Malouda drilled straight at Edwin van der Sar as Chelsea dominated the early stages, but steadily the Reds grew in stature. Rooney looked sharp as he narrowly failed to meet Patrice Evra's cross and then headed a half-chance off-target. Then he opened the scoring in style.

Collecting Nani's pass, the striker took advantage of criminally laid-back defending from the hosts by turning, striding forward and belting a low effort inside Petr Cech's right-hand post. The visitors had struck first.

The champions had little by way of riposte until the final moments of the first half, when van der Sar made a magnificent triple save, first parrying Lampard's low free-kick, then blocking Branislav Ivanovic's follow-up before clawing the loose ball to safety amid a whirlwind of boots and bodies.

There was nothing the veteran stopper could do when Luiz rifled home the equaliser on 53 minutes, however, as Chelsea started the second period in impressive fashion. The Brazilian pounced first on a loose ball after the Reds had failed to clear a Chelsea corner sufficiently and lashed a volley into the bottom corner.

United gradually weathered the hosts' storm, even after the introduction of substitute Didier Drogba, and might have retaken the lead when Rooney raced clear down the left but failed to shoot decisively or cross from a glorious position. Instead, he merely steered the ball between the far post and the onrushing Chicharito.

But, just as United appeared comfortable, Zhirkov tumbled over Smalling's outstretched leg in front of referee Atkinson, who pointed to the spot. Lampard slammed the ball into the roof of the net to darken United's mood, and the woe was compounded when Vidic saw yellow for a second time for hauling down Ramires in injury time.

The skipper would miss the Reds' trip to Anfield, where the league leaders would try to steady the ship on increasingly choppy waters.

The Teams

Chelsea: Cech, Ivanovic, Luiz (Bosingwa 81), Terry, Cole, Ramires, Essien, Lampard, Malouda (Zhirkov 71), Torres, Anelka (Drogba 61)
Subs not used: Turnbull, Mikel, Kalou, McEachran
Booked: Essien, Luiz, Ramires

Manchester United: van der Sar, O'Shea, Smalling, Vidic, Evra (Fabio 81), Fletcher, Carrick, Scholes (Berbatov 70), Nani, Rooney, Hernandez (Giggs 70)

Subs not used: Kuszczak, Brown, Rafael, Gibson
Booked: Giggs
Sent off: Vidic

'I think we defended badly on the first goal. That was a bad one to lose, but the penalty was so soft,' rued Sir Alex Ferguson. 'Dear me. That's three years in a row the referee's decisions have changed the game [at Stamford Bridge]. I'm pleased and proud of my players. They've endured a lot of decisions against them, they've carried themselves through it, they've done their best and they've created chances and played good football. They didn't deserve that.'

The manager made further comments about the referee's performance in another post-match interview. Although he quickly corrected an initial reference to Atkinson's fairness by instead calling into question the official's strength, Sir Alex was charged with improper conduct by the Football Association. The boss appealed the charge, while countless replays of the penalty incident continued to suggest it was a harsh decision.

'I was gutted,' admits Chris Smalling, who found himself on the wrong end of Atkinson's late call. 'We felt we controlled the game. It was disappointing not to get the second goal to open it up, but going into the second half we knew they'd have to come out a little bit more and they did. We still created chances, and then you've got the decisions. Quite often now you're getting big games being decided by a refereeing decision. Think what you will but, personally, I think it was a soft penalty. I felt I won the ball and he went over my standing leg. I didn't feel there was a lot more I could do.

'We didn't feel we deserved to lose. Then, luckily, or unluckily, it was Liverpool next up, and we looked at it like there was no better place to kick on and get back to winning ways. We looked at it as a positive. We were looking forward to trying to bounce back in a massive game.'

Smalling was assured of a start at Anfield, with the suspended Nemanja Vidic joining injury victims Rio Ferdinand and Jonny

Evans on the sidelines. Despite a worryingly concentrated level of absenteeism, the Reds' pre-match preparations were handed a quick-fire double boost when midfielders Michael Carrick and Darren Fletcher both extended their contracts.

'It's great news,' said Wayne Rooney. 'They have been great players for the team and have been very consistent for us over the last few years. It's always nice to see players sign new contracts because it's a big boost for the team.' Carrick and Fletcher had followed the example set by Nemanja Vidic, Patrice Evra, Ryan Giggs, Anderson and Rooney himself, although the striker was still irked that Edwin van der Sar could not be persuaded to follow suit. 'It's great to see all the lads sign new deals, but unfortunately Edwin hasn't,' he said. 'We'd like him to sign a new deal but obviously he's made his decision and we respect that.'

Fletcher was relishing the chance to visit Anfield – especially given his string of impressive displays in three successive wins over the Merseysiders – although he was wary of the impact his country-man, Kenny Dalglish, had already had in his second spell in charge of Liverpool.

'We know it is going to be a difficult game,' said Fletcher. 'Dalglish is a couple of months into the job now and he has rejuvenated the place. Performance levels have improved. He was only made the manager that weekend [when United knocked Liverpool out of the FA Cup in January], so he hadn't had a lot of time to put his stamp on the team. But he's done that now. I've noticed a slightly different formation. It's something we'll have to prepare for.

'Plus, it's part and parcel of football rivalry that they might have more incentive to stop us achieving stuff than to do it themselves. Liverpool are a proud club with a great tradition. They won't want to relinquish the record. It is going to be intimidating for us. Any corner, throw-in, or even glimpse of a chance for Liverpool is going to draw crazy cheers from their supporters. That's something we have to try to block out. We have to try to relish the pressure rather than be daunted by it. United fans will also do their best and it should make for a great atmosphere, one that should bring out the best from us.'

Barclays Premier League

Anfield | Sunday 6 March 2011 | KO 1.30pm | Attendance: 44,753 | Referee: Phil Dowd

Liverpool 3 (Kuyt 33, 38, 64)
Manchester United 1 (Hernandez 90)

United's quest to regain the Barclays Premier League title suffered a second successive setback as Dirk Kuyt's hat-trick gave Liverpool a deserved victory at Anfield.

The Dutch striker turned in a trio of close-range conversions to put the hosts out of sight with 25 minutes still to play. Meanwhile, United rarely looked like finding a route back into the game and had only Chicharito's injury-time header to clutch as consolation for a limp performance.

The Reds started slowly, reached a peak just before the hosts moved ahead and then tailed off in a key period before half time. Liverpool's energetic start had United on the ropes early, even though Dimitar Berbatov clipped the outside of Pepe Reina's post with an audacious swerving volley.

Just as Sir Alex's men began to settle, and Wes Brown had a deflected header cleared to safety, Liverpool forged ahead. The goal owed much to superb trickery from Luis Suarez, who turned away from Chris Smalling and Rafael, bypassed challenges from Michael Carrick and Brown and squared for Kuyt to smash in a finish from right on the goal-line.

Tails up, Liverpool soon pressed home their advantage as Nani misjudged Suarez's deep cross and headed back towards his own goal. Kuyt, deep inside the six-yard box, was more accurate with his own header and doubled the hosts' lead.

Nani's afternoon soon lunged from bad to worse, as Jamie Carragher planted his studs high into the winger's shin. As tempers flared on both sides, Nani leapt to his feet to show referee Phil Dowd his wound, then collapsed in agony before being stretchered from the field. Carragher was only booked. Soon afterwards, Rafael and Skrtel entered the book for a set-to after a strong challenge from the United defender.

The Reds started the second period with greater intent. Chicharito steered Berbatov's cross narrowly off-target, before Giggs did likewise from Wayne Rooney's centre. Berbatov then argued he had reduced the arrears, but the officials correctly ruled the Bulgarian's header had been blocked on the line by Raul Meireles.

United's cause was lost when Kuyt completed his close-range treble shortly after the hour. Suarez's free-kick bounced just in front of Edwin van der Sar, who couldn't clutch the ball, and his fellow Dutchman raced in to sweep home a finish.

Thereafter, United plugged away gamely but never looked like getting back into the match. The goal, when it came, was too late. Indeed, injury time had already begun when Chicharito nodded home Ryan Giggs' right-wing cross. The battle had long since been lost; now, the wider war was starting to hot up.

The Teams

Liverpool: Reina, Johnson, Carragher, Skrtel, Aurelio (Kyrgiakos 24), Meireles (Carroll 74), Gerrard, Lucas, Rodriguez, Suarez (Cole 89), Kuyt
Subs not used: Gulacsi, Spearing, Ngog, Poulsen
Booked: Carragher, Skrtel

Manchester United: van der Sar, Rafael (O'Shea 76), Smalling, Brown, Evra, Nani (Hernandez 45), Carrick, Scholes (Fletcher 84), Giggs, Berbatov, Rooney
Subs not used: Kuszczak, Fabio, Obertan, Gibson
Booked: Rafael, Scholes, van der Sar

There was no immediate reaction to the stinging defeat – not in public, at least, as neither the manager nor his players spoke to the media. Inside the away dressing room at Anfield, Sir Alex made his players aware that their display had fallen below the required standards.

'There have been a few occasions where the manager hasn't been happy afterwards and he really wasn't too happy after that game,' says Darron Gibson, an unused substitute at Anfield. 'If you lose a big game 3–1, I'd be surprised if any manager didn't go mad, but obviously we didn't play well and we knew we were in for it after the game.'

'We were so disappointed,' adds Edwin van der Sar. 'I think the last few years we haven't really played well there, and this year was no different. Somehow we weren't able to raise our game. We didn't really get going, they got a couple of scrappy goals, which were mistakes on our part, and I think Dirk Kuyt got the easiest hat-trick in world football over the last forty-five years. Hopefully the boys can change that bad run at Anfield over the coming seasons.'

Aside from the ramifications of United's meek display in terms of the title race, the game's major talking point was provided by Jamie Carragher's lunge on Nani. After the match, the veteran defender waited outside the away dressing room to apologise to the winger, whose wound was too gaping to stitch.

'It was a very bad tackle and I don't think the referee made the right call,' says van der Sar.

'To be fair,' Darron Gibson adds. 'He meant to go in hard, but he didn't go in to do what he did. I don't think any footballer means to hurt anybody else and it was nice to see him wait around to say sorry.'

Over the coming days, Carragher also telephoned close friend Michael Owen to check on Nani's progress. The winger, however, was still upset: 'He came to apologise after the game. But I was not happy. When I saw my leg for the first time, I thought my season was finished.'

Four days later, Sir Alex's next press conference, ahead of the FA Cup quarter-final against Arsenal, put him face to face with the nation's media, and the manager shed light on the extent of Nani's injury. 'We've managed to stitch the wound,' he explained. 'What we're guarding against now is infection. The swelling has gone down a great deal, which is good news. We have a two-week international break after next Saturday, but whether we can get him fit for the Bolton match is difficult to say.'

The real centre of attention at Carrington was the manager himself, so soon after receiving the FA misconduct charge and losing two major matches. Asked if he felt sorry for his Arsenal counterpart, Arsene Wenger, whose side had just exited the Champions League at the hands of Barcelona, Sir Alex replied: 'I have sympathy for myself. I've had a bad week! But you've got to look forward. We've got big opportunities and a lot of challenges ahead for the rest of the season. It's terrific to be involved at this time of year, when every game you play is of importance. We have Tuesday's match against Marseille and then we have Bolton in a league game.

'We've got the experience to recover from it [two successive defeats]. At any club, you don't go through a season where everything is rosy. When you get the bad moments, you have to recover. It's another day in the history of Manchester United. We take that history into games. Our ability to do that over the years has been a credit to every team I've had here.

'Games against Arsenal have always meant something and have always been competitive in my time here. Arsenal have always been there as one of our main contenders. There's an importance to any quarter-final tie and against Arsenal it's always exciting. There's an opportunity to get to the semi-finals, so we'll do our best and I'll pick my best available team. These games are never easy. We expect a difficult game and so will they.'

Within the squad, the visit of Arsenal had taken on huge significance. 'It was a massive game and everyone knew we needed to win,' recalls Darron Gibson. 'The manager, the players and the staff all knew what had to be done. I think everyone was a bit surprised by the team we put out, but we had a game-plan and I think the gamble the boss took paid off.'

FA Cup sixth round

Old Trafford | Saturday 12 March 2011 | KO 5.30pm | Attendance: 74,693 | Referee: Chris Foy

Manchester United 2 (Fabio 28, Rooney 49)
Arsenal 0

United made an invaluable return to winning ways, ringing the changes and still striking a psychological blow against title rivals Arsenal by booking a berth in the FA Cup semi-finals.

Close-range goals from Fabio and Wayne Rooney took a much-changed Reds side to Wembley as Arsene Wenger's side bowed out of a third competition in a fortnight, after their Carling Cup final defeat to Birmingham and Champions League exit to Barcelona.

The hosts' progress owed much to the brilliance of Edwin van der Sar, whose virtuoso performance prompted the entire home support at Old Trafford to urge him to renege on his retirement pledge. 'One more year' they bellowed, but got nothing but a string of excellent saves and bashful smiles in return.

Van der Sar was one of just five players who kept their place after starting at Anfield. Nemanja Vidic returned from suspension and Chicharito replaced Dimitar Berbatov, but it was Sir Alex's wholly new-look midfield that raised eyebrows. Fabio and Rafael started as marauding wingers either side of a central axis of Darron Gibson and John O'Shea, as the selection hinted that the boss had one eye on Marseille's Champions League visit.

The unfamiliarity in United's ranks was apparent early on as Arsenal bossed the opening exchanges. Andrey Arshavin struck wide from distance, while Robin van Persie and Abou Diaby both prompted routine catches from van der Sar as the Gunners passed and probed incessantly.

But they had also been warned. Rafael had headed Fabio's cross over the bar with United's only early opening and there would be no such profligacy second time around. A lightning break involving the twins culminated in Manuel Almunia pushing out Chicharito's header and Fabio was on hand to slide a finish high into the roof of the net. Advantage United.

Arsenal's response was swift. Van der Sar touched van Persie's low drive just past the upright, then plunged quickly to his right to stop Samir Nasri's shot from creeping inside the same post. After the interval came the passage of play that would seal the result. Van der Sar performed a heroic double save to prevent a Brown own goal and turn away Laurent Koscielny's follow-up, before substitute Antonio Valencia led a counter that brought United's killer second goal.

The Ecuadorian, warmly welcomed by the Old Trafford crowd, carried the ball 40 yards down the right flank and slipped it to Rafael. The Brazilian's cross for Javier Hernandez looped up off Johan Djourou and Rooney raced in to nod the loose ball in off the far upright.

Then it was over to van der Sar. Nasri, van Persie, Tomas Rosicky and substitute Marouane Chamakh all tested the Dutch stopper without finding a way past him, before Almunia took his turn to perform heroics. The Spaniard clawed away Djourou's errant intervention – in an incident that left the defender nursing a dislocated shoulder – then denied Chicharito in injury time with a wonderful double block.

An aggressive late cameo from Paul Scholes yielded a booking – the midfielder's tenth of the domestic season – that would rule him out of meetings with West Ham and Fulham. But no matter: United were back to winning ways and on the road to Wembley. Que sera, sera.

The Teams

Manchester United: van der Sar, Brown, Smalling, Vidic, Evra (Scholes 80), Rafael (Giggs 64), O'Shea, Gibson, Fabio (Valencia 46), Chicharito, Rooney
Subs not used: Kuszczak, Berbatov, Obertan, King
Booked: Scholes

Arsenal: Almunia, Sagna, Djourou, Koscielny, Gibbs, Arshavin (Ramsey 72), Denilson (Chamakh 59), Wilshere, Diaby (Rosicky 72), Nasri, van Persie
Subs not used: Shea, Eboue, Squillaci, Clichy

'We went out with a game-plan to get at them as quick as we could and press them as much as we could, and it worked,' reflects Darron Gibson. 'I think we surprised everyone on the day, but the gamble the boss took with the team he picked and the way we played paid off. It's the first time I've started against Arsenal, so I was pleased to win the game, and personally I was pleased to play well.

'When they had the ball it was tough for us. They're great on the ball, they pass and move well and they're great at attacking teams, but you have to flip the coin. When they had the ball we defended well, when we had the ball we attacked really well and I don't think they could handle us. I think our game-plan worked. We've got a good recent record against Arsenal. I don't know what it is – maybe they're scared of us – but we just know how to beat them. I think it's just because they're one of the best teams in the league and we've got to prove, every time we play them, that we're better than them.'

The occasion carried special significance for Antonio Valencia, who had looked sharp throughout his 45-minute cameo. Afforded a hero's welcome after a five-month spell on the sidelines, the Ecuadorian was predictably elated to have returned.

'It was a lovely moment, a great feeling, truly unforgettable,' he says. 'When you hear the support and the cheers of the supporters in a packed stadium you almost have an extra motivation. You don't want to disappoint them. It spurs you on even more. To get back was great, but that response made it even more special. It's funny . . . my sister was there and she said it sounded like David Beckham had just come on!

'You do worry about that first challenge – it's a big concern. You think: "I will take care, I will tread carefully for the first few games." But as soon as you're out there on the pitch in the heat of battle, you tend to get stuck in. My left foot did hurt a little, but once you're in the game you just forget about it. It's football and you get stuck in; that's what you have to do.'

The home support had made their mark on Valencia, but their efforts to persuade Edwin van der Sar to perform a U-turn and extend his United contract for 'one more year' were less successful. 'I don't hate the thought of retirement,' said the Dutchman. 'I am looking forward to it. It will be nice to finish at my peak. Maybe it is a weight off my shoulders. It's nice to get recognition from the fans and I will miss football and the buzz. But I have other good things, including a lovely wife and great kids.'

'The players are trying to persuade him to stay on,' confirmed Wayne Rooney. 'It's his decision so we've got to respect that, but he's such a great goalkeeper and despite the age he's at now, he's still the best goalkeeper in the world. He deserves credit.'

The Dutchman's heroics had booked a high-profile semi-final tie with local rivals Manchester City, while Stoke City and Bolton Wanderers would face off in the other Wembley meeting. England's national stadium was firmly in the Reds' sights on the European stage, too, as United prepared for a decisive clash with Marseille at Old Trafford. A goalless, eventless first leg yielded a recognisably iffy scoreline, with second-leg exits to Monaco and Real Madrid still fresh in Sir Alex's memory. The players were also well aware of the perils of conceding to Didier Deschamps' side.

'It's a dangerous scoreline with the way the away-goals rule works,' admitted Chris Smalling. 'It makes things interesting for the neutrals, but a bit nerve-racking for the players and the fans. You could see Marseille wanted to keep a clean sheet and they were well set up in that sense. They're a good side. It was an edgy game over there, with neither side wanting to give the other too much encouragement.

'From our point of view, we need to keep things tight at the back, because if they score it'll mean we need to score twice. You don't want to risk conceding the away goal, but I think the manager will want us to go at them. Being at home is a massive advantage for us and we're confident of going out there and getting the result.'

United's hopes of earning the required victory were aided by the rapid recovery of Nani, who had overcome the sizeable gash on his left shin, while Michael Carrick was also back in contention. The pair had trained the day after the FA Cup win over Arsenal and Sir Alex was buoyed by their return. 'We're in a better situation than we were at the weekend,' he said. 'Both will be involved on Tuesday night. It was also a fantastic bonus for us to get forty-five minutes out of Antonio Valencia against Arsenal. It was a great step forward considering he's been out for such a long time. The question is whether I can play him from the start or continue as I did on Saturday with him as a substitute. It's a great dilemma, a real selection poser for me.'

Such decisions were looking increasingly unavoidable. Ji-sung Park and Owen Hargreaves were back in training, albeit separately from the main group, while Jonny Evans, Rio Ferdinand and Anderson were all on the road to recovery. There was further good news when it was revealed the minor knock that ruled Nemanja Vidic out of pre-Marseille training was not expected to prohibit him from taking part in the match. Only Darren Fletcher, whose virus was worsening, found himself with no return date in sight, while Anders Lindegaard would undergo knee surgery just two appearances into his Reds career.

So it was with optimism that Sir Alex looked forward to pitting his wits against Didier Deschamps, not least because the growing stakes added a vital nervous edge to the fixture. 'It's nice to have a bit of apprehension about big ties,' said the boss. 'We've had that many times and it won't be any different on Tuesday. We're playing a very experienced, powerful Marseille team and we will have to play well. I've watched them twice away from home – against Monaco and Rennes – and they've showed the qualities we'll be up against.'

The manager also addressed his counterpart's claims that United were lacking 'fantasy' in the wake of Cristiano Ronaldo's 2009 departure, and in comparison to the fabled Treble-winning side of 1999. 'I hope we can show Didier Deschamps that despite his suggestion that our present side doesn't have as much "fantasy" compared with our team of a few years ago, we are still capable of producing our fair share of magic,' he said. 'I take his point because the side that captured the unique Treble was also something quite special, but don't underestimate the boys of today.'

Champions League second round, second leg

Old Trafford | Tuesday 15 March 2011 | KO 7.45pm | Attendance: 73,996 | Referee: Carlos Velasco Carballo

Manchester United 2 (Hernandez 5, 75)
Marseille 1 (Brown o.g. 83)

Sir Alex Ferguson's call for magic was answered largely by the penalty-box wizardry of Chicharito, who twice eluded the Marseille defence to slot home close-range finishes and book United's berth in the Champions League quarter-finals.

A late own goal from Wes Brown made for a jittery denouement against the Ligue 1 champions, but progress was secured by the predatory prowess of the Mexican, whose signing in April 2010 was almost lost in the foggy hangover of a Champions League quarter-final exit to Bayern Munich. Almost a year on, he had propelled United back to the same stage of the competition.

Recent outings against Chelsea, Liverpool and Arsenal confirmed Chicharito's rise to prominence since leaving Chivas, and Sir Alex

Ferguson again opted to deploy the 22-year-old alongside Wayne Rooney, leaving top scorer Dimitar Berbatov on the bench.

Marseille manager Didier Deschamps had struck a pre-match nerve with his assertion that the modern United's play lacked 'fantasy' and the hosts' lightning start to the game suggested the comments had resonated within the Reds' ranks.

Inside five minutes, United were ahead. Rooney, whose display oozed the zip and abandon most associate with his best play, magnificently controlled a difficult pass and spread play to Ryan Giggs. Upon receiving the return, Rooney drilled a perfect left-footed cross to the back post, where the lurking Javier Hernandez pounced.

Relief swept through Old Trafford and coursed through the Reds, as Giggs and Paul Scholes once more rolled back the years with eye-catching movement and possession play.

Marseille slowly began to creep into the game, with their athleticism and power proving increasingly problematic for United, and should have drawn level when Souleymane Diawara planted a powerful header wide. His marker, John O'Shea, was off the field with a pulled hamstring at the time, and the Irishman soon made way for Rafael, who would later succumb to the same injury and be replaced by his twin brother, Fabio.

The final chance of the half was volleyed over by Loic Remy as Marseille finished strongly, before an increasingly see-saw encounter swung back United's way with a powerful start to the second period. But still the scoreline carried menace, until a pivotal exchange with 15 minutes remaining.

Antonio Valencia neatly fed Giggs down the right flank and his measured pass across the area gave Chicharito another conversion rendered simple by the service and the Mexican's anticipation.

Though Marseille seemed bowed, substitute Mathieu Valbuena's vicious corner was inadvertently headed past Edwin van der Sar by Brown, under pressure from ex-Red Gabriel Heinze. Nerves gripped Old Trafford, but United held firm to progress into the quarter-finals for the fifth consecutive season.

The Teams

Manchester United: van der Sar, O'Shea (Rafael 36 (Fabio 70)), Smalling, Brown, Evra, Nani (Valencia 62), Scholes, Carrick, Giggs, Rooney, Hernandez
Subs not used: Kuszczak, Berbatov, Obertan, Gibson
Booked: Hernandez

Marseille: Mandanda, Fanni, Diawara, Heinze, Taiwo, Remy, Cheyrou, Mbia (J.Ayew 80), Gonzalez, A.Ayew, Gignac (Valbuena 69)
Subs not used: Hilton, Cisse, Abriel, Kabore, Andrade
Booked: Remy, Valbuena

'We thought he was a young lad who was going to progress and maybe have to get used to our training and English football, but he's been an absolute star and a real bonus for us,' said Sir Alex of Chicharito, who was fast making a case for being the signing of the season. 'His movement is fantastic, unbelievable. Did you see his movement for the opening goal? He has made three different types of run – in, out, in – and the boy has just got goals in him. He and Wayne are a good combination. Their partnership has been developing really well. Where Wayne has played in the last couple of games has really threatened teams. He's got such power and speed with the ball.'

While the squad's attacking options were giving Sir Alex a desirable headache, with Premier League top scorer Dimitar Berbatov on the bench and Michael Owen's return to consider, the manager had something of an injury crisis developing at the other end of the pitch. The loss of two full-backs to hamstring injuries, allied to calf injuries for first-choice central defenders Vidic and Ferdinand, constituted a real issue for the forthcoming visit of Bolton.

The boss confirmed he would have to 'wait and see' on Vidic, but hoped to have Jonny Evans back in contention. 'If we can get through the Bolton game I've then got two weeks during the international break to try to get some of them patched up,' he said. 'If you look at the games we've had over the last couple of weeks – Chelsea and Liverpool away from home, Arsenal in the FA Cup and then Marseille – it's a big demand on players. The speed of the game today catches you out.'

Michael Carrick was jokingly nominated in the dressing room for a reprisal of his 2009 defensive moonlighting, but the midfielder quickly played down the suggestion. 'It did get a mention in the changing room,' he smiled. 'I said to Mike Phelan: "I don't fancy that again." It's never nice to get injuries and it's disappointing when you pick up a number in a similar position. But I don't think we are that desperate yet and hopefully I won't be called upon.'

The post-match positivity that beams through Carrington after a victory was strangely tempered the day after the win over Marseille, as news filtered through the training ground that club legend Bryan Robson had been diagnosed with throat cancer. 'I couldn't believe it,' says Sir Alex. 'I've been in touch with him and he's positive. That's the important thing. We're all supportive of him because he is such a fantastic man. He's always been a fighter and he will be all right. I am sure of that.'

Sir Alex's mood was hardly helped by the Football Association's decision to hand him a five-game touchline ban for his comments about referee Martin Atkinson: three games for his recent actions and the activation of a two-game suspended sentence for previous criticism of referee Alan Wiley's performance in the Reds' 2009 draw with Sunderland. 'It is disappointing,' said the manager. 'I felt aggrieved and I now face an FA charge for what, to my mind, was simply telling the truth.'

The boss also used his pre-Bolton press conference to debunk growing suggestions that Rio Ferdinand's career was under threat after his latest injury setback. 'Rio has plenty of years ahead of him,' he assured the media. 'He's had a few injuries over the last few years that I'm sure are a concern for him. But he's still capable of coming back and playing at the top level. He's desperate to get back and he will.'

Shortly after the press conference, United were paired with Carlo Ancelotti's Chelsea in the Champions League quarter-finals, with a semi-final against either Internazionale or Schalke awaiting the winners of the all-English tie. The reaction at Carrington was largely one of detachment, with the vital visit of Bolton uppermost in everyone's thoughts.

'I think Bolton will come and have a go,' said Wes Brown. 'They're in the semi-finals of the FA Cup, which is a big boost for them and they've been doing well in the league. We all know how Bolton play – they're a big, powerful team and very dangerous in attack. So it'll be difficult. But beating Arsenal was a good win for us and I think it gives us an edge going into the last part of the season. After a disappointing run of results, it settled everyone down.'

Barclays Premier League

Old Trafford | Saturday 19 March 2011 | KO 3.00pm | Attendance: 75,486 | Referee: Andre Marriner

Manchester United 1 (Berbatov 88)
Bolton Wanderers 0

Just when it seemed United's resurgent form would be nipped in the bud by a magnificent defensive display from Bolton, up popped Dimitar Berbatov with a priceless late winner.

The Bulgarian poked home the rebound after Nani's shot had been spilled by Jussi Jaaskelainen just two minutes from time, snatching victory for the Reds, who had been reduced to ten men after a heavy challenge by Jonny Evans on Stuart Holden.

Led by inspired displays from Gary Cahill and David Wheater in the centre of defence, the Trotters rarely offered United a clear opening, but United overcame the personnel deficit, dug deep and once again demonstrated the resolve and bloody-mindedness that has characterised Sir Alex Ferguson's sides for more than two decades.

Bolton arrived at Old Trafford on the back of a six-game unbeaten run and, like United, fresh from booking a berth in the FA Cup semi-finals. There was a scare for the hosts within two minutes, as Evans' slip allowed Johan Elmander to tee up Fabrice Muamba, only for the midfielder to miscontrol and pass up the opportunity.

United were soon asking questions of the visitors, though. Wayne Rooney arrowed a 25-yard drive just wide of Jaaskelainen's top corner, before Cahill escaped censure for blocking Chicharito's close-range effort with his hand.

Neither defence was in the mood to concede chances, however. Rooney tried his luck from distance and Patrice Evra had to be alert to block Elmander's effort, but the interval prompted a rethink from Sir Alex, who was starting the first instalment of his five-match touchline ban. Berbatov and Fabio began the second period at the expense of Chicharito and Wes Brown.

Little changed. Both sides pressed for victory, only for attacks to fizzle out around both penalty areas. Then Berbatov almost broke the deadlock with 20 minutes remaining, steering a snapshot just past the top corner from 20 yards, before being hunted down by Cahill after latching onto Antonio Valencia's through-ball.

Just as the Reds were seemingly turning the screw and making chances, however, Evans and Holden contested a 50-50 challenge from which the Northern Ireland defender emerged to a red card from referee Andre Marriner. The American midfielder left the field on a stretcher with a deep gash below his knee.

Still United pressed, the danger of which was underlined when Trotters substitute Matty Taylor found himself free inside the penalty area. He could only head straight at Edwin van der Sar, though. Jaaskelainen then parried a Nani shot to safety, but moments later was less convincing in repeating the feat when the Portuguese winger again chanced his arm from outside the box. Pouncing at the perfect time, Berbatov steered the loose ball under the Finnish stopper to send Old Trafford into delirium and procure a huge three points.

The Teams

Manchester United: van der Sar, Brown (Fabio 46), Smalling, J.Evans,
Evra, Valencia, Carrick, Giggs, Nani, Hernandez (Berbatov 46), Rooney
Subs not used: Kuszczak, Owen, Park, Gibson, Gill
Sent off: J.Evans

Bolton Wanderers: Jaaskelainen, Steinsson, Cahill, Wheater, Robinson,
Elmander, Muamba (Klasnic 90), Holden (Taylor 78), Petrov, Sturridge
(Lee 60), Davies
Subs not used: Bogdan, Blake, Moreno, Alonso
Booked: Robinson

'We are fantastic when it comes to gritting our teeth and getting
something out of a dead situation,' beamed Sir Alex afterwards,
delighted his side had yet again demonstrated what sets them apart.
'We never gave in. It's the character of this club. It's a fantastic character. No other club in the country's got that.

'The only way I can judge today is that we had five massive
games in the last couple of weeks: two games against Marseille, we've
been to Chelsea and Liverpool, we beat Arsenal in the FA Cup. It's
a hell of a programme and these lads deserve praise for that. Players
had to play all over the place. Everyone's done a shift, worked their
socks off and I think we've got a deserved win out of it. The fans were
fantastic in the last twenty minutes, too. They got right behind us.'

The magnitude of the win was immediately apparent to Michael
Carrick, especially after second-placed Arsenal had drawn at West
Brom and were now five points behind, with a game in hand. 'It feels
like a huge three points,' said the midfielder. 'We were down to ten
men and up against it. To get the win is a massive lift for us and a
huge result. We kept pushing and believing we'd get the chance to
score. Thankfully we did and Berba's tucked it away. It would be nice
at the end of the season to be champions and look back and say today
was a good day.'

It wasn't such a good day for Stuart Holden. His knee injury would ultimately rule him out for six months, while Jonny Evans was left racked with guilt. The Northern Ireland international quickly contacted the American midfielder to apologise.

'I just said I was sorry and that I didn't mean to go in and hurt him,' revealed Evans. 'At the time I did think I'd gone in for a fair challenge and I'd won the ball. But looking back on it, when I went straight off the pitch and into the changing rooms and saw the tackle again, I realised it wasn't a good tackle and my concerns were immediately with Stuart.

'Bolton's doctor was keeping me informed and gave me a call on the Monday. It was disappointing to hear the news; I rang Stuart straight away to apologise. I think anyone appreciates a phone call if someone's caused them an injury. Not many footballers like to be on the treatment table – it's just unfortunate that someone else has caused an injury to you.'

Evans' red card would rule him out of the Reds' next three domestic ties: Premier League meetings with West Ham and Fulham, plus the FA Cup semi-final against Manchester City. Fortunately, Sir Alex expected to be able to welcome a host of players back after the intervening international break. 'It's come at an absolutely fantastic time for us,' said the boss. 'We've got the bonus of two weeks' rest to patch up the injuries and hopefully that'll be the biggest break of all.'

Only Wayne Rooney, Jonny Evans, Patrice Evra, Darron Gibson, Nani, Chicharito, Nemanja Vidic and Antonio Valencia left Carrington to join up with their respective national teams, although Sir Alex was also on international duty, jetting to America to help announce United's 2011 pre-season tour of the United States. There, he discussed plans to bring some new faces along for his next visit.

'We have certain [transfer] targets in mind at the moment,' said the manager. 'I think two or three will be fulfilled, there's no question about that. The Glazer family have always been very supportive of our desires to improve the team. We will continue without question, and when the opportunity does arrive and we identify the right young players, that's the way we'll go.

'What we are good at is bringing young players to the club, like Chicharito. If you look at how, over the last six to eight years, we've brought in young players like Ronaldo, Rooney – okay, one was seventeen, the other was eighteen – we're good at that. I don't see why we should change from what we're good at.'

Upon returning to Carrington, the manager was followed by a succession of his players, mercifully injury-free from their international exertions. Of those who remained at the training centre, Owen Hargreaves had suffered a shoulder injury and looked likely to miss the remainder of the season and Darren Fletcher's virus was showing no signs of abating. But there were positive signs in the recovery of Rio Ferdinand, Rafael and John O'Shea, who seemed likely to be available within a fortnight. Anderson and Ji-sung Park, meanwhile, were both fresh and raring for involvement at Upton Park in the first outing of April.

Entering the season's home straight, skipper Vidic was preparing for a hectic run of fixtures in typically professional fashion: by taking each hurdle as it came. 'I'm trying to think game by game and the first one is West Ham away,' said the Serbian. 'It's been a hard match for United over the last few years and we have to be ready, both physically and mentally. I always find the game there very physical because they are pushing hard and they want to beat Manchester United. But we have a good team and we are ready for the game.

'It's great to be in competition for three trophies, but obviously that doesn't mean anything if you don't win. It is not right to start thinking about trophies and playing City at Wembley [in the FA Cup semi-final] because one game can change everything. It would be a great achievement to win all three trophies but it will be very hard to do, especially if you look at the teams we are facing.'

10

April

The penultimate month of the season promised a glut of games to make or break United's campaign. On the agenda: four Premier League matches, an FA Cup semi-final derby and the small matter of a Champions League quarter-final double-header with Chelsea. Empty-handedness, a second Treble and all permutations in between were on offer.

Uppermost in every player's thoughts at Carrington was the Premier League title. Controversially snatched by Chelsea at this stage of the 2009–10 campaign, the Reds knew what was required in order to wrest it back from Stamford Bridge. There was, of course, the added bonus that success would render United the most prolific English champions in history, with 19 titles. Having helped draw the Reds level with Liverpool's long-standing record of 18, Wayne Rooney was desperate to help make history.

'I grew up an Everton fan, so to be part of the team to overtake Liverpool's record would be brilliant,' said the striker. 'It would mean so much to us players, as well as the fans. It is something I've been thinking about a lot. I know all the Everton fans want us to do it and hopefully we can. You look forward to every game at this stage and you've got to enjoy it, especially when you're in the running for a few trophies. It's exciting for the fans and it's exciting for the players knowing you are just a few weeks away from possibly winning a major trophy or two.'

Sir Alex Ferguson, overseer of so many hectic season finales in his time at Old Trafford, knew very well the need to chalk off victories with menacing regularity. With the ever-daunting trip to face West Ham looming large as United's first test in April, the boss wanted to return from Upton Park with three points ... even if his threadbare defence was missing Rio Ferdinand, Wes Brown, Rafael and John O'Shea.

'The big one is Saturday because we are depleted in one area of the pitch,' he said. 'With eight games to go, you can't exclude anyone. Whoever is the most consistent will win this league. But we should not over-stretch ourselves in terms of looking forward. This game is as important as any other.'

Come the final whistle, the importance of the Reds' trip to Upton Park would be lost on nobody.

Barclays Premier League

Upton Park | Saturday 2 April 2011 | KO 12.45pm | Attendance: 34,546 | Referee: Lee Mason

West Ham United 2 (Noble 11 (pen), 25 (pen))
Manchester United 4 (Rooney 65, 73, 79 (pen), Hernandez 84)

Test United's mettle and you usually get a response.

Having fallen behind to two Mark Noble penalties within the first half-hour at Upton Park, Wayne Rooney struck a stunning second-half hat-trick as the Reds roared back to claim a pulsating victory.

Noble's early double was set to deal the Reds' title hopes an untimely setback, before Rooney curled home a magnificent long-range free-kick, thundered in a superb leveller and converted a penalty in a breathless 15-minute spell. There was then time for substitute Chicharito to turn home a late clincher to cap another rousing fightback from Sir Alex Ferguson's side.

Edwin van der Sar was a precautionary absentee with a minor groin injury. His replacement, Tomasz Kuszczak, had little to do all afternoon but found himself facing two spot-kicks in the first 25 minutes. Noble dispatched both, the first of which was awarded for a clear handball by Patrice Evra, the second for a trip by Nemanja Vidic on Carlton Cole.

The Reds' first real opening fell to Ji-sung Park, whose stinging half-volley was somehow turned over the bar by Robert Green, but Vidic was fortunate to remain on the field after first seeing only yellow for hauling down Demba Ba, then escaping censure shortly after the interval for clumsily tripping the same player.

By then, Sir Alex had introduced Chicharito at the expense of Evra and moved Ryan Giggs to left-back. The changes worked beautifully, as the Mexican's menace drove the hosts deeper. When reward finally arrived for United's total dominance, it came stylishly as Rooney steered a wonderful 25-yard free-kick around the wall and inside Green's left-hand post. United's dander was up: game on.

Darron Gibson, Michael Carrick and Dimitar Berbatov all came close shortly afterwards, before Rooney hauled the Reds level by beautifully controlling Antonio Valencia's pass and unleashing a devastating low finish past Green. United's travelling contingent went wild and time remained for another notch of delirium.

Fabio's marauding run down the right flank culminated in a cross that struck Matthew Upson's arm, prompting the award of the game's third penalty, which Rooney duly slotted home to complete his own treble and United's comeback.

Still the Reds pressed for more. With six minutes remaining, Chicharito notched his now customary goal by sliding in from close range after Giggs' cross had deflected through the legs of two defenders.

'We shall not be moved,' roared the jubilant away support, who had witnessed yet another instance of the strength of character that has so often separated United from all the rest.

The Teams

West Ham United: Green, Jacobsen, Da Costa, Upson, Bridge, O'Neil (Obinna 83), Noble (Keane 83), Parker, Hitzlsperger, Cole (Piquionne 69), Ba
Subs not used: Boffin, Tomkins, Spector, Reid
Booked: Da Costa

Manchester United: Kuszczak, Fabio, Smalling, Vidic, Evra (Hernandez 46), Valencia, Carrick, Gibson, Park (Berbatov 64), Giggs, Rooney (Nani 88)
Subs not used: Amos, Owen, Anderson, Gill
Booked: Gibson, Vidic

'We've sent out a big message,' admitted Ryan Giggs. 'We've come back so many times and we've ground out results when we haven't played so well. No matter what the score is at half time or how badly we're playing, we're always capable of comebacks. It's a great characteristic to have.'

Giggs' surprise deployment as a makeshift full-back allowed the introduction of Chicharito from the bench, and that tactical re-jigging from Sir Alex was cited as a match-winning move by the player who ultimately played the role of match-winner.

'I think the substitutions were good ones and they won the game for us,' said Wayne Rooney. 'Chicharito is a massive threat and then Berbatov came on. And although he didn't get a goal, he was fantastic for us. He held the ball up brilliantly and allowed the runners to run off him.

'Upton Park is a difficult place to come, but we took encouragement from the first half when we got ourselves into good areas.

We didn't take our chances then, but we knew if we got the next goal we were capable of getting more.'

Rooney's breathtaking hat-trick propelled United's comeback and marked his final emergence from the shadows in what had been a long, trying season for the forward. 'I think everyone knew by the way he took the three goals that he was back,' says Darron Gibson. 'He had played well all season, just without scoring as many goals as he'd like. But then, when he is playing well and scoring goals, that's when he looks unstoppable.'

It seemed the only way to halt the England striker was to ban him. Rooney greeted his third goal at Upton Park by yelling two expletives at Sky Sports' pitchside camera and, although he swiftly apologised for his actions, the striker found himself under investigation by the Football Association. Within two days, he was charged with 'use of offensive, insulting and/or abusive language', an offence that carries a two-match ban. Fronted with the prospect of losing Rooney for the visit of Fulham and, most ominously, the FA Cup semi-final against Manchester City, United appealed the verdict and would have an answer before hosting Fulham.

In the meantime, a Champions League trip to Stamford Bridge beckoned. Though United had not won on Chelsea's patch since 2002, the Reds had played well there just a month earlier, only to be denied in controversial circumstances. For Patrice Evra, Stamford Bridge held only bad memories, having never tasted an away victory against the Blues and being banned for four matches for his post-match scuffle with a groundsman in 2008. 'It is something very strange,' he laughed. 'Always we have the sensation we have played very well against Chelsea but, in the end, we always lose. Five weeks ago, there was only one team on the pitch. One year ago, we lost to a strange decision. The key is our concentration. We can play better than them, but we must concentrate until the last minute.'

Sir Alex confirmed he hoped to welcome back Rio Ferdinand and Rafael for the gargantuan clash, and the former soon had his say on the furore over Wayne Rooney that threatened to overshadow the match itself.

'Wayne Rooney swearing on TV – as much as I don't condone it – is not front-page news,' said Ferdinand. 'There are bigger things going on in the world. There are things happening in Libya and Ivory Coast and we are talking about Wayne Rooney on the front page of newspapers because he swore at a camera. I don't feel sorry for him. He thrives off the attention. But he thrives off football attention rather than the stuff on the outside. That's what he wants to be judged on and talked about.'

It was up to Rooney to let his football do the talking at Stamford Bridge.

Champions League quarter-final, first leg

Stamford Bridge | Wednesday 6 April 2011 | KO 7.45pm |
Attendance: 37,915 | Referee: Undiano Mallenco

Chelsea 0
Manchester United 1 (Rooney 24)

The headlines again belonged to Wayne Rooney after a match-winning display, but it was a masterful collective show of resolve and discipline that put United on the brink of the Champions League semi-finals.

Reinforced by a surfeit of diligence in every position, the Reds stuck to a simple game-plan of retaining possession, then striking swiftly and clinically when the opposition had been drawn. The reward was a first win at Stamford Bridge since 2002, thanks to Rooney's calm finish that capped a flowing first-half move.

United escaped a strong late penalty shout when Patrice Evra hauled down Ramires, but referee Undiano Mallenco declined the award and offered the visitors an unusual dose of luck in West London.

Edwin van der Sar, Rio Ferdinand and Rafael returned to bolster the Reds' defence, but a sloppy start allowed both Fernando Torres and Didier Drogba to unleash efforts that van der Sar comfortably fielded. Before long, however, the hosts were nullified. Michael Carrick shone as a beacon of midfield intelligence, breaking up Chelsea attacks with regularity and ferrying possession about the United ranks.

As the Reds' attacking menace grew, aided by jittery possession play from the hosts, Rooney struck. Carrick arrowed a long, diagonal ball into the path of Giggs, who surged past the flat-footed Jose Bosingwa and cut back a perfect cross for Rooney to plant inside Petr Cech's far corner, via the base of the upright.

United's game-plan was unfolding perfectly and would have yielded another priceless strike before the interval had Rooney's cross not been fractionally too high for Chicharito. Instead, Chelsea almost went into the break undeservedly level. Drogba's deflected cross was missed by Torres but bounced against van der Sar's post and Frank Lampard's close-range rebound was heroically cleared off the line by Evra.

Soon after the restart, United were deprived of Rafael's services when he collided with Drogba and was replaced by Nani, prompting the surprise deployment of Antonio Valencia as a makeshift right-back. Early on, Nani looked set to tee up Javier Hernandez for a second goal but the Portuguese's cross was superbly shovelled away by Cech.

Despite impressive defensive resolve from United, Chelsea made late openings. Michael Essien volleyed wide from 20 yards and Torres drew a wonderful save from van der Sar with a header that appeared destined for the far corner, before Evra's late escape. Torres was also booked for a last-gasp attempt to win a spot-kick as Chelsea desperately sought parity.

United survived, with no small degree of irony after the controversial decisions that have tainted recent visits to Stamford Bridge. Had such an excellent performance yielded anything but victory, however, the Reds would again have suffered an injustice.

The Teams

Chelsea: Cech, Bosingwa (Mikel 78), Ivanovic, Terry, Cole, Ramires, Essien, Lampard, Zhirkov (Malouda 70), Torres, Drogba (Anelka 71)
Subs not used: Turnbull, Benayoun, Ferreira, Kalou
Booked: Essien, Ramires, Torres, Zhirkov

Manchester United: van der Sar, Rafael (Nani 51), Ferdinand, Vidic, Evra, Valencia, Carrick, Giggs, Park (Smalling 90), Rooney, Chicharito (Berbatov 78)
Subs not used: Kuszczak, Scholes, J.Evans, Gibson
Booked: van der Sar, Vidic

'The Ramires one looked like it could have been a penalty,' admitted Rio Ferdinand. 'But over the years I think they've ridden their luck against us a few times and had a few big decisions, so it's swings and roundabouts and it all evens itself out over the course of a couple of seasons. But we had a strong ref today and that was good for us.'

'If it was a break for us, it's our first one in seven years here,' smiled Sir Alex, before shifting focus back to an exceptional display from his side. 'I thought the players were great. Wayne was on tremendous form and he's given us a really great opportunity to get to the semi-final. His work-rate and desire to play were marvellous. He got a lot of abuse tonight and some late tackles, but he just got up again and just played his game. That shows the courage of the player.

'He's now more regular in his goalscoring, which, at this stage of the season, is going to be important. His goal tonight was another important one. But I think the whole team takes great credit. It's only half time, of course, but we've got our advantage, that away goal means something. But our biggest advantage is Old Trafford. Our support next Tuesday will be absolutely fantastic. I think our attitude must be to go and win the game at Old Trafford next Tuesday.'

From that soaring high, United arrived back in Manchester with a jolt, as the FA upheld Rooney's two-match ban and confirmed his absence from the meetings with Fulham and Manchester City. 'I am gutted to miss two matches, one of which is an FA Cup semi-final at Wembley,' a statement issued by the striker read. 'I am not the first player to have sworn on TV and I won't be the last. Unlike others who have been caught swearing on camera, I apologised immediately. And yet I am the only person banned for swearing. That doesn't seem right. Whatever, I have to accept that what's happened has happened and move on from here. That is what I intend to do.'

Carrington was stunned, according to Ryan Giggs. 'I'm not surprised by the furore surrounding it because of the profile Wayne has got,' says the winger. 'But a two-game ban? I'm surprised by that. There was no precedent and that's why we were bamboozled by it.'

Sir Alex, meanwhile, merely used the setback to galvanise his squad, saying: 'It will bring us together. It is a plus for us.'

Looking back, chief executive David Gill – also a Football Association board member – still feels Rooney was disproportionately dealt with. 'I do genuinely believe there have been some poor-ish decisions that, in my opinion, wouldn't necessarily have hit other clubs,' he says. 'That's not to say I'm condoning Wayne's comments, because I don't think they were correct, or what Sir Alex said [about referee Martin Atkinson in March], because it wasn't helpful. But at the same time, the actual punishments were harsh. We're possibly caught up in being one of the biggest clubs and the "Respect" agenda being there. What better way to demonstrate that the authorities are being tough than by hitting one of the biggest clubs the hardest?

'The club doesn't condone it, but Wayne recognised it was wrong and apologised almost immediately. We have various issues with the ban: one being consistency. What's going to happen now? Is the referee under pressure to send everyone off? I think sometimes in celebration people do swear, and all that means is that, to my mind, it's a dangerous course the FA have gone down, because consistent application is what's required and I'm not sure that'll necessarily happen. There are certain things you should wait until the start of a season to change.

'But it's a lesson to Wayne. He subsequently scored a great goal against Chelsea and smiled – that's what we want to see. There should be exuberance, but you look at the abuse he was subjected to and I know people say you've got to rise above it, but I defy anyone being vilified to that level to always retain your cool. I don't think the media helped, either, with the constant repetition of the footage, with his mouth blurred out.'

United's chief executive found himself joined in the stands by Sir Alex after the FA's decision to banish the manager from the touchline for five games, and Gill admitted the experience had been an eye-opener. 'It was interesting,' he smiles. 'I gave him a bit of advice! You think it was his idea to put Giggs at left-back against West Ham? I rest my case!

'Seriously, though, you don't interfere. I deliberately wouldn't enter into conversation with him. He might say something to me or make an observation, but I wouldn't ask questions or make comments because he's there concentrating.'

Gill's attentions in the run-up to Fulham's visit would switch to the future of Owen Hargreaves. Having been reduced to five appearances since securing the Double in Moscow, the midfielder's contract would end with the 2010–11 season, which he seemed likely to sit out the remainder of with a shoulder injury. Hargreaves met with United's chief executive for discussions and Sir Alex admitted the club had to consider its next move. 'I don't see Hargreaves playing this season,' he conceded. 'He's got this shoulder injury, which has put his season to an end, I think. He's carried bad luck all the time he's been here. His contract is up at the end of the season and we have to make a decision.'

Sir Alex's team selection for Fulham's visit was dictated in part by the enforced absence of Rooney, although the manager's options were nevertheless increasing. Anderson had emerged unscathed from a

Reserves outing, Wes Brown and John O'Shea were fit again and Darren Fletcher was back in full training and had regained some of the weight lost during his battle with a virus.

'Bit by bit we're getting players back,' said Sir Alex. 'It's just a question of what team I play, as I have to think about Tuesday. Fulham are a team who mirror their manager, Mark Hughes: they're very hard to beat. We need to perform. Our fans were fantastic at Chelsea on Wednesday and they will be at Old Trafford again tomorrow. They know the importance of being united at this time.'

Barclays Premier League

Old Trafford | Saturday 9 April 2011 | KO 3.00pm | Attendance: 75,339 | Referee: Mike Jones

Manchester United 2 (Berbatov 12, Valencia 32)
Fulham 0

The Reds moved three points closer to the Premier League title with a routine victory over Mark Hughes' Fulham, as Dimitar Berbatov and Antonio Valencia struck decisive early goals at Old Trafford.

Job done, United rarely expended more energy than was required for the remainder of the game, with the Champions League visit of Chelsea to consider. Still, another game chalked off, no injuries and a comfortable win formed a hugely positive afternoon's work for Sir Alex Ferguson's side.

The game may have panned out differently, however, had Fulham taken advantage of their powerful start and taken one of three presentable chances in the first ten minutes. Gael Kakuta, on loan from Chelsea, and Moussa Dembele both stretched Tomasz Kuszczak inside six minutes, before Bobby Zamora blasted wide after finding space inside the area.

United's slow opening might have been traceable to the eight changes Sir Alex had made to the side that won at Stamford Bridge.

Only Patrice Evra, Nemanja Vidic and Antonio Valencia survived. The highest-profile absentee was Wayne Rooney who, in commencing his two-match ban, gave Berbatov the chance to start for only the third time in 12 fixtures.

It was the Bulgarian who broke the deadlock on 12 minutes, reaping the benefit of wonderful approach work from Nani, who slalomed past several visitors and played a neat one-two with Anderson before teeing up Berbatov for a calm finish into the far corner.

The strike sucked the wind from Fulham's sails and gave the hosts new impetus. A procession of chances came and went, most notably when Anderson scuffed a shot wide after fine play from Valencia. But the Ecuadorian soon made the points safe for United.

Nani reached a long ball ahead of Mark Schwarzer, rounded the Australian goalkeeper and advanced on goal. The back-pedalling Aaron Hughes managed to divert Nani's shot away from goal, but it fell perfectly for Valencia to nod in from virtually on the goal-line.

United's tempo dipped markedly thereafter, but Fulham were unable to raise their own rhythm sufficiently to find a route back into the game. Substitute Eidur Gudjohnsen's shot was magnificently flicked around the post by Tomasz Kuszczak and Zamora curled a free-kick just over, but the Reds were rarely troubled. At the other end, John O'Shea was denied by Schwarzer and substitute Michael Owen was crowded out in a packed penalty area. But the points were long since secured.

With Chelsea's visit to consider, there was no reason for United to expend needless energy in the spring sunshine. Boxing clever gave the Reds a chance to deliver the Blues a knockout blow on two fronts.

The Teams

Manchester United: Kuszczak, O'Shea, Smalling, Vidic, Evra, Gibson, Scholes, Anderson (Fabio 77), Valencia (Owen 73), Berbatov, Nani (Carrick 87)
Subs not used: van der Sar, Brown, Park, Hernandez

Fulham: Schwarzer, Baird, Hughes, Hangeland, Salcido, Kakuta, Etuhu (Gera 68), Murphy (Greening 82), Dempsey, Dembele (Gudjohnsen 57), Zamora
Subs not used: Stockdale, Sidwell, Kelly, Halliche

'We weren't under instructions to ease off – that wasn't said – but I think the players knew the job was done and we just needed to keep the ball a bit and play the game out, obviously to try to save our legs for the Chelsea game,' says Darron Gibson. 'It was another great result. At this stage of the season you need to win, no matter what.'

The Reds' victory owed much to the trickery of Nani, who teed up both goals to extend his prolific run of goals and assists in a remarkable season that, perhaps most remarkably, had failed to yield a nomination for the PFA Player of the Year award.

'I am pretty amazed by that,' admitted John O'Shea. 'Maybe because he was still eligible for the young player award, people didn't vote for him for the senior player award. He is a constant threat. Defenders don't know whether he is going to go on his left or his right and his combination with Patrice Evra was excellent today.

'It is a classic cliché, but we are just chalking off one game at a time. The good thing is we feel so confident, especially at home. We have dropped only two points at Old Trafford this season and it would be very special if we could finish off the season keeping that record. You have to get excited. That is what you train all year for. You want to get to the latter stages of competitions.'

On a personal note, the Irishman had enjoyed a trouble-free afternoon against the Cottagers and he was in line to face Fulham's near-neighbours, Chelsea, in the Champions League as Rafael's recovery from his injury in the first leg continued to prove a hindrance. The young Brazilian was the only doubt, aside from long-term absentees Owen Hargreaves and Darren Fletcher.

Rio Ferdinand had been rested for Fulham's visit and was on course to return to the fold against Carlo Ancelotti's side. The defender joined Sir Alex Ferguson at Old Trafford for a pre-match press conference, where he was legitimately posed questions about United's chances of repeating 1999's unforgettable Treble.

'The Treble is not a motivation,' he assured the world's media. 'Our motivation is each competition. If that amounts to winning the Double, a single trophy each year or the Treble, so be it. I don't think the players who won the Treble were saying: "This is it; we want to win the Treble." It's about making sure this club wins a trophy every year. If you win one and you see another one, you want to try and win that.'

Ferdinand's insistence on giving each game due care and attention, rather than looking at the wider picture, mirrored the mood among his team-mates. 'We're not getting carried away,' Michael Carrick insisted ahead of the Champions League quarter-final second leg. 'We respect Chelsea. It was only last season that they beat us at Old Trafford in the league and a repeat of that result would knock us out. We are in the position we set out to be in, but it only counts for so much. Come Tuesday we need to perform again.'

Sir Alex, meanwhile, felt compelled to underline his side's will to win the Champions League for a fourth time given the highly publicised desire of Chelsea owner Roman Abramovich to see his club crowned European champions.

'It seems to be an obsession for them and that's certainly why they signed Fernando Torres,' said the boss. 'Roman Abramovich, the owner, has nailed his colours to the mast in that respect. I've thought that for quite a while with them. But, at the end of the day, it's a very difficult competition to win. All the best teams are there. To have an obsession to win it, you stretch yourself a wee bit. I had an obsession for a bit, when I lost a few semi-finals. You start thinking you're never going to do it. When we did it in Barcelona [in 1999], it was the greatest feeling of all time and it took the monkey off our back. I can understand [Chelsea's obsession], but it doesn't make them any more desperate than us. We'll be desperate to win tomorrow night.'

Champions League quarter-final, second leg

Old Trafford | Tuesday 12 April 2011 | KO 7.45pm | Attendance: 74,672 |
Referee: Olegario Benquerenca

Manchester United 2 (Hernandez 43, Park 77)
Chelsea 1 (Drogba 77)

There's something deep within United's genetics that compels Sir Alex Ferguson's team to put fans through the wringer before taking them to the heights of elation.

Seemingly coasting through to the Champions League semi-finals after Chicharito's goal had doubled the aggregate lead over ten-man Chelsea, a sloppy concession to Didier Drogba left the Reds at the mercy of an away-goals defeat for the final 13 minutes.

Not one of those had elapsed, however, before the danger had been extinguished. Ji-sung Park made the tie safe by lashing home a progress-sealing strike mere seconds after Drogba's effort had provoked a dose of the jitters around Old Trafford.

The South Korean's powerful finish at the Stretford End secured a semi-final clash with Bundesliga side Schalke, but much of the Reds' hard work had been done in earning a narrow first-leg win at Stamford Bridge. Wayne Rooney's solitary strike meant the Blues had to chase victory at Old Trafford and Carlo Ancelotti's side started the second leg intent on that outcome.

Nicolas Anelka skewed a shot just wide from the edge of the area, Frank Lampard side-footed wastefully at Edwin van der Sar and the Dutchman then had to sprint from his line to dispossess Anelka outside the area with a last-ditch tackle. United were also menacing on the counter-attack, however, with Rooney, Park and Chicharito all causing the visitors problems with their movement.

Those promising signs soon translated to tangible chances. Chicharito stooped to brilliantly head home Rooney's wickedly whipped cross from the right, only to have the goal correctly chalked off for offside.

So steady was United's wresting of control, it was no surprise when the Reds moved into the lead on the stroke of half time. Patient approach play culminated in John O'Shea sliding a pass through for Ryan Giggs, who strode into the Chelsea area and slipped a perfect ball across the box for Chicharito to stab a finish into the roof of the visitors' net.

Carlo Ancelotti's half-time response was decisive. He withdrew the ineffectual Fernando Torres and replaced him with Drogba, who immediately gave the Blues more menace in attack. It was the hosts, however, who posed the biggest questions in front of goal, as Petr Cech turned away Nani's stinging shot and fielded Giggs' tame header after more fine service from Rooney.

When Ramires was booked for a second time – a needless foul on Nani – the jig seemed up for Chelsea. Instead, United's concentration wavered just long enough for Drogba to strike. The Ivory Coast forward latched on to Michael Essien's lofted pass before drilling a low finish past van der Sar.

The visiting fans were still celebrating, however, when Park collected another Giggs pass – his third assist of the tie – and rifled home a finish to send the Reds to within touching distance of Wembley.

The Teams

Manchester United: van der Sar, O'Shea, Ferdinand, Vidic, Evra, Nani (Valencia 75), Carrick, Giggs, Park, Rooney, Hernandez
Subs not used: Kuszczak, Brown, Berbatov, Smalling, Scholes, Gibson
Booked: Evra, O'Shea

Chelsea: Cech, Ivanovic, Alex (Ferreira 82), Terry, Cole, Ramires, Essien, Lampard, Malouda, Torres (Drogba 46), Anelka (Kalou 61)
Subs not used: Turnbull, Mikel, Zhirkov, Benayoun
Booked: Malouda, Terry
Sent off: Ramires

'I think we've hit our form,' Sir Alex smiled afterwards. 'It's a great moment for us and I think the players are enjoying it. They're relishing the challenges they've got now, and I think you saw that tonight.

'Tonight we had some fantastic performers: Ji-Sung Park and Chicharito up front, Rooney played to his maximum. In the first leg he was outstanding and tonight he did his job right. But all over, no one let us down.'

'It was a very enjoyable night,' recalls Edwin van der Sar. 'It's always nice to win against great teams and Chelsea really are a great team. We've had many battles with them over the years and luckily we managed to win that one. It was tense, of course, and luckily Ji scored right after they equalised. It was a big sigh of relief for everyone. We didn't really have time to get nervous after they scored. If time had moved on and they'd gotten a corner or a free-kick then you never know what can happen, but Ji's goal was perfect timing and a great finish.'

The giant Dutchman smiles when reliving his race for a loose ball with Nicolas Anelka. 'I thought I was quicker than him,' he says. 'Which was obviously a misunderstanding of mine! I had to stop, otherwise I was risking something worse, but when he played the ball past me I followed him and managed to get my studs on the ball and I could play it out to safety. It was a good job I reached it!'

Fine margins make a major difference at the highest level – be they the length of a stud or the width of a post, as John Terry found in Moscow – and United's progress to the semi-finals provoked more media musings as to whether or not Sir Alex's side – atop the Premier League table and in the last four of both major cups – could repeat the 1999 Treble. 'You need a lot to do that,' said Sir Alex, playing down the suggestion. 'We've got an FA Cup semi-final on Saturday. It's a massive game and hopefully we can navigate that.'

Elsewhere in Europe, heavy wins for Barcelona, Real Madrid and Schalke confirmed their berths alongside United in the Champions League last four, with the Reds facing the Germans and *El Clasico* taking to the European stage. From one major game to the next, though, the players were taking it one step at a time. Finally their attentions could switch to a game over which the media had been frothing since the FA Cup semi-final draw: City at Wembley.

'It was just the same as every other week of the season,' says Darron Gibson. 'The players don't let the hype of the press and the fans get to us, although obviously we were buzzing going into the game. We were in really confident mood with high spirits. We were in a great position, coming off a win against Chelsea, and City were coming off a loss against Liverpool, so the momentum was on our side. It was a blow for us to be preparing for the game without Wayne Rooney, but they'd lost their main player in Carlos Tevez, who was injured.'

Aside from Rooney's suspension and the absence of Darren Fletcher, Owen Hargreaves and Anders Lindegaard, Sir Alex had the luxury of a bulging squad to select players from. 'I worry about the team I'm going to pick; I hope I pick the right team,' said the manager. 'I've got a group of players who are confident going into games. Their attitude is great and I couldn't ask for a better situation. The players are on form; the squad has got stronger with players back now and the bench reflected that on Tuesday night. I would say I'm lucky I've got the bunch of players I've got. It doesn't matter which game I'm going into, I would believe in these players.'

United were the undoubted favourites going into the Wembley meeting. This would be the Reds' ninth trip to 'new' Wembley since the stadium's 2007 reopening; for City, their first. Sometimes, though, the underdogs do bite.

FA Cup semi-final

**Wembley Stadium | Saturday 16 April 2011 | KO 5.30pm |
Attendance: 86,549 | Referee: Mike Dean**

Manchester City 1 (Y.Toure 52)
Manchester United 0

No excuses, no protests, no Treble.

United's hopes of a clean sweep of top honours were ended as Yaya Toure struck the only goal of a hard-fought Manchester derby at Wembley, and the Reds' misery was compounded by the dismissal of Paul Scholes for a high challenge on Pablo Zabaleta.

Sir Alex Ferguson's side were left to rue the spurning of early chances and a poor spell at the start of the second half in which Toure scored and City penned United back. Hindered by a numerical disadvantage when gearing up for the customary late charge, the Reds exited the FA Cup in relatively meek fashion.

With Wayne Rooney completing a two-match ban for his Upton Park indiscretion, Dimitar Berbatov was given the nod to start as a lone striker, and the Bulgarian came closest to breaking the deadlock in the first half with a pair of chances just seconds apart.

Neat one-touch football from Carrick, Scholes and Park on the edge of City's penalty area released Berbatov, but the striker saw his shot saved superbly by the onrushing Joe Hart. Then, from the resulting quickly taken throw-in, Nani advanced into the penalty area, passed low across the six-yard box and Berbatov stretched to meet the ball, but could only lift it over the bar from close range.

City began to emerge from their sluggish start around the half-hour mark, awoken by Gareth Barry's turn and shot that hit the side-netting. Mario Balotelli then forced a smart save from Edwin van der Sar with a 35-yard snapshot, Joleon Lescott volleyed over when unmarked and Vincent Kompany curled wide from 20 yards, as the Blues finished the half on top.

Roberto Mancini's side maintained the initiative in the early stages of the second period and struck the decisive blow seven minutes after the break. Van der Sar's errant clearance was tidied up by John O'Shea, but Michael Carrick was subsequently caught in possession by Toure, who burst into the United area and slid home a calm finish. The Blues in the stands went bananas and might have had a second goal to cheer had City capitalised on a further ten minutes of incessant pressure.

United weathered the storm, however, and belatedly set about overturning the scoreline. Nobody came closer to an equaliser than Nani, whose curling 20-yard free-kick clipped Balotelli and was instinctively turned onto the crossbar by Hart. Scholes' dismissal soon followed, and the numerical advantage allowed City to run down the clock comfortably and book a first FA Cup final berth since 1981.

The Teams

Manchester City: Hart, Zabaleta, Kompany, Lescott, Kolarov, Johnson (Wright-Phillips 79), De Jong, Barry, Y.Toure, Silva (Vieira 86), Balotelli
Subs not used: Taylor, Milner, Dzeko, Jo, Boyata
Booked: Balotelli, De Jong, Kompany, Zabaleta

Manchester United: van der Sar, O'Shea (Fabio 84), Ferdinand, Vidic, Evra, Valencia (Hernandez 65), Scholes, Carrick, Park, Nani, Berbatov (Anderson 74)
Subs not used: Kuszczak, Owen, Smalling, Gibson
Sent off: Scholes

One down, two to go. Not that the Premier League and Champions League provided much immediate consolation for United's despondent players after the Wembley defeat. Emerging from a dumbstruck dressing room, Sir Alex admitted the Reds' missed chances and second-half display proved the difference.

'The first fifteen minutes after half time cost us the game,' admitted the boss. 'Slack moments. Edwin van der Sar had a bad kick-out and Michael Carrick couldn't hold it and it was a goal. From then on, they were defending, apart from a couple of counter-attacks. It's disappointing as we should've been ahead in the first half as we were the better team. The first chance Dimitar Berbatov missed was a great save by the keeper but the second chance, from under the bar . . . if he'd had scored there, I had a feeling whoever scored first would win the match. We were a wee bit sloppy and it got them on the counter-attack against us.'

Sir Alex also sought to explain Paul Scholes' red card, even though he felt United's play had sharpened up for being forced to compete with ten men. 'Paul has had unbelievable moments and is a great player, one of the greatest ever at this club, but he has these red-mist moments and this was another one,' said the manager. 'He's a bit unfortunate as he went for the ball and it bounced up and he's gone through and caught the boy on the thigh.'

'We talked a lot about concentration, but today we didn't concentrate enough,' added skipper Nemanja Vidic. 'We had two or three chances in the first half, but didn't score the goal. All they had were shots from distance, but their goal has cost us the final. We didn't play as we should have in the second half. It was more open, they played a bit higher up the pitch and scored a goal. We had a few good situations from the right side that we should have done something with but didn't. We must forget the City game now and concentrate on winning the title. It will not be easy but we have to perform, play good football and try to win the league.'

Vidic was among four United players named in the Professional Footballers' Association Team of the Year, alongside Edwin van der Sar, Nani and Dimitar Berbatov. The Serbian was also nominated for the PFA Player of the Year award, but lost out to Tottenham's Gareth Bale, while Mexican starlet Chicharito finished third in the running for the PFA Young Player of the Year prize.

'I have done better than I thought I would, but I wouldn't say it has been easy. Nothing in life is easy,' said the little Mexican. 'Physically I have got a lot stronger. I go to the gym a lot. It is not because I like it. It is something I needed to do because the English league is quicker and more physical.

'It has helped my confidence a lot to score so many goals. But the most important thing for me has always been the results of the team.

Goals are merely a consequence of the work everyone does. Of course I am very happy to score, but if Manchester United win all their games, it doesn't matter who gets the goals.'

Chicharito was right. It wouldn't matter who scored in the next outing, at Newcastle, as the Reds sought to reignite a charge for the Premier League title. Victory would quickly bury the memories of Wembley, and Edwin van der Sar promised: 'It won't be difficult to pick ourselves up. We know how important the league is. We are in first position, so we just have to make the best of it. We have played a big number of games in the last three or four weeks and against Newcastle we must do better.'

Barclays Premier League

St James' Park | Tuesday 19 April 2011 | KO 8.00pm |
Attendance: 49,025 | Referee: Lee Probert

Newcastle United 0
Manchester United 0

United's post-Wembley bid to regain momentum in the Premier League title race was slowed by a resilient defensive performance from Newcastle, as spurned openings again proved costly for Sir Alex Ferguson's side.

Though the pepped-up hosts bossed the first half-hour, early opportunities for Chicharito and Wayne Rooney went begging, while Ryan Giggs might have done better with a pair of second-half chances as United finished in the ascendancy.

Both sides also implored penalty awards from referee Lee Probert: United for a dying-seconds tumble from Chicharito under pressure from Danny Simpson, Newcastle for Anderson's earlier trip on Peter Lovenkrands. Neither was given.

Sir Alex, perched up in the stands as he completed his five-match touchline ban, made five changes to the side that started the Reds' FA

Cup semi-final defeat three days earlier. Rooney returned from suspension, while Chris Smalling, Giggs, Anderson and Chicharito also reappeared.

Chicharito almost had United ahead inside two minutes. Rooney raced down the left flank and squared a perfect ball across the box for the Mexican, whose close-range effort was brilliantly smothered by Magpies goalkeeper Tim Krul.

Suitably warned, Newcastle soon had the visitors penned back, with Joey Barton slinging impressive service into Edwin van der Sar's area with unnerving regularity. The Dutchman clutched a close-range effort from Shola Ameobi and a 30-yard daisy-cutter from Cheik Tiote as the home support roared on their side.

Chicharito reminded Newcastle of the Reds' dormant threat with a neat touch and turn followed by a 25-yard effort that curled narrowly wide of Krul's top corner. He then released Rooney inside the box, but his goal-bound effort was deflected over by the Dutchman's shoulder.

The hosts had the final opening of the first half when Peter Lovenkrands planted a free header well wide from the penalty spot. Giggs then hit the target but headed straight at Krul from a similar position early in the second half.

Newcastle almost had a gift-wrapped opening when Anderson caught Lovenkrands inside the area, but referee Probert declined the hosts' appeals. Then came United's big chance. Chicharito released Patrice Evra down the left and the Frenchman's measured pull-back found Giggs, unmarked. Somehow, the winger steered his shot fractionally wide of Krul's post after a vital touch from the studs of Fabricio Coloccini.

Rooney repeatedly chanced his arm from distance as United pressed in vain, and the Reds' frustrations were compounded by referee Probert's injury-time decision to book Chicharito after the striker tumbled over Simpson's outstretched leg inside the home penalty area. There had been no goals, but the crowd went home after witnessing plenty of drama.

The Teams

Newcastle United: Krul, Simpson, Williamson, Coloccini, Enrique, Barton, Guthrie, Tiote, Gutierrez, Lovenkrands (Ireland 69), Ameobi (Ranger 72)
Subs not used: Soderberg, Perch, R.Taylor, S.Taylor, Kuqi
Booked: Tiote, Williamson

Manchester United: van der Sar, O'Shea, Smalling, Vidic, Evra, Nani (Owen 80), Carrick, Anderson (Valencia 70), Giggs, Rooney, Hernandez
Subs not used: Kuszczak, Park, Fabio, J.Evans, Gibson
Booked: Carrick, Hernandez

'It was a clear penalty, but it's an insult because he's booked him,' said an incredulous Sir Alex. 'The referee had a good game tonight. I thought he had an excellent game, but he lets himself down by booking the player. If he's not giving the penalty, fine, but to book him is an insult. I saw it myself and there was definitely contact, no doubt about that.

'I'm confident we'll be fine now as that was a hard game to get over. At this stage of the season, we're in a better position than we were on Saturday as there's one less game and five games left. Newcastle did exceptionally well in the first twenty minutes, but the longer the game went on I was sure we'd improve. We did really well in the second half. The passing was terrific and we got into great positions but just didn't trouble the keeper.'

'We thought we played well enough in the second half to score a goal at least,' concurred Michael Carrick. 'Giggsy had a chance or two and Chicha had the penalty shout. We came here to win the game, so we're obviously disappointed. At the moment the draw feels more like two points dropped [than one gained]. But we'll have to take it and move on. We're still in a good position and Saturday's game will be another big one for us.'

There was no respite in United's fixture list. Taxing trips to London and Newcastle had to be forgotten as Everton were due at

Old Trafford next, before a quickfire jaunt to Germany for a huge Champions League semi-final first leg. By virtue of Chelsea's surge in form and Arsenal's late-season collapse, United's nearest challengers for the title were the reigning champions, a shift in the chasing pack that did not surprise Sir Alex.

'I said a few weeks ago that Chelsea would be our main challengers and they are now above Arsenal,' he said. 'We recognise both are six points behind us, so both are challengers but I just have that slight preference for Chelsea. They have to come to Old Trafford, which is not going to be easy for them, but otherwise their fixture list is a bit easier than Arsenal's. Also, when you look at the two of them, I think Chelsea have far more experience. That is the difference. Arsenal have the better footballers but Chelsea are the stronger team.'

The manager was able to welcome back Rafael from his Stamford Bridge injury, but was unlikely to have Dimitar Berbatov available after a minor groin strain. Darren Fletcher was in line for a first-team return as soon as he regained full match fitness, while Paul Scholes missed out through suspension. The Toffees were ravaged by injury but arrived at Old Trafford in fine form, undefeated in seven games. Antonio Valencia was certainly well aware of their menace.

'We're wary of Everton because they are finishing the season strongly and we remember what happened at Goodison Park earlier in the season, when they scored two late goals,' said the Ecuadorian. 'We won't be taking them lightly, but it's a game we need to win and, in order to do that, we must continue to do the things we've been doing well in recent weeks.'

Barclays Premier League

Old Trafford | Saturday 23 April 2011 | KO 12.45pm | Attendance: 75,300 | Referee: Peter Walton

Manchester United 1 (Hernandez 84)
Everton 0

It's the plot twist that never tires: United in desperate need of victory, attacking the Stretford End and nabbing a winner in the dying minutes. The Reds rolled out the classic tale once more against Everton, as Chicharito headed home a priceless late goal to end the Toffees' stern resistance.

David Moyes' side had turned in a magnificently dogged display to frustrate the Reds for long periods before Chicharito popped up with six minutes remaining to nod home, perhaps symbolically, his 19th goal of the season and move United three points closer to a 19th domestic crown.

Though the Toffees arrived at Old Trafford as one of the Premier League's form teams, United's greater need for points was reflected in attacking dominance. How Sir Alex's men reached the interval without scoring was flummoxing.

The Reds repeatedly sprung the hosts' high defensive line. Nani dwelled and shot straight at Tim Howard after a three-on-three break, then Chicharito's cross was deflected into the American's arms after another swift counter led by Fabio. Chicharito soon drew a smart stop from the former United goalkeeper with a near-post effort and then forced him to beat another powerful effort behind after fine approach play from Wayne Rooney.

For all the trouble being caused by the little Mexican, he inadvertently helped the visitors escape the clearest opening of the half. Antonio Valencia out-muscled Leighton Baines and pulled back for Nani. Having slipped, Chicharito then sat helpless as he blocked the Portuguese winger's effort wide with his outstretched heel.

Mindful of the need to offer more attacking input, David Moyes introduced Tim Cahill and Victor Anichebe at the start of the second half, and the speedy Nigerian was soon appealing for a penalty after tumbling under pressure from Rio Ferdinand. Referee Peter Walton opted against an award.

United's frustration was growing, but the mood inside Old Trafford briefly became one of overwhelming relief when, with 23 minutes remaining, Jack Rodwell's deflected 25-yard shot was magnificently turned past the post by Edwin van der Sar.

That chance prompted a wave of United pressure, with both sides decamped to the visitors' half. Sylvain Distin sliced against his own post, Howard tipped over a Rooney free-kick and then saved a Chicharito header before the winner finally arrived.

Distin was caught in possession by Valencia, who then received the ball back from Anderson. The Ecuadorian's cross was deflected off Distin and fell beautifully for Chicharito to nod home from deep inside the six-yard box at the far post.

Cue widespread pandemonium inside Old Trafford and scenes that were repeated at full time. United were another 90 minutes closer to the end of an epic season, and three points closer to number 19.

The Teams

Manchester United: van der Sar, Fabio, Ferdinand, J.Evans, O'Shea (Evra 57), Valencia, Gibson (Giggs 74), Anderson, Nani (Owen 63), Rooney, Hernandez
Subs not used: Kuszczak, Brown, Carrick, Rafael
Booked: Anderson

Everton: Howard, Hibbert, Jagielka, Distin, Baines, Coleman (Gueye 75), Neville, Osman, Rodwell, Bilyaletdinov (Cahill 46), Beckford (Anichebe 46)
Subs not used: Mucha, Duffy, Mustafi, Vellios
Booked: Howard

'I could feel the goal coming,' grinned Sir Alex. 'We had the momentum and the crowd was up. When the crowd gets going, it sucks the ball in. We could have had the game finished by half time. But in the time-honoured fashion of Manchester United, we don't do that. We wait until the very end. It keeps everyone on the edge of their seat, but we get there. You say to yourself: "It's going to be another late one here." You can just smell the history of the club and so it was to be.

'The important thing is we never gave up. We took gambles, we took risks. We put Wayne Rooney in the middle of the pitch, we brought Ryan Giggs on, Michael Owen on. Jonny Evans has not had many games, neither has Fabio, but they both saw it through and showed great resilience and determination to get through it. It was a fantastic performance by the lads.'

While Sir Alex's faith never wavered, defender Jonny Evans concedes he feared the worst as Everton repelled attack after attack. 'I thought it was going to be one of those days,' he says. 'We hit the post and had quite a few chances in the first half, and you do sometimes fear the worst. I suppose you shouldn't at a club like this, at Old Trafford playing into the Stretford End. We've done it so many times over the years.

'Going into the last four games six points ahead is just an unbelievable feeling, as long as we keep ticking the games off. We've got hard games against Arsenal and Chelsea, and if we can get the points against them and not let them back into it we'll definitely go on and win the league.'

The Champions League was also in United's sights and the Reds barely had time to draw breath before boarding a flight to Gelsenkirchen for the trip to face competition dark horses Schalke. Once again Dimitar Berbatov and Darren Fletcher missed out, but Sir Alex could otherwise call on a full complement of players. The United manager was well aware of his side's poor record in Germany, with just three wins from 11 trips, and he was wary of facing Ralf Rangnick's outfit.

'They have beaten every team they have played in the Champions League at home this season, including Valencia and Inter Milan,' he said. 'Taken in isolation, that's fantastic form and there is no way Manchester United are going to be led into believing this is easy. This is a difficult game for us and we have no choice but to treat it that way.'

Nevertheless, the boss was brimming with cautious confidence, especially with a glut of experienced players available and in form, not least the influential England duo of Rio Ferdinand and Wayne Rooney. 'Rio's experience showed itself in the first leg against Chelsea,' Sir Alex said. 'He was immense. Experience and ability are vital in the situations we have at the moment. He's fresh and ready to play and it's a big boost for us.

'Wayne's form has been fantastic the last two months. More important is the freshness that has come into the team with players coming back: Anderson, Rio, Antonio Valencia and Ji-sung Park. Sometimes it happens that way. When big competitions come along, you find all your players are fit. It brings selection headaches, but they're the ones you want. This is a team that will not give in. There's absolutely no chance of that. That's a great quality. You saw that against Everton.'

With an incredible away record and having kept clean sheets in every European jaunt of 2010–11, the manager had every right to be confident in his side's abilities.

Champions League semi-final, first leg

Veltins-Arena | Tuesday 26 April 2011 | KO 7.45pm | Attendance: 54,142 | Referee: Carlos Velasco Carballo

Schalke 0
Manchester United 2 (Giggs 67, Rooney 69)

United turned in one of the finest European away displays of Sir Alex Ferguson's Old Trafford reign to take a huge step towards the Champions League final.

Ryan Giggs and Wayne Rooney struck quickfire goals midway through the second half, but the Reds could easily have been out of sight by that point had Schalke goalkeeper Manuel Neuer not turned in a wonderful one-man show of resistance.

The German international produced a string of superb saves in the first period to take his side into the interval on level terms, but United's patience paid dividends and even Neuer was powerless to prevent neat finishes from Giggs and Rooney in the space of three minutes.

It was the latter whose early effort set the tone for United's dominance. Although operating off Chicharito in an increasingly productive front pairing, Rooney found himself on the left wing before cutting in and unleashing a drive that nicked a defender and was top-corner bound until Neuer intervened.

The Schalke stopper then beat away a Ji-sung Park drive and held a low shot from Chicharito, who was then denied in two one-on-ones – first by Neuer's thigh, then by an uncharacteristically errant finish past the far post. As United continued to rampage forward, Neuer was on hand again to scoop away Giggs' back-post header.

Chicharito was again frustrated by the home goalkeeper with a fierce effort from the edge of the area, and Park's volleyed follow-up was blocked by Atsuto Uchida. The South Korean then teed up Fabio to volley over, before Neuer denied Giggs in a one-on-one to close the half.

The second period opened in similar fashion, as Neuer turned over a header from the peerless Michael Carrick and then Giggs fired wide after a superb shimmy to create room. Six minutes in, Chicharito fired past Neuer, only to find himself flagged marginally offside. The goal didn't stand, but United had made a key breakthrough in finding a route past the Schalke skipper.

The opening goal finally arrived on 67 minutes. Patrice Evra fed Rooney and the striker's brilliant disguised pass allowed Giggs to race through unchallenged to slip home an assured left-footed finish through Neuer's legs. Relief at last.

Scenting blood, United gambled and continued to press. Within two minutes, it paid off. Antonio Valencia touched the ball towards Chicharito and, with the Schalke defence crumbling, the Mexican helped it on intelligently to Rooney for a simple swept finish.

So total was United's dominance, Sir Alex was able to withdraw Park, Chicharito and Rooney to ensure their freshness for the looming trip to Arsenal. It looked likely that a subsequent jaunt to the capital would beckon the Reds, against either Real Madrid or Barcelona.

The Teams

Schalke: Neuer, Uchida, Matip, Metzelder, Sarpei (Escudero 73), Farfan, Papodopolous, Jurado (Draxler 83), Baumjohann (Kluge 53), Edu, Raul
Subs not used: Schober, Plestan, Charisteas, Karimi
Booked: Metzelder, Sarpei

Manchester United: van der Sar, Fabio, Ferdinand, Vidic, Evra, Valencia, Carrick, Giggs, Park (Scholes 73), Rooney (Nani 83), Hernandez (Anderson 73)
Subs not used: Kuszczak, Smalling, Rafael, J.Evans
Booked: Fabio

Inevitably, tongues were wagging post-match after Manuel Neuer's virtuoso goalkeeping display. 'He was fantastic,' rued Sir Alex. 'That is one of the best performances I've seen against Manchester United. Our concentration and the intensity of our play and speed of our passing were absolutely excellent tonight. It was a really top performance. I'm really pleased and every one of them has done fantastically well. We had fewer chances but were more dangerous after the break. The funny thing was that when Chicharito scored when he was offside, I think it told the players they could beat this goalkeeper.'

'When you're playing well and clicking like we did, it was very enjoyable,' says Rio Ferdinand. 'We played really well. In the first half, I don't think there are many teams in the world that could have dealt with us. We had people going long, we had people going short and dictating the play. We were snappy in the tackle and picking up second balls. If you're playing like that you're going to be a handful for anyone.

'We took the game by the scruff of the neck from minute one. We made sure we were on the front foot. At this stage of the tournament, that is what you have to do. It was more open than I expected. I thought it would be quite tight. But you can't say us creating chances was down to their performance or them freezing on the big stage. Some of our attacking play would have opened up anyone in the world.

'Part and parcel of being at this club is not having the time to dwell on days like this. We have big games every week. We have to make sure we don't get complacent. We are in a position in the league where it's down to us to perform and get the results. If we do that and stay focused we'll be champions. But there is a long way to go yet.'

After an overnight stop in Germany, United returned to Carrington with a daunting trip to the Emirates Stadium to face. Victory over the ailing Gunners would virtually end the title race, but Patrice Evra was wary of facing Arsene Wenger's side after such a poor run of results.

'Arsenal will play for pride,' he warned. 'They are at home. They will want to win. We have a great record at the Emirates, but it's a dangerous game. Arsenal want to show they still have a chance to win the title. If we lose there and Chelsea win, they are only three points behind us. We have to end the title race at the Emirates. We have to win.'

United's preparations were dealt a blow less than 24 hours before kick-off when Chelsea registered a late, come-from-behind win over Tottenham at Stamford Bridge. It was also drenched in controversy. Frank Lampard's equaliser was shown to have not crossed Heurelho Gomes' line, while Salomon Kalou was lurking in an offside position when he tapped in a late winner.

Was the tide beginning to turn?

11

May

Chelsea's controversial win over Tottenham had moved the reigning champions to within three points of United, and heaped extra pressure on the Reds ahead of the imposing trip to Arsenal.

Killing time in London ahead of the Emirates clash had, for some members of the squad, constituted watching Carlo Ancelotti's side on Sky Sports, and the manner of their victory had an impact on those who witnessed it.

'It doesn't give you nerves, but you start questioning everything and thinking about what could happen,' says Rio Ferdinand. 'Your emotions are all over the place. Me, Wazza [Rooney], Jonny [Evans] and Gibbo [Darron Gibson] sat and watched that game, and we were all thinking Chelsea would be lucky to get a point from it, then they ended up controversially taking three points and it can set you back a little bit.

'It can play with your emotions and your mind, especially when you've got a big, important game the next day. We were still confident that we could get a result, but sometimes it's hard when you know the entire season could be over if you win the next game. It can put a little bit more pressure on you sometimes.'

Barclays Premier League

Emirates Stadium | Sunday 1 May 2011 | KO 2.05pm |
Attendance: 60,107 | Referee: Chris Foy

Arsenal 1 (Ramsey 56)
Manchester United 0

Arsenal's own title ambitions may have imploded over the preceding weeks, but they rediscovered their best form in time to deal United's hopes a sizeable setback at the Emirates Stadium.

One-time United target Aaron Ramsey struck the only goal of the game, early in the second period, to secure a deserved victory for Arsene Wenger's side, who always looked the fresher team, as a result of having a week to prepare for the match.

The Reds, conversely, looked like they had expended too much energy in overpowering Schalke in Germany four days earlier. The visitors made scarcely any clear openings in North London, but nevertheless could have had a late penalty.

Not that Arsenal hadn't fallen foul of some questionable decision-making themselves, of course. Quite how Nemanja Vidic escaped censure for pawing Theo Walcott's cross away from Robin van Persie was a mystery, but the lack of a penalty for the hosts kept United in touch in a game Arsenal had clearly earmarked as a chance to silence their critics.

From the off, Arsenal created openings. Jack Wilshere and Walcott both fired wastefully off-target early on, while Vidic, Rio Ferdinand and Patrice Evra were all forced into alert blocks. Crucially, Edwin van der Sar was virtually unemployed for the entire half, though the same applied to Wojciech Szczesny at the opposite end.

The Pole was worked by a Wayne Rooney free-kick shortly after half time, and Evra slammed the rebound into Szczesny's side-netting, while Nani also curled a set-piece wide as United started the second period on top. Sir Alex sought to build on his side's improvement by introducing Antonio Valencia at the expense of Anderson, but Arsenal struck the killer blow within seconds of the Reds' reshuffle.

United were still reorganising when Wilshere fed van Persie on the right side of the area, and the Dutchman took stock before carefully teeing up the onrushing Ramsey to guide a shot through the legs of Michael Carrick and inside van der Sar's far post.

The visitors' response was one of jaded defiance. Arsenal were able to repel United's probing, with the majority of openings coming from set-pieces as Vidic headed a Nani corner wide and Rooney curled a free-kick straight to Szczesny. The Gunners looked to catch United on the counter-attack, but were almost undone as Nani led a Reds raid that culminated in Szczesny beating away the winger's shot.

Michael Owen, on for Carrick, was denied an apparently blatant penalty late on when he was crudely halted by Clichy inside the area, but referee Foy incorrectly waved away the claims.

The Emirates resounded with joy from the home support at full time – not least because they had thrown the Premier League title race wide open once more.

The Teams

Arsenal: Szczesny, Sagna, Djourou (Squillaci 69), Koscielny, Clichy, Ramsey, Song, Wilshere, Walcott (Eboue 78), van Persie, Nasri (Arshavin 46)
Subs not used: Lehmann, Bendtner, Gibbs, Chamakh
Booked: Ramsey, Song

Manchester United: van der Sar, Fabio, Ferdinand, Vidic, Evra, Nani, Carrick (Owen 85), Anderson (Valencia 56), Park, Hernandez (Berbatov 74), Rooney
Subs not used: Kuszczak, Smalling, Rafael, O'Shea
Booked: Fabio, Park, Rooney

'We didn't start particularly well and didn't create a lot in the first half,' admitted Edwin van der Sar, who ended up on the losing side after being beaten by Arsenal's solitary effort on target. 'We were quite solid at the back, we just didn't get the ball on the ground enough to hurt Arsenal. In the second half, we made some changes and, twenty seconds after that change, they scored a goal so we had to change our approach a bit more and created some chances to try and score an equaliser, but it never really happened.

'It's a tough place to come to, but we should've started it brighter and put them on the back foot. They're a quality team who also know how to play football – we wanted to get them on the counter-attack, but it didn't really happen. Unfortunately, I had no saves at all. It was a shame but, hopefully, it's not going to cost us too many things.'

As ever, Patrice Evra was in bullish mood post-match. The French defender displayed typical candour in evaluating United's display, but denied that the Reds had ceded the initiative to Chelsea in the title race.

'We have our destiny in our hands,' he said. 'We have a massive game against Chelsea. If we want to win the title then we have to beat Chelsea – it's as simple as that. If we don't beat them then we'll be in trouble. We just need to play the Man United way. I am not worried because we know we didn't do the things we normally do against Arsenal. We have three games left and need to win every game. Every game is a final.'

In the Premier League, at least, he was right. The Reds' next outing was a Champions League semi-final decider against Schalke, and their result and display at the Emirates, plus the first-leg lead established in Gelsenkirchen, meant Sir Alex would have plenty to consider in selecting his starting line-up to face the Bundesliga side. Carefully balancing the need to finish the job against Schalke, while still cultivating freshness in key players for Chelsea's visit was no easy feat. Nevertheless, the gaffer was upbeat about the overall state of play.

'Wednesday's a European semi-final second leg and then we've got the game on Sunday,' he said. 'We'll regroup and get them freshened up. I'll make some changes, without question, on Wednesday. We'll bring Paul Scholes back in. Dimitar Berbatov, Michael Owen: fresh players. We need to do that, but also I've probably got to keep experienced players at the back. We'll be all right.

'We're in as good a position as we could ever have wished for from the start of the season. We're in the semi-final of the European Cup in the second leg, with a two-goal lead, and we go into Chelsea with equal goal difference and a home game.'

Wayne Rooney was earmarked as a probable absentee with a tight hamstring, but the manager otherwise had a wealth of options at his disposal. One extra factor was the need to hand Darren Fletcher more playing time. The Scot had returned from his mystery virus in the Reserves in late April, and was now finally in line for his first senior outing since the start of March.

'Returning in the Reserves game against Arsenal had maybe been a bit too much, too soon,' admits Fletcher. 'But I was really delighted to be back in contention and was raring to get back to playing again after so long out. I was hoping to play a part against Schalke, but we all knew within the squad that whatever team was selected would be capable of winning the game, especially at Old Trafford, where we had been pretty formidable all season.

'I think the disappointment of the Arsenal result, and knowing we had the big game against Chelsea coming up, meant the manager had to take a calculated risk. He trusted the players. The manager appreciated that, yes, we wanted to achieve success in the Champions League and Premier League, but that was what we needed in order to give ourselves the best chance of doing that.'

Twenty-four hours before Schalke's visit, Barcelona hosted Real Madrid in the other semi-final. As widely expected, Pep Guardiola's side comfortably saw off their great rivals in another ill-tempered affair, drawing 1–1 to book a 3–1 aggregate victory. The Catalans would be waiting at Wembley for whoever emerged victorious from Old Trafford.

Champions League semi-final, second leg

**Old Trafford | Wednesday 4 May 2011 | KO 7.45pm | Attendance: 74,637 |
Referee: Pedro Proenca**

Manchester United 4 (Valencia 26, Gibson 31, Anderson 72, 76)
Schalke 1 (Jurado 35)

United booked a Wembley date with Barcelona after completing a double demolition job of Schalke at Old Trafford in a one-sided Champions League semi-final.

Already two goals clear after their exploits in Gelsenkirchen, the Reds duly thumped another four goals past the Bundesliga side in Manchester, while the visitors could muster only a solitary response.

With one eye firmly on Chelsea's looming visit in a Premier League decider, Sir Alex made eight changes to the side that lost at Arsenal – yet that tinkering did nothing to detour his side's march to Wembley.

Antonio Valencia broke the deadlock with the hosts' first opening. Atsuto Uchida surrendered possession to Anderson in dangerous territory and the Brazilian quickly found Darron Gibson. The midfielder slid a marvellous pass into the path of the onrushing Ecuadorian, who took a touch before sliding a finish under Manuel Neuer to send Old Trafford wild.

Gibson then crashed home United's second goal six minutes later to effectively end the tie. Teed up by the scorer of the first goal, Gibson smashed in a low shot, which thudded off Neuer's leg and rebounded in off the post. The Schalke stopper had kept his side in the tie with his first-leg heroics, but should undoubtedly have done better with Gibson's blockbuster.

The visitors briefly rallied when Jurado lashed a magnificent effort into the roof of Edwin van der Sar's net, but a recovery was never on the cards. Benedikt Howedes cleared Valencia's effort off the line almost immediately and Neuer made a wonderful fingertip save from Anderson's arced effort as United continued to dominate, and further goals arrived midway through the second period.

A beautiful, flowing Reds move culminated in Uchida blocking Anderson's sliding effort, only for the midfielder to regain his feet quickly, swivel and direct a left-footed shot underneath the dive of Neuer.

Within three minutes, the Brazilian had doubled his career tally for United. Again Valencia was involved, releasing Dimitar Berbatov with an incisive through-ball which tore Schalke's ragged backline apart, and the Bulgarian squared for Anderson to tap home.

The biggest semi-final aggregate victory in Champions League history had been secured, as had the most tantalising of finals: Barcelona at Wembley. The Reds would have another crack at ruling Europe. First, however, was the small matter of domestic rule, with Chelsea's visit just four days away.

The Teams

Manchester United: van der Sar, Rafael (Evra 60), Smalling, J. Evans, O'Shea, Gibson, Scholes (Fletcher 73), Anderson, Valencia, Berbatov (Owen 77), Nani
Subs not used: Kuszczak, Giggs, Hernandez, Vidic
Booked: Anderson, Gibson, Scholes

Schalke: Neuer, Uchida, Howedes (Huntelaar 70), Metzelder, Escudero, Jurado, Papadopolous, Farfan (Matip 75), Baumjohann (Edu 46), Draxler, Raul
Subs not used: Schober, Sarpei, Schmitz, Karimi
Booked: Escudero

'I didn't sleep last night thinking about it,' smiled Sir Alex Ferguson, when asked about the risks of making wholesale changes to his team for a Champions League semi-final. 'I woke up four times, picking different teams. When I analysed each individual who was playing,

I think "why can't I play them?" The semi-final thing and the fact that it's such an important game does create a certain bit of doubt in your mind about whether you're doing the right thing but I'm glad we were vindicated.'

'Some of the performances that the lads put in really showed how strong the squad is,' added stand-in captain John O'Shea. 'We could have scored a few more goals, but we are very happy with the end result. We lacked the same level of intensity we normally have against Arsenal at the weekend, as the boys had put in such a great performance in Schalke. The manager did take a risk but he also had faith in the squad.'

Both the skipper and manager confirmed that the squad had watched Barcelona sidle past Real Madrid and into the final. 'I think they are definitely the team of the moment – there's no question of that,' said Sir Alex. 'It's a fantastic type of football they play, it's a pleasure to watch and I think it will be a fantastic final.'

'We watched the game closely against Madrid,' continued O'Shea. 'They got through it quite well, but we can put it to one side now. We have three huge games in Manchester United's history before another massive match.'

No sooner had a Wembley berth been booked, than thoughts had turned to the visit of Chelsea. Schalke was a mere memory, albeit one that could fuel the Reds as the reigning Premier League champions rode into town.

'The dressing room was fantastic after we beat Schalke,' says Darren Fletcher. 'But we'd only reached the final, and at this club we're quite reserved in our celebrations even when we win things. It was a great achievement to get to another final, but we were so aware of the Chelsea game at the weekend. I think that's why this team and this club are so successful: yes, we enjoy success, but we never get carried away with it and we know we always have big games to come.'

They didn't come any bigger, in domestic terms at least, than United against Chelsea at Old Trafford. The champions-elect were up against the reigning champions, just three points ahead and with almost identical goal difference. A win for Carlo Ancelotti's side would draw them level on points and overturn United's solitary goal advantage. Coming little more than a year after the Blues had overhauled the Reds in M16 en route to claiming the Premier League title, the similar circumstances were regularly being flagged up in the media as the game edged closer.

There were, of course, key differences. Wayne Rooney was fit again, whereas he missed the 2010 meeting and, unlike a year earlier, United had been able to rest a glut of key players in readiness for the head-to-head. Still, the public perception that the Blues were set to pip the Reds for the second year running rankled at Carrington.

'There was big pressure on us to get something from the game and you got the sense that a lot of people fancied Chelsea to get a result. It didn't wind us up, but it made us more determined,' recalls Ryan Giggs.

'People expected us to lose to Arsenal and Chelsea, and then it would be a shootout over the last two games between us and Chelsea,' adds Darren Fletcher. 'But we knew it was still in our hands and we knew we were capable of winning the game. Having beaten them twice in the Champions League and played really well down there in the league game, we were supremely confident going into the game. I think all the neutrals wanted them to win because it would make for an exciting last couple of games, but we weren't thinking of that. We were only thinking of the win.'

Barclays Premier League

Old Trafford | Sunday 8 May 2011 | KO 4.10pm | Attendance: 75,445 | Referee: Howard Webb

Manchester United 2 (Hernandez 1, Vidic 23)
Chelsea 1 (Lampard 68)

Insatiable, energetic, dominant: if there had been any doubt over which team deserved to rule England, it was blown away by a whirlwind United display that left champions Chelsea in tatters.

Chicharito opened the scoring with a cool finish inside the opening minute, then skipper Nemanja Vidic capped a stunning start from the Reds with a close-range header. Chelsea had no response, bar a second-half consolation from Frank Lampard, and at full time Old Trafford reverberated with joy as a 19th league title edged into view.

The din in M16 took just 37 seconds to reach a crescendo, as Ryan Giggs fed Ji-sung Park, whose through-ball was diverted into Chicharito's path by the sliding David Luiz. The Mexican steadied himself, slotted a finish inside Petr Cech's near post and provoked scenes of mass hysteria among the home support. The tone for an unforgettable afternoon had been set.

The visitors were rocked, while the hosts set about them incessantly. Ji-sung Park appeared omnipresent, Giggs and Michael Carrick dictated the game's tempo and Antonio Valencia offered Ashley Cole one of his most uncomfortable afternoons. Wayne Rooney forced a fine flying save from Cech with a 30-yard screamer, Chicharito narrowly missed Park's tantalising cross and Rooney dragged just wide from the edge of the area before the lead was doubled by skipper Vidic.

Park's screeching effort was fended behind by Cech and, from the resulting corner, Giggs sidestepped Salomon Kalou's feeble challenge and crossed into a packed area. Vidic raced into space among static blue figures and nodded the ball down, past Cech and into the roof of the net.

Stung into life, Chelsea almost hit back when Edwin van der Sar clawed away Kalou's header and kept out Didier Drogba's free-kick, but the visitors were fortunate to go into the interval with a full team on show, after the already-booked Branislav Ivanovic controversially escaped a second caution for a clear foul on Rooney.

Carlo Ancelotti sought to add zeal to his side in the second period with the introduction of Ramires and Alex for John Obi Mikel and Luiz, but United rarely looked troubled. Instead, the visitors were fortunate to escape penalty claims against Lampard for handling Valencia's cross and John Terry for a clear trip on Valencia, as referee Howard Webb denied both strong shouts.

The Blues halved the arrears when Ivanovic climbed to head a Ramires cross goalwards and Lampard stabbed home from close range, but such was United's mood that Rooney almost instantly restored the cushion, only for his effort to be cleared off the line by Alex.

Chelsea realistically needed two more goals to prolong their title hopes, but instead the chances all fell to Rooney, who delayed one shot too long, then watched on as another effort was deflected onto the roof of Cech's net. Chicharito headed Valencia's driven cross over the bar from close range as time ticked away, but the misses ultimately counted for nothing.

Webb's final whistle marked the end of a sterling afternoon's work for United. With only a point required from games against Blackburn and Blackpool to clinch a 19th title, it also effectively marked the end of Chelsea's brief reign as champions.

The Teams

Manchester United: van der Sar, Fabio (Smalling 88), Ferdinand, Vidic, O'Shea (J. Evans 45), Valencia, Carrick, Giggs, Park, Rooney, Hernandez
Subs not used: Kuszczak, Anderson, Berbatov, Nani, Scholes
Booked: Giggs, Rooney

Chelsea: Cech, Ivanovic, Luiz (Alex 46), Terry, Cole, Essien, Mikel (Ramires 46), Lampard, Kalou (Torres 62), Drogba, Malouda
Subs not used: Turnbull, Ferreira, Benayoun, Anelka
Booked: Drogba, Essien, Ivanovic

There was no disguising the significance of the result. Sir Alex Ferguson bowed to the Stretford End as he made his way from the field. Behind him, jubilant squad members huddled in a scrum of triumph. Handshakes, high-fives and hugs all round. Nobody could deny United's claim to be the best team in England now.

'We were brilliant,' grinned Sir Alex. 'We made a fantastic start and it was a good team performance. When we gave the goal away it was understandably a bit nervous, but the fans helped us a lot. We just need one point now and I think, knowing the players, they'll get their point – there's no doubt about that.

'To win the nineteenth title would be fantastic. To be the most successful team in the country in terms of championship victories . . . The minute we won for the first time in 1992–93, the door opened for us. It's an incredible achievement.'

'We were relieved to get the win,' says Rio Ferdinand, looking back. 'But in saying that I think the result flattered them a little bit. It could have been four or five. A few decisions went their way, they got a lucky goal, really, and we had countless opportunities to score goals; enough chances to win two or three games. But it was nice. The last three games we've played against Chelsea, we've beaten them every single time. It got the monkey off our back, really, in terms of results against them over the last few years.

'It was the best atmosphere at Old Trafford that I've known for a long time. The fans were up for it. They knew what that result meant and they knew it could be a pivotal moment in the season. The roar before the game kicked off, the chanting in the warm-up . . . there was just a really good buzz about the place and the early goal managed to pump things up even more. Everything clicked and it was good to be a part of it.

'The dressing room was enjoyable afterwards, but there's a sense of professionalism at this club where you don't get too ahead of yourself. There were loads of people coming up to us and congratulating us that night and over the following days, and we hadn't even been crowned champions. We just had to take each step as it came.'

Even so, it was extremely feasible to expect a solitary point from the games against Blackburn and Blackpool, with both sides still firmly entrenched in a compelling relegation battle that threatened several teams. Barring an almighty collapse, United would end the season as champions – the perfect riposte to those who had criticised the Reds for the majority of the season, according to skipper Nemanja Vidic.

'Compliments are not always good for you,' said the Serbian. 'Criticism can help a team. Back in early season, there were people always trying to compare this team to other United teams. They were saying we didn't have the individuals like we used to and that we weren't as good. But you look at the names in this team and you think, "How could they say that?"

'We have never been focused on what people have been saying about us, but you can still get benefits from it. It can be a positive. Sometimes criticism can help a side. It can drag you forward. You have to work harder to prove to your critics that anything they say is not true. It pushes you to work harder. If you are getting compliments then that can have the opposite effect. It can relax you. You start believing what people are saying about you and you are not on top of your game. If we win the title, we will have proved to everyone that we are a very good team and will have proved them wrong.'

Darren Fletcher had something else to prove: his fitness ahead of the Champions League final. The Scot had missed previous finals in Rome and Moscow through suspension and non-selection respectively, and seemed unlikely to recover in time to feature at Wembley. 'I'm desperate to play,' he said. 'But so is everybody else.'

After another Reserves outing – as Warren Joyce's side won their league group – Fletcher looked likely to play a part at Ewood Park. But, with no injuries elsewhere in the squad, Sir Alex had a multitude of options as he sought the point that would finally, as he had wished so many years ago, knock 18-times champions Liverpool off their perch.

Speaking just before he was charged by the Football Association for complimenting referee Howard Webb before the previous weekend's win over Chelsea, the boss confirmed that he would rest Edwin van der Sar but would otherwise field his strongest team.

'The most important thing is to approach this game the right way,' he said. 'It's always a difficult game at Blackburn. They're also fighting. They're going to try their utmost to get a point or even beat us. We must put in the same effort. It's a hard game for both teams. But we're going there with the confidence of last Sunday, which was a great performance by us and we need another win like that.'

Barclays Premier League

Ewood Park | Saturday 14 May 2011 | KO 12.45pm | Attendance: 29,867 | Referee: Phil Dowd

Blackburn Rovers 1 (Emerton 20)
Manchester United 1 (Rooney (pen) 73)

Champions! After a long, agonising season of twists and turns, United finally wrapped up the title and, for a record 19th time, loomed large over all of England.

Wayne Rooney's second-half penalty secured the crown-clinching point in a hard-fought encounter with Blackburn at Ewood Park, but even in making history, the Reds insisted on going about it the hard way.

Brett Emerton had fired Rovers ahead, and the hosts might have established a two-goal lead at Ewood Park when Martin Olsson headed against Tomasz Kuszczak's post, before Paul Robinson hauled down Chicharito and gave Rooney the chance to seal United's coronation.

Though it was, at times, an afternoon of undiluted agony, the Reds began the game in encouraging fashion. As the prospect of becoming champions dangled before them, the visitors bossed possession. Less than four minutes had passed when the first chance arrived, but Nani could only thump a header against Robinson's crossbar from Rooney's tantalising cross.

But, against the run of play and in sloppy circumstances, Blackburn took the lead.

Emerton's ambitious chip was touched away by Kuszczak, but Olsson retrieved the ball before it crossed the byline, exchanged passes with Junior Hoilett and picked out Emerton at the back post to steer a fine finish back across goal.

The hosts were galvanised. Steve Kean's side charged into challenges, doubled up on United's wingers and packed the penalty area. Carving open the Rovers defence was no easy task for the champions-elect, who were also given a let-off when Kuszczak's clearance was charged down by Hoilett and ricocheted wide.

The Reds should have nabbed a leveller just before the interval after Chicharito was robbed by a fine sliding challenge from Phil Jones, but Nani steered the inviting loose ball over the crossbar. That woodwork was rattled midway through the second period at a key time, with the game still finely balanced.

Olsson rose to meet Emerton's cross, but the Norwegian could only nod against Kuszczak's post from close range. Moments later, Chicharito raced on to Ryan Giggs' pass, touched the ball past Robinson and tumbled under the goalkeeper's challenge. Dogged by vehement appeals from both sides, referee Phil Dowd sought the opinion of his linesman before awarding the spot-kick.

Rooney held his nerve and crashed an unstoppable penalty high into Robinson's right-hand corner to prompt scenes of utter delirium in the Darwen End. 'We shall not be moved,' cried the 8,000 travelling supporters, who also unfurled a banner which simply read: 'Top of the perch.' Rarely has the view looked so good.

The Teams

Blackburn Rovers: Robinson, Salgado, Samba (Andrews 78), P.Jones, Givet, Emerton, J.Jones (Dunn 74), N'Zonzi, Olsson, Hoilett (Pedersen 59), Roberts
Subs not used: Bunn, Kalinic, Santa Cruz, Benjani
Booked: J.Jones, N'Zonzi, Salgado

Manchester United: Kuszczak, Fabio (Scholes 62), Ferdinand, Vidic, J.Evans, Valencia, Carrick, Giggs, Nani (Berbatov 81), Rooney, Hernandez
Subs not used: Amos, Evra, Owen, Anderson, Smalling

'It was terrifying!' shouted penalty hero Wayne Rooney, struggling to make himself heard over the United supporters revelling in their side's success. The striker then quickly added: 'It's a great feeling after the year I've had, with the ups and downs, so for me this is for the fans. Winning the Premier League is an incredible feeling and to get that nineteenth title to become the most successful English club is brilliant. Of course for me personally, being an Everton fan, it's even more special [to overhaul Liverpool]. It's a great feeling for the whole club, the team, the fans, everyone.'

'For nineteen years we've been competing for the [Premier] League – it's an amazing feat,' added Sir Alex, who quickly shifted his focus forward. 'It's an incredible achievement, and every young player that comes to the club gets ingrained into the fabric of that. Chris Smalling's got his first medal, so have Darron Gibson and Chicharito. It's a wonderful experience for them because they are the future.

'There's a responsibility as the manager of Manchester United that doesn't go away. I'm not going to take it easy because we won the title today. Hopefully, we'll be better next season. Hopefully, we'll be adding two or three players in the summer. We've got some young players coming back, like Danny Welbeck, Tom Cleverley and Mame Diouf and we want to be better. I think the ambition of the club doesn't alter.'

The manager's smile, however, betrayed his desire to savour the present, just for a moment. Grins clustered in one end of Ewood Park, shared by players, staff and fans alike. A deflated replica trophy was passed among the players, who joined the Red Army in their singing and were quickly armed with bottles of champagne. The away dressing room was soon awash with it, and the celebratory drinks flowed throughout the course of a long evening at Rosso, the

247

Manchester restaurant part-owned by Reds defender Rio Ferdinand. Suffice to say, a good time was had by all.

'Those are the nights you love,' says Ryan Giggs. 'It's a relief and you can let everything go and enjoy yourself with the players and staff. Obviously, you've been through so much together and fought so hard throughout the season, it's just a great celebration. We've had some good nights down the years, and this was another good one.'

The legacy of Saturday's excesses had passed in time for the following week's return to training. A conversation between Sir Alex and his coaches immediately after the Blackburn game, however, had concluded that the sessions would be largely geared towards the Champions League final, rather than the Premier League finale against Blackpool. Detailed plans were outlined as to how best maximise the Reds' chances of upsetting Pep Guardiola's tournament favourites, but Sir Alex was still keen to stress that he would be going for victory against Ian Holloway's Seasiders.

'Obviously everybody expects me to leave players out, and that will be the case. I have to think about next week,' he said. 'I have to juggle the balls and make sure I get the right mix and keep the right energies for Barcelona. There are players who need a game anyway. Darren Fletcher, Paul Scholes and Anderson will all play. So will Berbatov, Evra and van der Sar.

'We'll do our fairest to make sure there's no criticism of the club. The only thing you could be criticised for is if you lose a game and it affects other teams. That's when you should be put under scrutiny for the team you picked. Against Hull [in 2009] we played all the young players and we won 1–0, so there was no reason to criticise the selection on that occasion. This time it will be the same again. We have to make sure we win.'

The Reds' preparations for their two remaining games were punctuated by further cause for celebration at the club's annual awards bash. In hotly contested categories, Chicharito was named the Sir Matt Busby Player of the Year, as voted by supporters, while the dressing room vote for Players' Player of the Year went to Nani. The least surprising outcome of the evening was Wayne Rooney's Goal of the Season gong for his overhead kick against Manchester City, while youngsters Oliver Gill and Ryan Tunnicliffe were named as star men for the Reserves and Under-18s respectively.

As the week wore on, there was much to consider for Sir Alex, who, like Chelsea counterpart Carlo Ancelotti, escaped with a Football Association warning for his pre-match praise of Howard Webb. Firstly, he met with Owen Hargreaves to confirm that the injury-jinxed midfielder would not be offered a new contract. 'This has been a difficult decision knowing how hard the lad has worked to win back his fitness,' he solemnly said. 'But we have made it in the hope he will be able to resurrect his career elsewhere.'

Hargreaves' departure had been on the cards, as the midfielder has missed nearly three of his four years at Old Trafford through injury. Less predictable was a knock on the door from Edwin van der Sar. 'Edwin decided he wants to go out at the top, though he did have a wobble,' revealed the manager. 'Edwin came to see me and told me he was thinking about changing his mind. I had to tell him to be quick about it because we were in the middle of concluding a deal for a new keeper. He came back a couple of days later to say he would be sticking with his original decision to go, which I think at his age, forty-one next birthday, is the right thing for him to do.'

The big Dutchman would indeed be sticking to his guns, and he was relishing the chance to sign off with one final appearance at Old Trafford. 'Last weekend felt a bit awkward,' he said. 'I didn't feel like a champion dressed in my shoes and suit, but hopefully I will after the Blackpool game.'

Barclays Premier League

Old Trafford | Sunday 22 May 2011 | KO 4.00pm | Attendance: 75,400 |
Referee: Mike Dean

Manchester United 4 (Park 21, Anderson 62, Evatt o.g. 74,
Owen 81)
Blackpool 2 (Adam 40, Taylor-Fletcher 57)

United's coronation was preceded by a fittingly entertaining spectacle, as the Reds rounded off their Premier League campaign with a win that relegated Blackpool at Old Trafford.

Ji-sung Park's early opener was overturned by goals either side of half time from Charlie Adam and Gary Taylor-Fletcher, before goals from Anderson, Ian Evatt – at the wrong end – and Michael Owen secured United's highest ever home points total in a season.

Pre-match suggestions that Sir Alex Ferguson's team selection would be scrutinised by the FA were rendered farcical by the imposing line-up from the hosts; although Blackpool should have forged ahead inside 30 seconds when Keith Southern sidefooted hopelessly off-target from Adam's centre.

Taylor-Fletcher was close to turning in another cross from the Scot, before United clicked into gear. Rafael's thunderous volley was padded down by Matthew Gilks, who then turned away Dimitar Berbatov's low, guided effort. The Bulgarian had better luck soon afterwards as a provider for Park, who lofted a delightful finish over the onrushing Gilks to open the scoring.

Blackpool were rocked. Berbatov spurned a chance to double the lead when firing against Gilks' legs after more defensive hesitancy, while misjudged challenges from Adam on Park and Alex Baptiste on Berbatov might both have been punished with penalties, only for Mike Dean to wave away United's appeals.

The referee was central to the visitors' leveller just before half time, as he overruled his assistant to award a Blackpool free-kick just outside the United area. Adam superbly thumped home a shot in off the base of Edwin van der Sar's post to level the scores. There would be no farewell shutout for the Dutchman, and United had conceded a Premier League home goal in the first half for the first time in 2010–11.

Scenting a great escape, Ian Holloway's side took the lead shortly before the hour mark – again making their mark as the first side to lead United in the Premier League at Old Trafford all term. David Vaughan broke forward and played a one-two with Jason Puncheon before crossing for Taylor-Fletcher to touch home off the far post. With scores elsewhere also favourable, the Seasiders were temporarily safe.

The dream would soon become a nightmare, however, as Anderson swapped passes with Park before sweeping home the South Korean's accurate cross. United piled on the pressure and forged a succession of chances before Chris Smalling, on as a substitute, drilled in a cross which Evatt shanked past Gilks to put the hosts ahead.

Evatt almost atoned by storming through at the other end, only to be denied by van der Sar, with the Dutchman making a brave stop, before substitute Owen sprinted on to Anderson's through-ball and cracked a shot emphatically inside Gilks' near post. Thereafter a succession of opportunities were fired narrowly off-target as Berbatov tried in vain to become the sole winner of the Golden Boot, but instead he had to settle for sharing it with Carlos Tevez.

Blackpool, along with Birmingham and West Ham, who had dropped a week earlier, were left relegated by the result. Their players were afforded a warm send-off by the Old Trafford crowd, but the main event was still to come.

The Teams

Manchester United: van der Sar, Rafael (Smalling 46), Vidic (Rooney 84), J.Evans, Evra, Nani, Scholes, Anderson, Fletcher, Park (Owen 63), Berbatov
Subs not used: Lindegaard, Ferdinand, Valencia, Gibson
Booked: Fletcher, Owen

Blackpool: Gilks, Eardley, Baptiste, Evatt, Crainey, Southern (Ormerod 87), Vaughan, Adam, Taylor-Fletcher (Varney 76), Campbell, Puncheon (Phillips 75)
Subs not used: Kingson, Beattie, Grandin, Cathcart
Booked: Vaughan

The roar that greeted Nemanja Vidic's Premier League trophy lift may have been audible in Merseyside, so long and loud did it hang in the Manchester air. Flanked by bouncing, grinning team-mates, the Serbian skipper held aloft the fruits of another season of graft, gumption and guile, and couldn't contain his joy.

'This has been our main target: to win the league,' he said. 'But we won't stop now. We want to improve and get better. I was very proud when I was given the captaincy and, I have to say, I'm enjoying this role. But at the end of the year, if you don't lift the trophy it's not a great feeling. I'm very glad we've won the trophy this year, especially because it's such an important trophy.

'Since I've arrived every year has got better and better. It's amazing. I've been here five years and we've won the league four times and played in three Champions League finals. It's a dream and to be part of this team, this club, is amazing. We're getting better and better.'

Each player beamed as he posed with the trophy. 'As they say, if you can't beat them, join them,' grinned Michael Owen. 'I won a lot of trophies with Liverpool, but to win the Premier League is the pinnacle of anyone's career. I'm very proud today.'

'This is what you play football to do: to win trophies, to win medals,' concurred Wayne Rooney, who had earlier marked the title win by shaving '19' into his chest hair.

The occasion carried special significance for departing goalkeeper Edwin van der Sar, who addressed the crowd and thanked them for their support, as did Sir Alex. Both men were united in their sign-off: vowing to do their utmost to add the Champions League trophy to its Premier League counterpart.

That steely focus gripped the squad. After parading the trophy around Old Trafford with family and friends, there would only be thoughts of Barcelona thereafter. Training sessions increasingly took the players into a specific approach of pressing and maximising possession against the game's leading exponents of the passing game.

'We've played against Barcelona three times and there's always a solution to every good player,' Sir Alex told a Carrington press conference, two days after Blackpool's visit. 'We hope we can find a solution for Lionel Messi on Saturday. You also have to recognise they have other good players and we have other good players. That's why it's such a thrilling game on Saturday.

'We'll find a solution to the game. It's about what's best for us; what's the best way for us to win the match. It will be down to how we operate in the attacking part. I'm sure Barcelona are aware of the threats we have. We have to rely on our players to perform. I think we're ready and we've prepared very well.'

Those preparations would include the Gary Neville testimonial, which gave the boss a chance to keep several players' fitness ticking over. The farewell to one of Old Trafford's favourite sons climaxed three successive days of major events in M16.

After the first team's coronation, Paul McGuinness's Under-18s won the FA Youth Cup at the expense of Sheffield United, completing a 6–3 aggregate win to secure the trophy for a record tenth time. The most vaunted winners of the competition, the Class of '92, would reunite for one last time on Neville's special night. The star of the show was joined by brother Phil, Nicky Butt and David

Beckham, while Ryan Giggs and Paul Scholes both completed half an hour as United were beaten 1–2 by Juventus.

With almost all of a bulging squad fully fit and attuned for a specialised gameplan, the boss had some major selection decisions to make. He had virtually settled on his starting line-up, but would have to leave some experienced professionals out of his squad entirely.

'It's not easy because you're dealing with the human side of the game,' he said. 'Players have worked hard all season, and it's been a squad game for us this year. It can't be easy. Unfortunately, one person has to tell them and that's me. It's not an easy job, but we have to win the game; they all understand that. They've all contributed and that doesn't make it easy for me. I hope I pick the right team and the right substitutes.'

The spotlight was soon trained on those jostling for involvement, as Carrington hosted a media open day. Talk inevitably concerned memories of United's last meeting with Barcelona: the 2009 final in Rome.

'It's something you don't forget,' said Rio Ferdinand. 'You remember the bad times more than the good times, and that defeat is definitely still fresh in our minds and we have a good chance to put that to bed. It's huge for us. We've got some unfinished business there with them. We went off the pitch last time with loads of questions; plenty of ifs, buts and maybes, things we didn't do and probably should have. This time we want to make sure we give it our all and leave everything out on the pitch.'

'Defeats like Rome stay with you for a long time,' added Ryan Giggs. 'We didn't produce the football we were capable of and gave bad goals away. If you play brilliantly and the other team plays brilliantly and you lose, you can hold your hands up, but we didn't really play as well as we know we can. You look back on the game and it's always the case that when you've played well you were never as good as you thought, and when you've played badly you were never as bad as you thought.

'There have been some great teams we've played against. Real

Madrid around 2000, the 1996–97 Juventus team were very good, and Barcelona are there. They're a talented side and they've had success in the last five or six years, both at home and abroad. It won't be easy, but you have to beat the best teams to win the Champions League.'

Having fulfilled their media duties and prepared meticulously in training, United headed to London via train, arriving two days after Barcelona, whose journey to the capital had been hastened by the resurgence of an Icelandic ash cloud. Having checked in to their hotel, Sir Alex was joined by Rio Ferdinand and Nemanja Vidic in UEFA's obligatory pre-match press conference. Pep Guardiola, meanwhile, was flanked by his captain, Carlos Puyol, in their later media address, which took place while United trained on the Wembley turf.

The mood among the Reds was light-hearted, but focused. Every player, when pressed for a word by a passing fan or journalist, confirmed that everybody was ready for the following day's match. Sir Alex had settled on his team. The players were primed and raring to go into battle with the hot favourites – not that the manager was concerned with talk of odds.

'I don't think it matters if we're underdogs,' he said. 'You don't care what the betting says or the experts say . . . that doesn't matter. It's what happens on the pitch and we go out there with a genuine chance whether we're favourites or not favourites.'

UEFA Champions League final

**Wembley Stadium | Saturday 28 May 2011 | KO 7.45pm |
Attendance: 87,695 | Referee: Viktor Kassai**

Barcelona 3 (Pedro 27, Messi 54, Villa 69)
Manchester United 1 (Rooney 34)

There's no shame in being beaten by the best, especially when they're this good.

For the second Champions League final in three seasons, United were overrun by Pep Guardiola's masterful Barcelona side, who clinched their fourth term as kings of Europe with goals from Pedro, Lionel Messi and David Villa. Though the Reds went into the interval on level terms after Wayne Rooney's delightful leveller, there was no answer to the Catalans' second-half masterclass.

Sir Alex Ferguson said pre-match that there was a solution to every problem, when referencing how he planned to combat the threat of Messi. Alas, Barcelona created too many problems to counter, and none was greater than that posed by the little Argentine sorcerer.

As widely predicted, the boss went for the same starting XI that strode to semi-final victory in Schalke. It was a selection of bold intentions, even if it was soon apparent that United counter-attacks would be sporadic interludes in an evening of Barcelona probing. The Reds started brightly enough and pressed high, while defending stoutly in the early exchanges, with Nemanja Vidic making a series of heroic interventions.

Slowly but surely, however, the Spanish champions' movement began to pull open weaves in the United fabric, and the deadlock was broken when Xavi expertly found Pedro inside the area, and the youngster steered an unerring finish inside Edwin van der Sar's post.

The legacy of United's defeat in Rome was a gnawing sense that the Reds never recovered from falling behind. There would be no repeat this time around. Seven minutes after conceding, the Premier League champions were level in sublime fashion. Rooney neatly swapped passes with Michael Carrick and Ryan Giggs before hitting one home high past Victor Valdes. Game on.

Rooney's leveller didn't change the flow of the game, but it did stem it temporarily. United survived just one more scare before the interval, as Messi narrowly missed sliding home Daniel Alves' cross. Halfway through, the Reds could reflect on a job largely well done. The second period, however, would be a different matter.

From the off, Barca pressed with greater urgency and intent.

Their high tempo, pass-popping approach had United's backs to the wall and it was no surprise when they retook the lead within ten minutes. It was a mistake to leave Messi unattended to take Andres Iniesta's pass; and a bigger one still to let the little maestro advance to virtually the edge of the area from where he unleashed a low, dipping shot that evaded van der Sar's dive.

As United had seen in Rome, mistakes are seldom unpunished by Pep Guardiola's side. The Reds had been reminded of it by Messi, but the point was hammered home once more as Villa killed the contest with 21 minutes remaining. Messi's weaving run into the area was halted, but Carrick's touch was mis-controlled by substitute Nani. Sergio Busquets recovered the ball and teed up Villa, who took a touch before arcing a magnificent finish high inside van der Sar's left-hand post.

Time remained for one more chance of an unlikely salvage act. Rooney – United's star performer – again picked his way through the Catalans' defence, but could only curl his effort from the edge of the area onto the roof of Valdes' goal. Thereon, Barcelona sat back, soaked up all the pressure the Reds could muster and counted down to the final whistle. When it came, the United half of Wembley Stadium warmly applauded the winners. The Red Army recognises true class, and their side had just been beaten by the very best in the business.

Disconsolate, white-clad figures littered the pitch, just as they had in Rome two years earlier. The champions of England could only look on as the new kings of Europe ascended to their rightful throne, casting a mighty shadow over the rest of the continent.

The Teams

Barcelona: Valdes, Alves (Puyol 88), Mascherano, Pique, Abidal, Xavi, Busquets, Iniesta, Villa (Keita 86), Messi, Pedro (Afellay 90)
Subs not used: Oier, Bojan, Thiago, Adriano
Booked: Alves, Valdes

Manchester United: van der Sar, Fabio (Nani 69), Ferdinand, Vidic, Evra, Valencia, Carrick (Scholes 77), Giggs, Park, Rooney, Hernandez
Subs not used: Kuszczak, Owen, Anderson, Smalling, Fletcher
Booked: Carrick, Valencia

'I think they are the best team we have ever played,' sighed Sir Alex Ferguson, deep within the bowels of Wembley Stadium. 'They are at a tremendous peak in the cycle of their team and you get teams who elevate themselves to that status. We were well beaten. There is no other way to address the situation. We were beaten by the better team, a fantastic team of course, but I expected to do better. We expected to do better, it's as simple as that.'

So did the players. Numbness gripped the United dressing room, and gradually subdued players filtered through the UEFA mixed zone to offer their thoughts on the evening's events. Not one took issue with the result. Magnanimity oozed forth as they headed towards their coach. Amid it all, however, the perpetually forthright Patrice Evra shone as a beacon of defiance, finding the voice to outline the squad's collective verdict.

'We always want to be the best team in the world, but for the moment, we have to accept that for the last three years Barcelona have been the best team in the world and United are second,' said the Frenchman. 'The consolation is that Manchester United had a good season. Not a great season because we didn't win here, but a good season.

'I want to come back to the final again and play against Barcelona. We are not afraid. We just have to give them credit tonight and say they are better than us. But we will keep going. We have still won the league and we are going to win the league again next year, and make sure we win the Champions League as well. I know what we have to do. Go on holiday, have a rest and come back because Manchester United never die.'

Epilogue

Regardless of the Champions League final, the club's first trophy parade since 1999 had been arranged since the Reds had clinched the Premier League title at Ewood Park. But, coming so soon after the events of Wembley, and on a Bank Holiday Monday typically saturated by the Manchester rain, some of the players were sceptical about the turnout among supporters.

As the open-top bus headed out of the Manchester Evening News Arena into the teeming elements, however, any doubt was swiftly doused. Upon turning onto Deansgate, the players met a sea of umbrellas, banners and scarves. The mood on board turned from trepidation to excitement, as the squad took in their audience.

'It's amazing,' said John O'Shea. 'The lads were obviously wondering if many people would turn up, but we never should have doubted the fans. We realise now how important that nineteenth league title is to the fans. We want to really cherish these moments. We're disappointed, obviously, from the weekend, but I think this will help the players get over it.'

'I can't believe the turnout,' added Darren Fletcher. 'I think all the lads are genuinely surprised and humbled, and realise what great fans we've got. I think if we'd have left after the Champions League final and not done this then the lads would've been really down, but it's given us another boost and sends us out on a high.'

The Premier League trophy was perched on the very front of the bus initially, safeguarded by Rio Ferdinand and Nemanja Vidic, before being passed among the larking players who posed for pictures and revelled in the occasion. Wembley was, for two hours at least, a distant memory.

Slowly but surely, the Reds headed towards Sir Matt Busby Way. The players – when they could wrest the microphone from Patrice Evra, at least – took turns singing songs en route, before they paused amid the thronging crowd at Old Trafford. Sir Alex addressed the supporters to thank them for their input to the season.

'I think what this shows is their fantastic loyalty,' said the boss. 'What really is impressive is the number of children who are here. There are a lot of fathers here with kids who are as young as one or two years of age sitting on their shoulders. That's the future of Manchester United: young people.'

At the opposite end of the age scale – in playing terms – Ryan Giggs was similarly focused on what lay ahead. 'There'd be something wrong if we weren't disappointed by Saturday,' he said. 'But taking everything into account, if you'd said at the start of the season that we'd have got the nineteenth title, everyone at the club would have taken it. After today it's not about nineteen, it's about pushing on into the twenties. That's what this club is about: not standing still, but moving forward.'

As an embodiment of the investment in youth that had spawned such success for Sir Alex, Giggs had shown making history was all about looking to the future. So too had Paul Scholes over the course of an epic Reds career, which was curtailed when the midfielder announced his retirement the morning after the parade.

Crucially, his services were retained as a coach. Steeped in United's winning culture, Scholes can imbue his experience in future crops of burgeoning talents rising through the club's ranks – including 2011's Youth Cup winners. With an inspirational new teacher secured for their education, plus a Premier League title to defend and a new European benchmark to aim for, United's prospects burn brightly as the 2011–12 season looms tantalisingly on the horizon.

Appearances and Goals

Appearances

	Premier League		FA Cup		League Cup		Champions League		Other		Total	
	Apps	Sub	Apps	Sub	Apps	Sub	Apps	Sub	Apps	Sub	Apps	Sub
Nemanja Vidic	35		2		0		9		1		47	
Patrice Evra	34	1	3		0		9	1	0		46	2
Edwin van der Sar	33		2		0		10		1		46	
Nani	31	2	2	1	0		9	3	0	1	42	7
Michael Carrick	23	5	3		1		11		1		39	5
Wayne Rooney	25	3	1	1	0		9		1		36	4
Dimitar Berbatov	24	8	2		0		6	1	0	1	32	10
Darren Fletcher	24	2	1	1	1		5	2	0	1	31	6
John O'Shea	18	2	4		1		5	1	1		29	3
Rio Ferdinand	19		2		1		7		0		29	
Javier Hernandez	15	12	4	1	2	1	6	3	0	1	27	18
Ryan Giggs	19	6	1	2	1		6	2	0	1	27	11
Ji-sung Park	13	2	1		2		8	1	1		25	3
Rafael	15	1	3		1	1	6	1	0		25	3
Paul Scholes	16	6	2	1	0		4	3	1		23	10

	Premier League		FA Cup		League Cup		Champions League		Other		Total	
	Apps	Sub	Apps	Sub	Apps	Sub	Apps	Sub	Apps	Sub	Apps	Sub
Chris Smalling	11	5	2	2	3		7	2	0	1	23	10
Anderson	14	4	2	2	2		4	2	0		22	8
Jonny Evans	11	2	2		2		2	1	1		18	3
Fabio	5	6	3	1	2		5	2	1		16	9
Antonio Valencia	8	2	1	1	0		5	2	1		15	5
Darron Gibson	6	6	3		2		3		0		14	6
Wes Brown	4	3	2	1	2	1	2		0		10	5
Tomasz Kuszczak	5		1		2		2		0		10	5
Gabriel Obertan	3	4	2		2	1	1	2	0		8	7
Federico Macheda	2	5	0		2	1	1	1	0		5	7
Michael Owen	1	10	1	1	1	1	0	2	1		4	13
Bébé	0	2	1		2	1	0	1	0		3	4
Gary Neville	3		0		0	1	0		0		3	1
Ben Amos	0		0		1		1		0		2	
Anders Lindegaard	0		2		0		0		0		2	
Owen Hargreaves	1		0		0		0		0		1	
Ravel Morrison	0		0		0	1	0		0		0	1

Goals scored

	Premier League	FA Cup	League Cup	Champions League	Other	Total
Dimitar Berbatov	20	0	0	0	1	21
Javier Hernandez	13	1	1	4	1	20
Wayne Rooney	11	1	0	4	0	16
Nani	9	0	0	1	0	10
Ji-sung Park	5	0	2	1	0	8
Nemanja Vidic	5	0	0	0	0	5
Michael Owen	2	1	2	0	0	5
Ryan Giggs	2	1	0	1	0	4
Anderson	1	0	0	3	0	4
Darren Fletcher	2	0	0	1	0	3
Antonio Valencia	1	0	0	1	1	3
Fabio	1	1	0	0	0	2
Bébé	0	0	1	1	0	2
Darron Gibson	0	0	1	1	0	2
Patrice Evra	1	0	0	0	0	1
Federico Macheda	1	0	0	0	0	1
Paul Scholes	1	0	0	0	0	1
Wes Brown	0	1	0	0	0	1
Gabriel Obertan	0	0	0	1	0	1
Chris Smalling	0	0	1	0	0	1
Own goals	3	0	0	0	0	3

Acknowledgements

MUTV
ManUtd.com
United Review
Inside United
Photographs: John and Matt Peters

Sincere thanks to everyone at the club for their co-operation and support during the writing of this book, especially Sir Alex Ferguson, his staff and players for ensuring a truly historic season.

Thanks to: Nick Coppack, Rhea Halford, Ian Marshall, Karen Shotbolt and James White for your collective input and patience.